ALL THAT FITS A WOMAN

ALL THAT FITS A WOMAN

TRAINING SOUTHERN BAPTIST WOMEN FOR CHARITY AND MISSION, 1907-1926

T. Laine Scales

MERCER UNIVERSITY PRESS
Macon, Georgia
2000

ISBN 0-86554-668-1   MUP/H497

The paper used in this publication meets the minimum requirements of American National Standard for Information Sciences—Permanence of Paper for Printed Library Materials, ANSI Z39.48-1984.

Library of Congress Cataloging-in-Publication Data

Scales, T. Laine
    All that fits a aoman: training Southern Baptist women for charity and mission, 1907-1926
        p. cm.
    Includes bibliographical references and index.
    ISBN 0-86554-668-1
    1. Womans Missionary Union Training School for Christian Workers (Louisville, Ky.)—History. 2. Southern Baptist Convention—Education—Kentucky—Louisville—History—20th century.   3. Women missionaries—Training of—Kentucky—Louisville—History—20th century. 4. Missionaries—Training of—Kentucky—Louisville—History—20th century. 5. Baptist women—Education (Higher)—Kentucky—Louisville—History—20th century. 6. Baptists—Education(Higher)—Kentucky—Louisville—History— 20th century.

BV2093.W66 S33 2000
286'.132'082—dc21
                                                           00-033931

In Memory of my Mother
Barbara Clem Scales
1936-1999

CONTENTS

PREFACE

This work began as a dissertation project and my deepest gratitude goes to the committee at University of Kentucky that advised me in shaping the project and prompted me when I got stuck. Most especially, I want to thank Richard Angelo and Beth Goldstein for consistent encouragement and confidence in me. Beth offered me the extraordinary care and attention she gives so generously to students and took me in as one of her family when I needed it most.

The Carver School of Church Social Work at the Southern Baptist Theological Seminary, Louisville, Kentucky hosted me as a visiting researcher from 1990-1992. I was inspired to tell this story by its first dean, Anne Davis who first introduced me to the school's history. Two colleagues at Carver School, Donoso Escobar and Diana Garland, were especially supportive, listening and reading.

Many people made information available to me: Ron Deering of the Southern Baptist Theological Seminary provided access to photographs as well as a helpful library staff. Lynn May headed up the staff of the Southern Baptist Historical Library and Archives at Nashville. I am grateful to that group for providing me access to their materials as well as financial assistance. The Woman's Missionary Union of Birmingham opened their library to me and Elgee Bentley and Betty Hurt were particularly resourceful. I am also grateful to Cindy McMurtry for help with photographs. Other individuals who helped locate resources were Paul Debusman, Paulette Moore Catherwood, Elgee Bentley and Bill Sumners.

Sherry Scales Rostosky and Roger Aker gave feedback on the manuscript at important times. I am particularly grateful to Melody Mazuk who was a careful reader as well as a true friend and supporter through every phase of the project.

Sarah Canoy Parker, alumna of House Beautiful and WMU leader in my childhood church inspired my interest in the culture of WMU. Her stories of student days, particularly her courtship with her husband LeRoy, ignited my interest in student life at House Beautiful.

My parents, Charles and Barbara Scales gave spiritual guidance to me and my sister Sherry, all the way from "Jesus Loves Me" to seminary and beyond. They have never limited us, as little girls or as women, while we respond to God's call to ministry.

Most of all I thank my husband Glenn Blalock for his encouragement and tangible support in this project, and in every aspect of our life together.

1. Students in the Training School home, circa 1912 (Photograph courtesy of the Southern Baptist Theological Seminary [SBTS])

2. "Woman's Missionary Union Royalty," Nashville, 1919 (Photograph courtesy of Woman's Missionary Union)

3. Eliza Sommerville Broadus, founder of the WMU Training School (Photograph courtesy of SBTS)

4. Fannie Exile Scudder Heck, founder of the WMU
Training School and president of WMU (Photograph
courtesy of SBTS)

5. Emma McIver Woody, founder of the WMU Training School (Photograph courtesy of SBTS)

6. Anna Eager, founder of the WMU Training School
(Photograph courtesy of SBTS)

7. Maude Reynolds McLure, principal, 1907-1923 (Photograph courtesy of SBTS)

8. Training School students walk to class, circa 1912 (Photo-graph courtesy of SBTS)

9. House Beautiful, completed 1917 (Photograph courtesy of SBTS)

10. Frost Memorial Staircase, House Beautiful (Photograph courtesy of SBTS)

11. Dining room of the Training School, circa 1917 (Photograph courtesy of SBTS)

12. The Goodwill Center: workshop for social work and missions training (Photograph courtesy of SBTS)

13. Students with young women of the Goodwill Center
(Photograph courtesy of SBTS)

14. Jewell Legett (second row, second from left) with her
class, 1909 (Photograph courtesy of SBTS)

15. Juliette Mather, WMU employee, 1921-1955
(Photograph courtesy of WMU)

16. Juliette Mather (front row, second from left) with Training School classmates (Photograph courtesy of SBTS)

17. Carrie Littlejohn, principal, 1930-1951 (Photograph courtesy of WMU)

18. Training School students, circa 1912 (Photograph courtesy of SBTS)

19. Student body, 1917-1918, with principal Maude McLure
(Photograph courtesy of SBTS)

20. Old Testament Class 1915-1916. (Photo courtesy of the Southern Baptist Theological Seminary.)

21. Students in parlor, circa 1908. (Photo courtesy of the Southern Baptist Theological Seminary.)

22. "The Big Four." The first four students to move into rented home, 1904 (Photo courtesy of the Southern Baptist Theological Seminary.)

INTRODUCTION

O n February 3, 1909, Jewell Legett was having a bad day at the Training School, as she recorded in her diary:

> The cook left suddenly today; the gas bill came in much larger than it ought to be; the house committee came and reported the rooms to poor, sick Miss Brown as something aw-ful—every one of them nearly; Miss Wise and I like never to have gotten supper ready, even with Sandlins and Miss Moseby's aid; and I can't decide whether to move into Corbitt's room or not; and Mr. Cornelius is sick; and I can't get all the N.T. lesson, and I think "I'll go off in the garden and eat worms."[1]

Legett entered the Woman's Missionary Union Training School in the fall of 1908 to prepare for service as a foreign missionary. A few months later, perhaps when she was having a better day, Jewell noted that the "beautiful home-school had done wonders" for her as she had learned about prayer and Christian fellowship. In addition, the school experience had made her "willing, even glad, to take up her life work. . . ."[2]

The Woman's Missionary Union Training School for Christian Workers was established in 1907 "to train women for efficient service in foreign, home, and city missions and as church and Sunday School workers." The school provided courses in missionary methods, social work, fine arts, and domestic science. Students also completed theological studies in the neighboring classrooms of the Southern

---

[1]Jewell Legett, Personal Diary, February 3, 1909, in Woman's Missionary Union Archives, Birmingham, Alabama.

[2]*Foreign Mission Journal* 60 (August 1909): 41.

Baptist Theological Seminary, founded in 1857 to educate male ministers. The controversy of the ideological struggles of turn-of-the-century Southern Baptists concerning the place of women in Southern Baptist life surrounds the formation of this women's school and the entry of women into theological education. The Training School provided both formal course work and a home life designed to socialize women students into roles considered by Southern Baptists to be appropriate for their gender. As the school attempted to evangelize women and children on the mission field and in the United States, graduates of the Training School passed on the values and attitudes concerning women's proper sphere of Christian service.

Historian Gregory Vickers noted that while most late-nineteenth and early-twentieth century Southern Baptists considered women's primary roles to be domestic, Southern Baptist women enlarged their domestic sphere to include themselves as homemakers for all of society. "Mother and homemaker," wrote Vickers, "were made functions of the more inclusive worker and were redefined as world mother and community homemaker."[3] He further argued that this missionary endeavor was the leading force for women to develop alternatives to images Southern Baptist men used to limit women's sphere of activity to the home.[4]

The use of this broader domestic responsibility called women to serve in the entire world and was seen as the primary undercurrent of the education offered by the WMU Training School. The words from Jewell Legett's diary demonstrate how students' daily lives were centered on domestic concerns. For instance, each student shared in

---

[3]Gregory Vickers, "Models of Womanhood and the Early Woman's Missionary Union," *Baptist History and Heritage* 24 (January 1989): 52. Many nineteenth century leaders of the women's movement, most notably Frances Willard of the Woman's Christian Temperance Movement, argued for an enlargement of women's sphere on the idea that "the world is our home." See Ruth Bordin, *Woman and Temperance: the Quest for Power and Liberty*, 1873-1900 (Philadelphia: Temple University Press, 1981).

[4]Ibid., 41, 52. See also, Barbara Epstein, *The Politics of Domesticity*, (Middletown: Wesleyan University Press, 1981); Lori Ginzberg, *Women and the Work of Benevolence: Morality, Politics, and Class in the Nineteenth Century United States*, (New Haven: Yale University Press, 1990).

the responsibilities of home life. The school's formal curriculum trained Christian women for the spiritual, physical, and educational nurturing of other women and children around the globe. In this way, the curriculum prepared a woman student for her future vocation as homemaker and church worker.

As Vickers points out, the missionary concern of WMU women was the force that prompted the women to quietly challenge their limited roles in Southern Baptist life. By both preserving and molding WMU culture, the WMU Training School participated in opening doors for Southern Baptist women. Driven by their desire to go overseas as missionaries, the first Training School students entered the male Seminary classroom in search of a quality theological education never before offered to Southern Baptist women.

Women students of the WMU Training School had much in common with other pioneering college women. In her historical overview of higher education for women, Barbara Miller Solomon writes: "Educated women may not have been consciously trying to redefine womanhood; yet all along their actions did extend its definitions."[5] The women of the Training School lived in a world where definitions of womanhood were influenced by their identities as southerners and as evangelical Christians. At a time when Americans were struggling with questions concerning "woman's proper sphere," the students and faculty of the Training School negotiated their roles as women within the traditionally masculine domains of theological education and church-related vocations. At times Training School women attempted to change the practices that limited their sphere of service, but often the women insisted upon preserving customs that were accepted by the larger denomination of Southern Baptists. An overview of issues facing American women in the nineteenth and early twentieth centuries will provide a context for the Training School story.

---

[5]Barbara Miller Solomon, In the Company of Educated Women: A History of Women and Higher Education in America (New Haven: Yale University Press, 1985)xix.

"The Woman Question"

At the turn of the twentieth century, when women knocked at the doors of the Seminary, the entire nation was struggling with "the woman question." Traditional roles for women were challenged by women's involvement in reform efforts of the Progressive Era. The roots of this woman's movement reached back into the 1700s, but the movement had gained a great deal of momentum in the late nineteenth century as women began to find meaningful involvement outside the home through women's clubs, mission societies, philanthropic organizations, political involvement, and higher education. Linda Kerber calls the period between 1870 and 1920 the "high-water mark" of women's public influence.[6] This movement climaxed in 1920 with the ratification of the Nineteenth Amendment, which allowed women to vote.

While women across the nation were affected by these changes, the experiences of African-American, poor, and southern women differed from those of northern white women, upon which most accounts of the movement are based. Few scholars have given these groups of women serious treatment. Their stories are typically found in separate works and are rarely if ever integrated into accounts of the women's movement as a whole. While Southern Baptist women are the focus of this study, a brief sketch of the women's movement across the nation will provide a context for the main discussion.

While the women's movement of the late-nineteenth and early-twentieth centuries may have climaxed with the suffrage victory, the original goals of the movement were much broader than women's desire for the vote. The early feminists of 1848 who passed the Declaration of Sentiments and Resolutions at Seneca Falls, New York called for the elimination of divisions that separated the activities of men and women. Their demands included the "overthrow of the monopoly of the pulpit," and equal opportunities in education and the

---

[6]Linda Kerber, "Separate Spheres, Female Worlds, Woman's Place: The Rhetoric of Women's History," *Journal of American History* 75 (1988): 27.

professions. Claiming that God created men and women as equals, these feminists demanded an end to the treatment of one sex as different from and inferior to the other.[7]

In the 1890s, Elizabeth Cady Stanton organized an effort challenging the theological premise that women were inferior to men by writing a *Woman's Bible*. Stanton's vision was "to make woman a self-supporting equal partner with man in the state, the church and the home."[8] At the turn of the twentieth century, Charlotte Perkins Gilman articulated what William H. Chafe calls the "full elaboration of the feminist impulse." While creating a plan to carry out the goals of Seneca Falls, Gilman suggested ways women could gain economic equality with men. Gilman further believed that economic equality was needed for women to be free. She recommended the organization of community kitchens, child-care facilities, and housekeepers to free women from domestic responsibilities and allowing entrance into the workplace.[9]

Radical thinkers like Stanton and Gilman were part of an "isolated fringe group," according to Chafe. The changes they proposed had little chance of being accepted by a society that revered the institutions these women criticized: family, marriage, and the church. Furthermore, by challenging the idea of separate spheres of appropriate activity for men and women, early feminists alienated the mainstream of American society and encountered hostility from many corners.[10] As Chafe points out, social movements typically attract individuals with contrasting points of view: those who insist on radical reform and those who are willing to compromise to bring about change. The early women's movement was no exception. After the Civil War, feminists divided themselves into two groups: the more conservative American Woman's Suffrage Association that limited its goals to winning the ballot, and the more liberal National Woman's

---

[7]William H. Chafe, *The American Woman: Her Changing Social, Economic, and Political Role, 1920-1970* (New York: Oxford University Press, 1972) 5-6.

[8]Ibid., 7.

[9]Ibid., 7-9.

[10]Ibid., 10.

Suffrage Association that aimed at broader institutional reform. The continued hostility toward the more radical feminist demands caused the more liberal position became untenable. In 1890, the two groups reunited as the National American Woman's Suffrage Association (NAWSA) focusing on "the most respectable and limited feminist demand": winning the suffrage.[11]

As the twentieth century arrived, the emphasis on special roles for females continued. Women in higher education heard rhetoric in accord with Dean Briggs who claimed in an address to Smith College alumnae that women's colleges existed "not for the competition of women with men, but for the ennobling of women as women. . . . If women's colleges . . . teach women to compete with men, they will fall—or what is worse, they will make women ignoble."[12]

In spite of their limited choices in higher education, women managed to make progress toward changing the attitudes of the public. Educator Sally Schwager argues that although women's education was conservative in its preservation of domestic and subservient roles for women, it nevertheless provided women with the knowledge and attitudes they needed to bring about change toward nontraditional values.[13]

African-American Women

While white women were writing the "Declaration of Sentiments" demanding equal rights, many black women were still slaves. For African-American women, battles for property rights, education, and suffrage were only part of a complex struggle against oppression based on race, class, and gender. In her book, *Righteous Discontent*, Evelyn Brooks Higginbotham notes that black women made great strides in the years between 1890 and 1920. As the nineteenth century was

---

[11]Ibid., 12.

[12]Shelia Rothman, *Woman's Proper Place: A History of Changing Ideals and Practices, 1870 to the Present* (New York: Basic Books, 1978) 40.

[13]Sally Schwager, "Educating Women in America," *Signs: Journal of Women and Culture in Society* 12 (1987): 332-334.

coming to a close, black educator Anna J. Cooper had published her feminist critique; A *Voice From the South* and Ida B. Wells completed *On Lynchings*.[14] The National Association of Colored Women had been organized. Periodicals such as *The Woman's Era*, published in Boston, facilitated communications.[15] Yet during this same period despite all the steps forward, the heightened racism that followed Reconstruction brought about an all-time low in American race relations.[16] Higginbotham notes, "the cynical era of Jim Crow and the optimistic woman's era stood entangled one with the other."[17]

One of the most pressing issues for black women was lynching. Not only were black men lynched, but also studies conducted in the 1920s revealed that eighty-three women had been lynched since 1892. In 1895 Ida B. Wells began an antilynching movement that was continued in the 1920s by leaders like Mary B. Talbert. Southern white women, appalled that lynchings were often rationalized as a means of protection, cooperated with black women in antilynching campaigns during the Progressive Era.[18]

African-American women were also concerned about education. The obstacles they confronted were great. As Eleanor Flexner points out, white society had set the pattern of valuing the education of men and boys above that of women. Although schools for African-American children included both boys and girls, boys were in the majority and typically stayed in school longer than girls. In 1851, Myrtilla Miner opened the first school to train African-American girls as teachers in Washington, DC. Miner was a white woman educated at a Quaker women's seminary at Rochester. By 1857, Miner had

---

[14]Evelyn Brooks Higginbotham, *Righteous Discontent: The Woman's Movement in the Black Baptist Church, 1880-1920* (Cambridge, MA: Harvard University Press, 1993) 13.

[15]Eleanor Flexner, *Century of Struggle: The Woman's Rights Movement in the United States* (New York: Atheneum, 1972) 118-19.

[16]Higginbotham, *Righteous Discontent*, 4.

[17]Ibid., 14.

[18]Glenda Riley, *Inventing the American Woman: A perspective on Women's History, 1607 to the Present,*. 2 Vols (Arlington Heights, IL: Harlan Davidson, Inc., 1986)vol 2: 198-199.

created a school that supported three departments: primary teaching, domestic economy, and teacher training.[19]

In the years following the Civil War, many colleges for African-American men became coeducational. For example, Shaw University in North Carolina began admitting women in 1872. With the cooperation of Baptist white women of the North, Atlanta Baptist Female Seminary (later renamed Spelman) opened in the basement of a church to provide education for black women of the South.[20] In spite of these opportunities, only thirty African-American women had received college degrees by 1890. Anna Cooper blamed the men of her race who "do not yet think it worthwhile that women aspire to higher education . . . . Let money be raised and scholarships be founded in our colleges and universities for self-supporting, worthy young women."[21]

African-American women were interested in many of the same causes as white women: temperance, education, and social reform. However, black women formed separate clubs and organizations, partly because they were excluded from white women's groups. For example, the Woman's Christian Temperance Union (WCTU) allowed African-American women to affiliate with the union but only within their own separate units.[22] In July 1895, Josephine St. Pierre Ruffin addressed a group of twenty club representatives in Boston, challenging the white women's organizations that excluded African-American women. She noted that the type of organization needed was "for the benefit of all humanity, which is more than any one branch or section of it . . . we are not drawing the color line; we are women, American women . . . cordially inviting and welcoming any others to join us."[23]

While most historians focus on the women's clubs as the African-American woman's avenue to activism, Higginbotham argues that the

---

[19]Flexner, *Century of Struggle*, 98-101.
[20]Higginbotham, *Righteous Discontent*, 21-22.
[21]Flexner, *Century of Struggle*, 128.
[22]Ibid., 192.
[23]Ibid., 190.

church provided the foundation that allowed women to enlarge their sphere of activity:

> The club movement among black women owed its very existence to the groundwork of organizational skill and leadership training gained through women's church societies. . . . More than mere precursors to secular reform and women's rights activism, black women's religious organizations undergirded and formed an identifiable part of what is erroneously assumed to be "secular."[24]

Higginbotham notes that black women supported women's suffrage, demanding not only the right to vote, but also full inclusion in public life. Typically, African-American women formed their own suffrage organizations such as the Tuskegee Woman's Club of Alabama and the Colored Woman's Suffrage Club of Los Angeles.[25] Often viewed as "a weapon to right racial wrongs," African-American women also saw the vote as a way to improve their condition as women.[26] Gertrude Rush, a black lawyer from Iowa, argued that the vote would empower women to improve their working conditions, wages, and business opportunities.[27]

Southern White Women

For nineteenth century white women of the South, there was no "blatant call to action," like the Declaration of Sentiments written at Seneca Falls. Southern women were different from their northern sisters and their "woman movement," as it was known in the South, took on a regional distinctiveness. In the North, notes Jean Friedman, modernization and urbanization had contributed to the development of an autonomous women's culture, which fostered a greater sense of

---

[24]Higginbotham, Righteous Discontent, 16.
[25]Riley, Inventing the American Woman, 157.
[26]Ibid., 12, 226.
[27]Ibid., 226.

self-worth and heightened militancy. However, in the "rural, kin-oriented, church-related" southern society, family loyalty, rather than an autonomous women's culture, remained a basis for women's self-identity.[28]

According to southern women's historian Anne F. Scott, the southern cultural patterns that reinforced gender roles "remained the most rigid in any part of the country."[29] Traditional institutions of chivalry and "the myth of the Southern Lady" reinforced legal and social discrimination of women. Scott describes the context as characterized by

> . . . a widespread legal and theoretical acceptance of the premise that woman was an inferior creature and a widespread expectation that she would perform as a superior one. The acceptable goals for southern women were to please their husbands and to please God, and to this end they were supposed to be beautiful, mildly literate, gracious, hardworking, and church-going.[30]

During the antebellum years the Southern Lady "became a distinct type among American women," and because of the Southern Lady myth, the struggle of the southern woman to free herself was more complex than for women of other regions.[31] These ideas were not peculiar to the American South; a similar myth is found in the image of the lady of Victorian England. However, the South held a firmer grip on the image, which has been slow to die. In fact, Scott maintains

---

[28]Jean Friedman, "Title," in *Sex, Race, and the Role of Women in the South,* edited by Joanne Hawks and Sheila Skemp, 3-13. (Jackson: University Press of Mississippi, 1983). Q-missing Reference info

[29]Anne F. Scott, *Making the Invisible Woman Visible* (Urbana and Chicago: University of Illinois Press, 1984) 220.

[30]Ibid., 212.

[31]Anne F. Scott, *The Southern Lady: From Pedestal to Politics, 1830-1930* (Chicago: University of Chicago Press, 1970), x-xi.

that the image of the Southern Lady has never completely disappeared.[32]

During the Civil War, southern white women found themselves with new responsibilities in both the private and public realm. The concept of separate spheres became more elastic during war years as women managed whole plantations and were cast into new leadership and decision-making roles in churches. During Reconstruction, a time when women outnumbered men, all hands were busy rebuilding the South and "the lady herself had not much time for acting her prescribed role."[33]

Through organizations such as Woman's Christian Temperance Union (WCTU) and church-affiliated mission societies, women learned to lead, make speeches, keep records, and organize. Scott asserts that women used such seemingly conservative organizations as "protective colorations" for their desires for independence, noting that husbands and fathers could hardly object because it seemed very respectable.[34] The WCTU was founded in 1874 and became the largest woman's organization in the nation during the 1890s. The organization did not become active in South until the 1880s when its leader Frances Willard began touring the region. The organization grew rapidly in the South, due to Willard's extraordinary personal appeal.[35] She used the rhetoric of what historian Barbara Welter has called "the Cult of True Womanhood" to convince women to become involved. Affirming the popular notion that woman's primary sphere was domestic, Willard used the watchwords *mother* and *home*. She assumed that women were pure and belonged "to the less tainted half of our race." At the same time, Willard encouraged women to expand their definitions of home to include the larger society. She called upon

---

[32]Scott, *Southern Lady*, 14-15; 221.

[33]Scott, *Invisible Woman*, 213; and Leon McBeth, *Women in Baptist Life* (Nashville, TN: Broadman Press, 1979) 63. See also Drew Gilpin Faust, *Mothers of Invention : Women of the Slaveholding South in the American Civil War* (Chapel Hill: University of North Carolina Press, 1966).

[34]Scott, *Invisible Woman*, 215.

[35]Flexner, *Century of Struggle*, 184; and Scott, *Invisible Woman*, 204

women to "make the whole world homelike," proclaiming that "mother-hearted women are called to be the saviors of the race."[36] A deeply religious woman herself, Willard appealed especially to churchwomen. Meetings of the WCTU were typically held in churches with hymns, Scripture readings, and prayer as a part of the program.

Anne Scott notes the irony that, although the WCTU was such a respectable organization in the eyes of southerners, "no group did more to subvert the traditional role of women, or to implant in its southern members a sort of unself-conscious radicalism which would have turned the southern male speechless if he had taken the trouble to listen to what the ladies were saying."[37] Through the WCTU, women expanded their involvement in other social issues such as prison reform, child labor regulation, and compulsory education. Eventually, they moved into the battle for suffrage, reasoning that women could bring about prohibition if they had the vote.

At the same time, a few white southern women were changing the way they viewed the world and emerging as leaders of the southern women's movement. Twenty-five-year-old Laura Clay was convinced that Christianity carried a message of emancipation for women. Her Protestant faith was her inspiration as she led the women of Kentucky to work for the right to vote. The sisters of the Clay family, Mary Barr Clay and Sallie Clay Bennet, along with their mother, Mary Jane Clay, constructed an effective woman suffrage network in Kentucky. Leaders of the women's movement in the South, like the Clay women, typically came from prominent families. Therefore they enjoyed the freedom of being somewhat radical with less risk. They were well-educated and had traveled outside the South, encountering women leaders from other parts of the country. Their contemporaries described these women as beautiful, charming, and intelligent,

---

[36]Scott, *Invisible Woman*, 204-205; See also, Barbara Welter, *Dimity Convictions; The American Woman in the Nineteenth Century* (Athens: Ohio University Press, 1976) 21-41.
[37]Scott, *Invisible Woman*, 215.

representing perfect southern lady behavior. These women were also deeply religious.[38]

Throughout the South many opposed or were indifferent to the women's suffrage issue. Kentucky's Henry Watterson, for example, warned that voting women would imperil the whole human species.[39] Tennessee, Arkansas, and Texas were the only three states of the former Confederacy to ratify the Nineteenth Amendment. Other states either rejected woman suffrage or failed to take action until forced to do so after the final ratification of the amendment in August 1920.[40] In addition to the anti-suffrage rhetoric heard across the nation, which claimed that suffrage was unwomanly, southern opponents posited an additional argument unique to their region. The main anti-suffrage argument presented in the South was based on the notion of white supremacy. Woman suffrage, opponents warned, would reopen the question of the Negro vote, which had effectively been denied through poll taxes, qualifying tests, and the white primary.[41] A large majority of southern Democrats moved to block the proposed Nineteenth Amendment down to the closing battle. Senator Ellison Smith of South Carolina chastised the few southerners that supported the amendment:

> I warn every man here today that when the test comes, as it will come, when the clamor for Negro rights shall have come, that you Senators from the South voting for it will have started it here this day.[42]

Scott notes that the dividing lines for and against woman suffrage were not those of gender. Men like Desha Breckinridge in Kentucky

---

[38]Claudia Knott, "The Woman Suffrage Movement in Kentucky, 1879-1920" (Ph.D. diss., University of Kentucky, 1989) 42-43; Scott, *Invisible Woman*, 214.

[39]Scott, *Invisible Woman*, 213.

[40]Ibid., 220

[41]Flexner, 295; Catherine Allen, *The New Lottie Moon* Story (Nashville: Broadman Press, 1980) 236-237.

[42]Flexner, *Century of Struggle*, 303.

and Luke Lea in Tennessee supported women's rights, while many southern women feared change, believing that emancipation of women threatened the stability of the home. Other women were silent, perhaps privately sympathetic with the cause but not willing to do battle with public opinion or to suffer ridicule.[43]

In 1919, seventy years after Seneca Falls, Congress finally initiated the Nineteenth Amendment to the constitution allowing women to vote. Next, ratification by three-fourths (thirty-six) of the states was required. Eleven states ratified within the first month and others followed. By August of 1920, thirty-five states had ratified the amendment when the Tennessee legislature called a special session leading to the ratification necessary to win the final victory.[44]

The myth of the Southern Lady was held up as an ideal for women of prominent families as well as the poor and working class. In spite of this, white women of the South made slow progress toward expanding definitions of appropriate spheres of activity. Scott cautions us not to view southern women as a monolith, since a great deal of variety existed among them:

> We have realized that there is no such thing as "the southern woman," for she came in many varieties of class, race, and ability. The reality, we have discovered, is neither so simple nor so glamorous as the myth. People have a disconcerting ability not to fit into the historian's categories, much less to fit the legends their descendants like to relate. The reality, when it finally emerges, is no less interesting and far more helpful in understanding ourselves, than all the myths and fictions ever were.[45]

---

[43]Scott, *Invisible Woman*, 219.

[44]Anne F. Scott and Andrew M. Scott, "One Half the People: the Fight for Woman Suffrage" in *Women's America: Refocusing the Past*. 2nd ed. Edited by Kerber and Matthews, 307-308 (New York: Oxford University Press, 1987).

[45]Scott, *Invisible Woman*, 110.

Gaining Access to Theological Education

The struggle of Southern Baptist women to gain access to theological education begins before 1900 and is still being fought. This study, however, is limited to the Training School's formative years of 1907 through 1926. In 1900, missionary E. Z. Simmons launched a campaign to convince Southern Baptists that women missionaries needed theological studies in order to serve on the foreign field. The Training School grew out of this need and thrived in a coordinate arrangement with the Southern Baptist Theological Seminary. Women attended classes with the male students until 1926, when the Seminary moved to a suburban location, leaving the Training School in downtown Louisville.

The principle sources that informed this discussion were minutes and reports of the school's board of managers and of the annual meetings of Woman's Missionary Union. Diaries and letters of Training School students and faculty were very useful as well as scrapbooks assembled by individual students and the school's supporters. *The Baptist World, the Foreign Mission Journal, Royal Service* and a variety of state Baptist newspapers were also key resources. While there are many groups of Baptists in the South, the term "Southern Baptist" is used here to describe persons associated with the denomination that calls itself the Southern Baptist Convention (SBC).

The story of the Training School is set at the turn of the twentieth century. Yet at the beginning of the twenty-first century, many Southern Baptist women still find themselves severely limited by a denominational culture that does not recognize their ability for and calling to types of ministry that lie outside rigidly defined definitions of woman's place of service in the church. The fear of today is the same as it was in 1907 when the Training School was formed: that women will preach and serve as leaders of men. Many women inclined toward the ministry are baffled that even in the twenty-first century, Southern Baptists open their seminary classrooms to women, yet do not encourage the denomination's sisters to enter all forms of

Christian ministry. While women of other denominations have been able to move into these areas of service, Southern Baptist women continue to find change very slow in their denomination. Perhaps this narrative will provide historical perspective into why this remains so even today.

1

ORGANIZING FOR SERVICE
Southern Baptist Women
and the Woman's Missionary Union

Controversies surrounding the formation of the Woman's Missionary Union Training School at the turn of the twentieth century illustrated the complexity of an ongoing debate among Baptists: the place of women in church life. Concerns about appropriate roles of women in Baptist churches have existed since the denomination's seventeenth century beginnings. A brief historical sketch of Baptist beliefs and practices concerning the role of women will provide a context for the story of the Woman's Missionary Union and its Training School.

Baptists in England

Baptists emerged in seventeenth century England amid the various dissenting movements preaching the purification of the church and the return to a New Testament Christian model. One group of English Baptists believed in the doctrine of the general atonement of Christ who died for all. Known as General Baptists, this group formed the first Baptist church in England around 1611 or 1612 at Spitalfield, near London. They numbered about forty churches by 1644. Particular Baptists, who organized their first church about 1638, were more strictly Calvinist in theology, believing that Christ's death allowed for a limited or particular atonement available only for the elect.[1]

A common link between these differing groups was the insistence on religious liberty for each individual, claiming the freedom of each person to approach God without interference from secular authority. Individuals, however, were not without accountability to a congregation; yet unlike other groups, church discipline came from within the congregation, rather than from outside authorities. Baptist historian Robert Torbet noted that early Baptists emerged from a Free Church tradition, viewing the church as "a gathered fellowship of believers bound together in a covenantal relationship to God to witness fearlessly to their faith wherever they might be."[2] Baptists rejected infant baptism and, by the time they published their 1644 London Confession, they had identified immersion as the appropriate mode of believers' baptism. [3]

Baptist historian Leon McBeth has demonstrated that women played a very active role in English Baptist churches, serving as deacons and sometimes as preachers. They contributed to the business of the church, giving money, voting, testifying of their Christian experience, and disciplining church members. The public role of Baptist women in England, however, declined over the years. Although quite active in the seventeenth and eighteenth centuries, women of the mid-nineteenth century found churches questioning their right to vote or speak out on church matters.[4]

The middle of the seventeenth century found English Baptists migrating to America in search of religious freedom. In spite of these hardships, Baptists organized churches in New England and eventually migrated to other colonies. Separating from their Puritan neighbors, Baptists were persecuted, as they were in England, for their

---

[1]Robert Baker, *The Southern Baptist Convention and Its People: 1607-1972* (Nashville: Broadman Press, 1974) 18-19; and Leon McBeth, *The Baptist Heritage*, (Nashville: Broadman Press, 1987) 39-42.

[2]Robert Torbet, *A History of the Baptists* (Valley Forge: Judson Press, 1950), 30.

[3]Ibid, 33-43.

[4]Leon McBeth, *Women in Baptist Life* (Nashville: Broadman Press, 1979) 36-37.

beliefs about baptism and their refusal to support the established churches in the colonies. The Calvinist Particular Baptist tradition soon predominated in the American colonies.[5]

Baptists in the American South

Baptists from New England migrated to the southern colonies. In 1696, the First Baptist Church of Charleston was established in the Carolina colony by a group of Baptists moving from Kittery, Maine. This was the first Baptist church organized in the South and was soon followed by others in the Carolinas and Virginia.[6] The Charleston church followed the tradition of the Regular Baptists, emphasizing a concern for theological, ecclesiastical, and liturgical order.[7]

A second group to migrate south was the Separate Baptists, emerging in the mid-eighteenth century from Separate Congregationalism. In response to the First Great Awakening, the Separate Baptists left New England to spread Christianity across the American frontier. One group of sixteen people, led by Shubal Stearns and Daniel Marshall, headed south in 1754, later establishing the Sandy Creek Baptist Church in Sandy Creek, North Carolina.[8] Unlike Regular Baptists, this group was uneducated and had an aversion to education, especially theological training, stemming from the belief that such reflection might lead to spiritual pride.[9] McBeth notes that the lack of formal schooling among ministers and laity may have been an

---

[5]McBeth, *The Baptist Heritage*, 143-170; and Nancy Tatom Ammerman, *Baptist Battles: Social Change and Religious Conflict in the Southern Baptist Convention* (New Brunswick, NJ: Rutgers University Press, 1990) 23.

[6]Robert Baker, *SBC and Its People*, 32-35.

[7]Bill J. Leonard, *God's Last and Only Hope: The Fragmentation of the Southern Baptist Convention* (Grand Rapids, MI: Eerdman's Publishing, 1990) 32.

[8]Robert Baker, *SBC and Its People*, 47-49.

[9]William Mueller, *A History of Southern Baptist Theological Seminary* (Nashville: Broadman Press, 1959) 5.

advantage, allowing them to identify immediately with the common folk who were their converts.[10]

In contrast to the more orderly Regular Baptists, the Separate Baptists had a worship style that "tended toward spontaneity, enthusiasm, and emotional outburst, and they often experienced dramatic conversion and expressed it with shouts, tears, groans, and spirited singing."[11] The evangelistic impact of this small group of Separate Baptists in Sandy Creek was remarkable, spawning forty-two area churches and nurturing 125 ministers within seventeen years. While Regular Baptists were located mainly in the cities and along the tidewater areas of Virginia and the Carolinas, Separate Baptists were scattered throughout the rural areas of the same colonies, and also moved west into Tennessee, Kentucky, Arkansas, Louisiana and Texas.[12]

Disagreeing on a number of theological issues, Regular and Separate Baptists also differed over the practical matter of women's roles in the church.[13] Separate Baptists drew from the traditions of early English Baptists, allowing women to speak and vote in congregational meetings. They also ordained both men and women as deacons and preachers. Margaret Clay of Virginia was an eighteenth century preacher of the Separate Baptist tradition. She first became known as a woman of public prayer, and her home was a center for Baptist preachers. Arrested in Virginia for unlicensed preaching, she was sentenced to a severe public whipping. A supporter paid the fine, however, and spared her the beating.[14]

Regular Baptists, on the other hand, began early to disapprove of women speaking and voting in church, and by the mid-eighteenth century, the number of women serving as deacons and elders was

---

[10]Leon McBeth, "Southern Baptist Higher Education" in *The Lord's Free People in a Free Land: Essays in Baptist History in Honor of Robert A. Baker*, edited by William R. Estep, 117 (Fort Worth: Southwestern Baptist Theological Seminary, 1976).

[11]Leonard, *God's Hope*, 33.

[12]Robert Baker, *SBC and Its People*, 49-56; McBeth, *Women in Baptist Life*, 45.; and Leonard, *God's Hope*, 33.

[13]McBeth, *Women in Baptist Life*, 45.

[14]Ibid., 44.

declining. There was a range of practice among Regular Baptists. Some churches that banned women from preaching and teaching did allow them to vote; other churches banned women from voting as well.[15]

Unification, Expansion and Organization

Although there was early distrust and even open antagonism between Separate and Regular Baptists, the two groups united in the late eighteenth century in order to fight for religious liberty. In Virginia and North Carolina, Baptists published formal statements of union, while in other states they gradually eliminated their distinctions without taking formal actions.[16] Baptists supported the Revolutionary War at least in part because they saw it as a necessary step toward religious liberty. With the birth of the new nation came the Constitution and Bill of Rights, which guaranteed religious freedom. Although Baptists had been scorned and vilified in the pre-Revolutionary period, their rapid growth, their support of the patriot cause, and their leadership in securing religious liberty improved their status among other religious groups.[17] The adjectives Regular and Separate were eventually dropped and Baptists entered the nineteenth century strengthened and unified, although the unification of these regional groups did not obliterate their theological and liturgical differences.[18] Certain traits of each group survived among the united body. The Regulars' concept of doctrine and ministry survived along with the fervent evangelism and informal services of the Separate tradition. The Separate tradition of leadership roles for women, however, disappeared with the merger of the two groups. After about 1800,

---

[15]Sarah Frances Anders, "Tracing Past and Present," in *The New Has Come: Emerging Roles Among Southern Baptist Women*, edited by Anne T. Neil and Virginia G. Neely, 11-12 (Washington D.C.: Southern Baptist Alliance, 1989).

[16]Robert Baker, *SBC and Its People*, 56.

[17]Ibid., 102.

[18]Ammerman, *Baptist* Battles, 24, 342, n.20.

Baptist women preachers are unheard of in the South, although a few churches continued to ordain deaconesses.[19]

Baptists turned to the task of missionary expansion, both on the American frontier and overseas. The entire nation was caught up in a wave of missionary zeal, and Baptists were at the forefront. William Carey, an English Baptist who sailed for India in 1792, launched the foreign missionary movement. The Baptists organized mission societies to support Carey and the other missionaries who followed him. One of the first of these societies was the Boston Female Society for Missionary Purposes begun by Mary Webb.[20] These early mission societies provided opportunities for women to learn organizational and leadership skills within their own groups.

Baptists Organize

Although many early mission societies were composed of women, there were also societies organized for men only and for mixed groups. Sociologist Nancy Ammerman has noted the importance of these early mission societies in fostering a new form of organization: "By adopting a cause bigger than any one locale, Baptists in America began to develop organizational structures that would soon transform them into a denomination."[21] The first national organization of Baptists in America was formed in order to provide support for three missionaries: Adoniram Judson, Anne Hasseltine Judson, and Luther Rice. These three left Massachusetts in 1812 to serve as missionaries in India. They had been commissioned by Congregationalists but during the voyage were converted to Baptist beliefs. When they arrived in India they were promptly baptized by immersion and sent their resignations to the Congregational mission board. [22]

Rice returned to the United States and traveled across the nation seeking support for Baptist mission work in India. In response to his

---

[19]McBeth, *Women in Baptist Life*, 46.
[20]McBeth, *The Baptist Heritage*, 183-187, Ammerman, *Baptist Battles*, 26.
[21]Ammerman, *Baptist Battles*, 26.
[22]McBeth, *The Baptist Heritage*, 345.

plea, thirty-three Baptist men convened in Philadelphia in May 1814 to form the General Missionary Convention of the Baptist Denomination in the United States for Foreign Missions. Planning to meet every three years, the group became more commonly known as the Triennial Convention. Electing a southerner, Richard Furman, as president of the newly formed body, they also appointed the Judsons and Rice as their own missionaries. Made up of delegates from mission societies, churches, and other groups, the Triennial Convention was for men only. Thus women's mission societies, comprising over half of the 200 existing Baptist mission groups, sent male representatives.[23]

Early Baptists and Higher Education

In addition to raising money to support missions, Luther Rice also invested energy into providing higher education to Baptists. He viewed this as a prerequisite rather than as a rival to missions. Rice saw a need for colleges to train missionary appointees, pastors, and laymen in order to improve leadership in the churches. However, not all Baptists shared his vision. Albea Godbold noted among Baptists "a pronounced prejudice against education," especially theological education.[24] Many associated education with the persecution that had been suffered at the hands of well-educated clergy in England and Colonial America. Baptists of the frontier feared that education would lead to spiritual pride or world damage faith.[25] McBeth noted, however, that this anti-education sentiment began to moderate during the nineteenth century, and enthusiasm for missions, both domestic and foreign, spurred the creation of Baptist colleges as a means of furthering the missions cause. John Mason Peck, who went to St. Louis in 1817 as a frontier missionary under the Triennial Convention, articulated the need for educated ministers in the west:

---

[23]McBeth, *The Baptist Heritage*, 344; Ammerman, *Baptist Battles*, 27. See also, McBeth, *Women in Baptist Life*, 81.

[24]Albea Godbold, *The Church College of the Old South* (Durham: Duke University Press, 1944), quoted in Leon McBeth, "Southern Baptist Higher Education," 116-117.

[25]Mueller, *History of Southern Seminary*, 4-5.

"I cannot bear that our preachers . . . should continue as ignorant as some of them are now."[26]

Evangelism in the South

Although overseas missions occupied a great deal of attention and effort from Baptists, evangelism at home was not ignored. In the North, the Second Great Awakening added many new converts to the ranks of Baptists as well as other denominations. In the South, revival of a different sort swept the region. Southern groups held "camp meetings" to which great crowds of people would come to hear preaching. Camp meetings were characterized by "excessive emotional display including the jerks, the barks, dancing, rolling, shouting, fainting, and similar exercises."[27]

This method of evangelism began in Kentucky with the Presbyterians and was soon adopted by Methodists and Baptists. Southern Baptist historian Robert Baker notes that the climax of these meetings came in August 1801 at Cane Ridge, Kentucky, when the crowd numbered between twenty and thirty thousand.[28] Ammerman suggests that these gatherings, often called "protracted meetings," were a form of organized religion naturally suitable to the scattered population on the frontier. Protracted meetings served a social function, providing an opportunity for association in a land where the nearest neighbor might be miles away.[29]

As a result of these evangelistic efforts, the number of Baptist churches grew rapidly and membership grew at a rate of three times the population. Along with the Baptists, Methodists and Presbyterians also experienced remarkable growth and eventually established in the South an evangelical ethos centering on evangelical conversion and pious living. Ammerman argues that what emerged was "more a religious culture than a religious community, an ethos more than an

---

[26]McBeth, "Southern Baptist Higher Education," 116.
[27]Robert Baker, *SBC and Its People*, 94.
[28]Ibid.
[29]Ammerman, *Baptist Battles*, 28.

institutional structure." From this religious culture emerged "a growing Southern regional consciousness. With evangelicalism at the center of the culture, Baptists in the South began to proclaim theirs as the best possible way for a Christian to live, a model for humanity."[30]

Conflict and Division

As Baptists in the North became involved in the national movement to abolish slavery, Baptists in the South worked to defend the institution of slavery. Each side used Scripture and Baptist doctrine to defend its position. According to Torbet, as abolitionist developments emerged among Northern Baptists, Baptist leaders tried to avoid conflict through the 1820s and '30s by promoting a policy of moderation. The issue was successfully suppressed until the American Baptist Anti-Slavery Convention met in New York City in April 1840, deciding to take a clear abolitionist stance. As a result, a strong segment of Baptists in the North began efforts to take over the Foreign Mission Board and prevent the appointment of slave owners as missionaries. Eventually they prevailed and announced in 1844 that slaveholders would no longer be appointed.[31]

The Alabama state convention addressed a resolution to the Convention in November 1844, demanding that slaveholders enjoy the same privileges as non-slaveholders, especially with reference to the appointment of missionaries. The reply came back from the board in December that if anyone having slaves should seek appointment as a missionary "and should insist on retaining them as his property, we could not appoint him. One thing is certain: we can never be a party to any arrangement which would imply approbation of slavery."[32] The Virginia Foreign Mission Society called for a meeting in May for Baptists of the South to decide a course of action.[33]

---

[30]Ibid., 30-31.
[31]Torbet, A *History of Baptists*, 282-291.
[32]Ibid., 291.
[33]Ibid., 293.

On May 8, 1845, the suggested meeting convened in Augusta, Georgia. Three hundred and twenty-seven male delegates, primarily from Georgia, South Carolina, and Virginia, gathered to organize the Southern Baptist Convention (SBC). They created two mission boards (foreign and domestic) and convinced a few existing missionaries to work for the new denomination.[34]

The new body inherited an ecclesiastical pyramid, based on four levels of organization, which had been developing since 1707. At the base was the *local church*; churches within the geographical area of a county or two formed an *association*. Baptists within state organized state conventions, while the *Southern Baptist Convention*, at the apex, coordinated southwide denominational efforts. The organizational structure, however, was non-hierarchical, leaving individuals and local congregations with a great deal of autonomy in matters of doctrine and practice.

By the late-nineteenth century, white Southern Baptists had left behind earlier Baptist dissenter status and had become the mainstream of southern society. Like other southerners, the majority of Southern Baptists lived in rural areas and was "of humble birth and modest means." By 1900 they composed the largest white denomination in the South.[35]

The Southern Baptists

The formation of the SBC illustrates several points regarding the denominational culture that congealed among Southern Baptists. First, women held church leadership roles among early Baptists of the Separate tradition. Women were allowed to speak and vote in church

---

[34]McBeth *The Baptist Heritage*, 388-391. See also, Rufus B. Spain, *At Ease in Zion: Social History of Southern Baptists, 1865-1900* (Nashville: Vanderbilt University Press, 1967) 6-7. Torbet, *A History of Baptists*, 293. Torbet reports 328, rather than 327 delegates whereas McBeth notes that an actual number of only 293 men were present, as some were representing more than one congregation or society, and therefore were counted more than once.

[35]Spain, *At Ease in Zion*, 10, x.

meetings and were ordained as both deacons and preachers. However, as earlier divisions between Separate and Regular traditions were erased, Baptists followed the Regular tradition of male dominance.[36] As the two groups united, the role of women became a very real problem. The desire for unity, however, was stronger than these tensions and the traditions of Separate Baptists who allowed a larger role for women did not last in the new group.[37]

Second, Baptists are historically a very diverse group of people due to a strong insistence on the accountability of each individual before God (soul competency) and the autonomy of the local congregation. Churches have therefore followed a variety of practices regarding the participation of women. In spite of great diversity, Baptists have found a surprising amount of unity in response to the missionary imperative. Southern Baptist historian Walter Shurden asserts that the missionary cause, rather than doctrinal unity, held the SBC together. Bill J. Leonard expands upon Shurden's thesis, noting that in order to unite as many Southern Baptists as possible in fulfilling the mission task, the SBC operated under a "Grand Compromise" in which doctrinal positions remained general enough to include many diverse traditions. This compromise contained the seeds of controversy, which have emerged whenever those who adhere to a particular theological viewpoint attempt to impose their views on all Southern Baptists.[38] With such diversity within the denomination, local churches have historically followed a variety of practices regarding the participation of women. Controversy emerged as congregations criticized one another's practices.

Third, the story of the SBC reveals the intense regionalism felt by members of the newly formed denomination. Leonard asserts that this regionalism was far more important than the missionary cause in uniting Southern Baptists. The missions cause was not a new one for

---

[36]Sarah Frances Anders, "Woman's Role in the Southern Baptist Convention and Its Churches as Compared With Selected Other Denominations" *Review and Expositor* (Winter, 1975) 11-12.

[37]McBeth, *Women in Baptist Life*, 44-46.

[38]Leonard, *God's Hope*, 37-39.

the emerging denomination; Baptists of the South had been united with their northern counterparts in mission activity since the formation of the Triennial Convention in 1814. According to Leonard, what united Southern Baptists was "a common rejection of earlier ecclesiastical alignments."

> To remain in union with the Triennial Convention meant that Baptists in the South could no longer be appropriately southern. This they would not do. Their unity around certain sectional issues—particularly slavery—was the basis for their break from the North and their decision to form a new denomination. The SBC was therefore southern before it was missionary.[39]

The myths that helped form southern self-identity were many: genteel society of educated persons, a sense of neighborliness, the relationship between the sexes, and the myth of white supremacy.[40] Each of these myths influenced the people involved in working out appropriate roles for Southern Baptist women. But perhaps the notion most integral to the role of women in the denomination is what Anne Firor Scott calls "the myth of the Southern Lady." Emerging in the nineteenth century as a distinct American type, the image was reinforced by evangelical theology. It required that women be submissive to God, submissive to their husbands, and dependent on male protection.[41]

As Southern Baptists rejected former northern alliances, they expressed intense regionalism in formulating an understanding of women's roles in the denomination. Southern Baptist author Catherine Allen identifies this regionalism as the main cause of early opposition to a missionary organization for Southern Baptist women: "The woman's rights movement arose in the North; it was rejected.

---

[39]Ibid., 18.

[40]Ibid., 13.

[41]Anne Firor Scott, *The Southern Lady: From Pedestal to Politics, 1830-1930* (Chicago: University of Chicago Press, 1970) xi, 5, 10.

Woman suffrage arose in the North; it was spurned. The first women public lecturers were Northerners; they were ridiculed."[42] Southern Baptists were tightly intertwined with southern culture.

Fourth, the missionary imperative has always been vitally important to Southern Baptists. When women first attempted to enter denominational life, they did so in the missions arena, arguing that women could make a great contribution to the missions cause by evangelizing other women and raising funds for missionaries. Nineteenth century women who wanted more opportunity to participate in Southern Baptist life did not put forth the arguments heard today, those of equality of persons or the dissolution of separate roles for men and women. Rather, they insisted that they would do women's work to further the Southern Baptist goal of evangelizing the world. After much controversy, the claim that they could aid the missions cause earned women a place among Southern Baptists through their own organization, the Woman's Missionary Union.

Finally, by the nineteenth century, Southern Baptists had begun to value formal education, particularly for their ministers. Their anti-education sentiments passing away, Southern Baptists through their state conventions were establishing colleges. Before the SBC was formed, Baptists in the South had already seen a need for a central institution to educate preachers.

The Southern Baptist Theological Seminary

The need for a seminary to train ministers was evident long before the creation of the Southern Baptist Convention in 1845. As early as 1788, Virginia Baptists formed a committee of ten persons "to forward the business respecting a seminary of learning."[43] The first half of the nineteenth century saw the creation of numerous Baptist colleges across the South to provide educational opportunities for young male

---

[42]Catherine Allen, A Century to Celebrate: History of Woman's Missionary Union (Birmingham: Woman's Missionary Union, 1987) 31.
[43]Mueller, A History, 5.

ministers. In 1825, South Carolina Baptists founded the Furman Academy and Theological Institute.[44] In Georgia, Baptists supported the Mercer Institute but also participated with South Carolinians in an effort to establish a southwide seminary. The proposed seminary would have support beyond the individual states, as noted in the 1837 report to the South Carolina Convention:

> The Seminaries are not *State* but *Southern* Seminaries, and this fact being affectionately and *publicly* recognized by their respective officers, will induce a similar recognition on the part of the friends of the Institutions in the different States which may be interested in their success.[45]

The need for a southwide seminary became more urgent with the denominational split between Baptists of North and South. With the creation of the Southern Baptist Convention in May 1845, Baptist preachers in the South no longer traveled to the North for ministerial education. However, not all Baptists supported the trend toward education for Baptist ministers in either colleges or seminaries. The anti-education sentiment found among Baptists of an earlier time persisted in some quarters. The Towaliga Baptist Association of Georgia articulated this suspicion of seminary education in 1838:

> We believe that Theological Seminaries are calculated to aid and abet, in the corruption of the church, by offering induce- ment to designing characters to seek after and obtain the advantages derived from the same; and through their exer- tions as false teachers, corrupt the church, of whom our Lord bids us beware.[46]

---

[44]McBeth, "Southern Baptist Higher Education," 124.

[45]Roy L. Honeycutt, "Heritage Creating Hope: The Pilgrimage of the Southern Baptist Theological Seminary," *Review and Expositor* 81 (Fall 1984): 370.

[46]Ibid., 370.

In spite of some opposition, the movement to establish a south-wide institution to train male ministers continued with strong leadership coming from South Carolina and Georgia.[47] Leaders in Baptist higher education were clergymen of the privileged class. For instance, Richard Furman spent his formative years on his family's South Carolina plantation and later became a leading clergyman in Charleston.[48] Jesse Mercer pastored in Washington, Georgia, and founded Georgia's Baptist state paper, *The Christian Index*. Mercer showed support for education among Baptists by making liberal financial contributions to Baptist educational enterprises although he lacked formal schooling himself.[49] James Pettigru Boyce, of Furman University, was the son of the wealthiest man in South Carolina.[50] These leaders used their resources to further the cause of higher education among Baptists.

Boyce rallied support for centralized ministerial training. He was convinced that Southern Baptist ministers should be brought together and educated in an institution with southwide support, rather than in religion departments of state Baptist colleges. Before he was thirty years of age, Boyce was using his influence as a leader in Southern Baptist circles to create support for the proposed seminary. He envisioned a theological seminary based on three principles. First, a seminary should not be reserved for college graduates but should also admit men without college experience. Second, the seminary should offer "further and special courses" for advanced students, preparing them for original scholarship in order to "make our country less dependent upon foreign scholarship." Finally, the seminary should create and adhere to a belief statement called the "Abstract of Principles" which every professor would sign, "so as to guard against

---

[47]See Mueller, *A History*, 19, 17.

[48]James Rogers, *Richard Furman: Life and Legacy* (Macon: Mercer University Press, 1985) 47,67; and Joe M. King, *A History of South Carolina Baptists* (Columbia: South Carolina Baptist Convention, 1964) 21.

[49]B. D. Ragsdale, *Story of Georgia Baptists*, Vol.1 (Atlanta: Georgia: Baptist Convention, 1932) 35; and William H. Brackney, *The Baptists* (New York: Greenwood Press, 1988) 227.

[50]McBeth, "Southern Baptist Higher Education," 119.

the rise of erroneous and injurious instruction in such a seat of sacred learning"[51]

In 1857, at the annual meeting of the Southern Baptist Convention held in Louisville, Kentucky, the Southern Baptist Theological Seminary was voted into being. The first academic session of the Seminary opened October 3, 1859, at Greenville, South Carolina.[52] Four professors instructed twenty-six men, with Boyce appointed Chairman of the Faculty. The young school was in operation for only three years before the Civil War forced its closing in October 1862. When the Seminary was reopened in 1865, only seven students were in attendance, and efforts were made to relocate to an area less ravaged by war. Louisville, Kentucky was selected as the next location, and in 1877 the Seminary moved into rented space owned by the Louisville Public Library. Eighty-nine men were enrolled that session.[53]

By 1886, the school had received several endowments, allowing for the purchase of property in downtown Louisville and the construction of its first building, New York Hall, named to honor John D. Rockefeller and other Baptist supporters from New York City. By 1888, the Seminary was enrolling 164 men, and Boyce was formally given the title of President of the Seminary. Boyce died that same year, and in 1889 John A. Broadus, a noted preacher and professor of homiletics, as well as a member of the original Greenville faculty, was elected the Seminary's second president.[54]

The campus of the Seminary began to take shape as a second building, Norton Hall, was completed in 1893 to house classrooms and faculty offices. This building was needed to accommodate the 316 students attending Southern in 1895, making it one of the world's largest theological institutions. The Seminary's third president,

---

[51]Honeycutt, "Heritage Creating Hope, 374.

[52]The name of the Southern Baptist Theological Seminary will be referred to as "the Seminary" throughout the remainder of this book.

[53]"Southern Baptist Theological Seminary: A Brief Historical Sketch," *Review and Expositor* 81 (Fall, 1984): 363-66.

[54]Ibid.

church historian William H. Whitsitt, took office that same year and was soon swept up in controversy over his historical investigations. Whitsitt's studies convinced had him that seventeenth-century Baptists did not initially practice baptism by immersion but began that practice in 1641. This assertion undermined the beliefs of Landmarkism, a form of Southern Baptist primitivism that emerged in Kentucky and Tennessee, gaining prominence in the 1850s. Landmarkism claimed that Baptists could trace the practice of immersion in an unbroken line all the way back to John the Baptist's immersion of Jesus. J. R. Graves, a leader of the Landmark movement, not only denounced Whitsitt but also the Seminary that employed him: "We do not want German Rationalism and infidelity to be taught to our young ministers."[55] Under pressure from Seminary trustees, Whitsitt resigned, although he maintained strong student support. Contemporary Baptist historians generally accept his views of the history of baptism by immersion.[56]

In 1899, in the midst of this controversy, E. Y. Mullins came to Louisville to serve as the Seminary's fourth president. Mullins had been a pastor in Massachusetts, and although he was sympathetic with Whitsitt's views, his location outside the South had allowed him to remain somewhat removed from the Whitsitt controversy. According to Baptist historian Bill Leonard, this made Mullins an ideal candidate for maintaining the Grand Compromise that allowed a diversity of doctrinal positions in order to unite as many Southern Baptists as possible in the missions effort. In fact, Leonard asserts that Mullins himself was a personification of the Grand Compromise, maintaining denominational unity through his leadership as a preacher, professor, and theologian. Walter Shurden describes

---

[55]Leonard, God's Hope, 132.

[56]Bill J. Leonard, "Student Life at Southern Seminary," Review and Expositor 81 (Fall 1984): 447; Leonard, God's Hope, 49, 132-133; Honeycutt, "Heritage Creating Hope," 380-381.

Mullins's skill: "Denominational politics was something he loved and the art of politics something in which he excelled."[57]

Mullins's political prowess was of great benefit to those proposing a training school for women in connection with the Seminary. He became an important figure in the initial creation of the school for women, using his influence within the denomination to gather support for the cause. Mullins clearly articulated ways in which the training of women would benefit the missions cause and skillfully managed the opponents of the idea, particularly Annie Armstrong of the Woman's Missionary Union. A brief history of the formation of Woman's Missionary Union, and an overview of WMU's position concerning the role of women in denominational life, will provide a context for the Training School story.

The Women Organize

In the second half of the nineteenth century, Southern Baptist women began a long struggle to form a centralized missions organization to unite local mission groups. They were successful in 1888 when the Woman's Missionary Union (WMU) was formed as an auxiliary to the SBC. The story of the women's attempt to organize reveals the resistance of many Southern Baptists to women who desired a larger role in church life. A brief review of the activities of other evangelical women of the nineteenth century will place the women of WMU in context.

The evangelical movement was liberating to some women, according to Nancy Hardesty. Women like Angelina and Sarah Grimké found inspiration in the concept of human beings as free moral agents who are equal in the sight of God.[58] The nineteenth century saw the birth of many new religious groups in America. Women were founders or leaders of many of these new groups such

---

[57]Walter B. Shurden, "The Pastor as Denominational Theologian in Southern Baptist History," *Baptist History and Heritage* 15 (July 1980): 10.

[58]Nancy Hardesty, *Women Called to Witness: Evangelical Feminism in the Nineteenth Century* (Nashville: Abingdon Press, 1984) 67.

as the Shakers, founded by Mother Ann Lee, and the Seventh Day Adventist Church, founded by Ellen Harmon White. On September 15, 1853, Antoinette Brown became the first American woman whose ordination was documented. She had been preaching since 1848 after graduating from Oberlin and studying theology for three years.[59] Other women, many who were not officially ordained by their denominations, served as traveling evangelists. Maggie N. Van Cott was a successful evangelist among the Methodists. In one year she preached 399 sermons and won 1,735 converts. Although the Methodist bishop refused to ordain her, Van Cott continued her ministry. One day she attended a prayer meeting in New York attended by influential businessmen. Moved by the spirit, Van Cott prayed and testified. One man reprimanded her, saying that this was a men's meeting and women should not speak. Vann Cott responded, "I thought I felt the Spirit of the Lord; and I am taught that, where the spirit of the Lord is, there is liberty."[60]

In contrast to Van Cott, other nineteenth century evangelical women did not claim their right to speak and instead felt it more proper to keep silent. Even during the latter half of the nineteenth century in South Carolina, it was feared that the women of a Southern Baptist mission society would soon be speaking in public and joining the women's rights cause. The women vehemently denied the accusation, demonstrating their sentiments about such an activity:

> The idea of calling us woman's rights! Why our cheeks are made to tingle with blushes. . . . Let us say to those who antagonize our Woman's Missionary Societies that never with God's help will the women of South Carolina ascend the rostrum or let our voices be heard save in our own retreats.[61]

---

[59]McBeth, *Women in Baptist Life*, 58.
[60]Ibid., 61.
[61]Allen, *Century to Celebrate*, 330.

Luther Rice's and the Judsons' 1812 missionary journey inspired more women to form missions societies and to support the missions cause through prayer and contributions. According to Joan Jacobs Brumberg, the mission of Anne Hasseltine Judson validated the claim of nineteenth century women to activity in the religious sphere:

> Their feminist concerns were expressed in their support of foreign missions, which promised the social elevation of heathen women through Christianity, rather than the political feminism that put a knife to the heart of "True Woman-hood."[62]

By the time the Baptist Triennial Convention was formed in May 1814, Baptist women had begun seventeen women's mission societies; eight of these were located in the South. When the SBC was organized in 1845, the number of women's mission societies in the South had grown to over 100.[63] However, the Triennial Convention had encouraged these efforts by women, whereas the SBC did not. The Triennial Convention also appointed single women missionaries; the SBC would not do so for nearly thirty years.[64] This resistance to the women's efforts demonstrates the strong effect of southern culture on the role of women in the newly formed SBC. An intense regionalism that rejected all northern trends such as women organizing clubs or societies and speaking in public, combined with a determination to uphold southern myths concerning women's roles, impeded the formation of a central women's organization among Southern Baptists. Northern Baptist women from churches that had previously been a part of the Triennial Convention organized an independent mission board, which appointed its own missionaries in 1871, a full seventeen years before Southern Baptist women had succeeded in

---

[62]Joan J. Brumberg, *Mission for Life: The Story of the Family of Adoniram Judson* (New York: The Free Press, 1980) xiv.

[63]Allen, *Century to Celebrate*, 17.

[64]Ibid., 18, 26.

forming a central organization. However, this tardiness paralleled other women's organizations in the South. The Woman's Christian Temperance Movement was eight years old by the time it moved into southern territory in 1882. The woman's club movement gained momentum in the South a full decade after it originated in the North in 1890.[65]

Formation of Mission Societies

The Woman's Missionary Union (WMU) traces its origins to the efforts of a Baltimore woman named Ann Jane Graves. Typical of other leaders of nineteenth-century women's organizations, Graves was well educated and wealthy, "with the advantages of an extensive social influence." She was a widely known author who wrote on women's roles in society, advocating education of women "so they could rear competent children and manage wholesome households."[66]

Although Graves herself was Methodist, she reared two sons who chose to be Baptists; one was appointed a Southern Baptist missionary to China in 1856. Roswell Graves believed that only women could evangelize the women in China and convinced his mother, his aunt, and his wife to provide funds for a Chinese "Bible woman" to read Scripture to women in Chinese homes. Ann Graves organized a society to support other Bible women, and by 1848, when Southern Baptists came to Baltimore for the annual convention, Graves called together the wives of SBC delegates and challenged them to form similar organizations. Graves eventually became a Southern Baptist and led a group of Baltimore women to form an organization called Woman's Mission to Woman in October 1871. The society's purpose was to employ native Bible women to work under the supervision of Western Christian missionaries. They used the method of "mite

---

[65]Ibid., 32.
[66]Ibid., 23-24.

boxes" to raise funds, asking each member to put at least two cents per week into the little box in her home.[67]

Meanwhile, in Newberry, South Carolina, women of the First Baptist Church organized a similar society with the support of their pastor who corresponded with Ann Graves. Graves sent him mite boxes. Soon after, a group in Society Hill, South Carolina had organized a society using the same name and constitution as Woman's Mission to Woman of Baltimore. As women raised more money for the missions cause, Graves sought to clarify the relation of women's societies to the SBC Foreign Mission Board (FMB). Southern Baptist women might work independently, as Northern Baptist women had done, or they might cooperate with the FMB. Henry Allen Tupper, the newly appointed corresponding secretary to the FMB, encouraged the women to cooperate with the Board. He showed his support for women by leading the FMB to appoint its first single women missionaries, Edmonia Moon and Lula Whilden who set sail for China in 1872. The FMB made three promises to the women's societies: that women's contributions would be kept in separate accounts, that the FMB would help women to form mission societies across the South, and that the evangelization of women would be emphasized. The next year the FMB showed a seventy-five percent increase in contributions. The commitments made to the women had paid off.[68]

For the next sixteen years, the FMB continued to support the women's efforts and to encourage approval between Southern Baptist brethren by presenting reports of the women's work each year at the convention meeting. These reports caused considerable debate as some objected to women taking a larger role in church life. However, some were supportive of the women's desire to organize the scattered mission societies into one body. John Williams recommended that the 1872 annual meeting of the SBC endorse the Woman's Mission to Woman movement and encourage women to organize in local churches. The motion eventually passed, but the debate was appar-

---

[67]Ibid. 24.
[68]Ibid., 26-27.

ently heated. Offering a word of comfort, Ann Graves advised Williams: "Do not be discouraged; you are only in advance of your brethren; in a few years they will be with you."[69]

Objections

The formation of a centralized organization was delayed another sixteen years. What were the reasons behind the objections to women's organizing? Allen describes a "climate of hostility" with arguments falling into three categories: Church organization, women's rights, and southern pride. Some feared that the organization of a woman's group in a local church would give the women too much economic control. The mission groups would compete with, rather than aid, other church activities by diverting funds outside the local church.[70] Secondly, men feared that women would leave the home and enter the pulpit, violating norms about proper behavior for Southern Baptist women. As one opponent commented: The only four things any Christian can do for missions are to pray, to give, to talk, to go. . . . Three of these are open to women. . . . They may give and pray and go to their heart's content."[71] Finally, Allen notes that the men's objections may have stemmed from an effort "to glue the shattered southern culture back together." The instability following the Civil War caused southerners to be protective of traditional norms and values that included the confinement of women to their own arena of activity.[72]

Although Allen villainizes men as the chief objectors, there is indication that some Southern Baptist women also may have objected to the movement to organize women's missions groups. She reports that men often stated that southern women did not want change but that only "outside agitators" could be pushing these ideas. While Allen presents these statements as rationalizations put forth by male

---

[69]Ibid., 28.
[70]Ibid., 30.
[71]Ibid., 31.
[72]Ibid.

opponents, it is possible that the wives, mothers, daughters, and sisters of these men were most comfortable in their designated sphere of activity and sincerely did not desire to participate in organizational activities.[73] Since Southern Baptist women of this era rarely spoke in public or wrote editorials, their opinions on the matter are not easily discerned.

During this period other denominations also experienced a new wave of opposition to the idea of women's leadership. This was perhaps a reaction to the temporary emergence of women's leadership in the Civil War years, during a shortage of available men. As women attempted to form missionary societies, American men often viewed them as "churchly versions of the suffragette movement." The sheer numbers of women involved was also threatening, argues Leon McBeth. "To deal with a few women preachers was one thing, but the arousing of millions of women in the missionary societies was something else."[74]

Building Support

The FMB assisted the women in becoming more structured in 1874 by appointing central committees in each state that would coordinate the operations of scattered local groups. The appointed women were typically wives of SBC pastors or women of economic privilege. In some states (North Carolina, for example) Southern Baptist men used the power of their own state conventions to block the women from networking through central committees.[75] Although the FMB encouraged the women in certain aspects, its support had limits. The Board pulled back in instances considered too controversial. In 1882 the SBC suggested that the FMB employ a woman to supervise the State Central Committees, collecting and disseminating information, "and in other ways to stimulate and strengthen woman's

---

[73]Ibid.
[74]McBeth, *Women in Baptist Life*, 61-63.
[75]Allen, *Century to Celebrate*, 28

work for women in all lands."[76] The FMB chose not to employ such a woman representative, fearing that "a false step now might entail fatal embarrassments for years to come." According to McBeth, the FMB predicted that placing a woman in such a leadership position would alienate too many Southern Baptist supporters. Thus the first opportunity for women to hold a significant leadership position in the SBC failed.[77]

Following this setback, Southern Baptist women founded their own monthly newspaper to support their cause. *The Heathen Helper* was first issued in November 1882 in Louisville, Kentucky. Although the Central Committee of Kentucky operated it, each state was invited to send material through a "contributing editress." Women also found ways to publish information about their work through a regular column or page in some of the state Baptist papers. The papers published missionary testimonies, Bible study lessons, and letters from missionaries.[78]

In 1882 the Home Mission Board (HMB) began asking women's societies for financial contributions. Isaac Taylor Tichenor began heading the HMB the year that only thirty-one women's societies contributed to the HMB while over 500 societies supported the FMB. Tichenor asked an energetic woman in Baltimore, Annie Armstrong, to help by clothing American Indians in a school run by the HMB. Armstrong inspired other women to cooperate with the HMB, instilling a commitment to both domestic and foreign missions among Southern Baptist women.[79]

The five years leading up to the organization of the Woman's Missionary Union in 1888 were critical. Each year's annual convention brought controversy as women continued to meet and plan while their husbands deliberated the business of the denomination. Waco, Texas was the first host city officially to invite women to attend. The host city customarily provided free lodging and meals to official male

---

[76]McBeth, *Women in Baptist Life*, 88.
[77]Ibid.
[78]Ibid., 89.
[79]Allen, *Century to Celebrate*, 29-30.

delegates but did not allow for women visitors. In 1883, however, Waco Baptists brought in 1,000 cots and lined them up in churches for the men, while every woman was entertained in a home. The Southern Baptists who descended upon Waco numbered 3,000, at least 700 of whom were women. Texas towns sent in wagons laden with food supplies for the guests. The women had an inspiring meeting in the Methodist church, featuring hymns, prayers, and women speakers, while the men conducted business in the Baptist church. At the next year's annual meeting, Baltimore women hosted their Southern Baptist sisters and the women's meetings became an annual event.[80]

The 1885 SBC annual meeting began with controversy as two women from Arkansas, Mrs. J. P. Eagle and Mrs. M. D. Early, appeared as authorized delegates to the SBC. Due to the variety of practices concerning women's roles in Southern Baptist life, women had been serving as delegates at some state conventions. Kentucky was the first to adopt this practice in 1869. Therefore, it is likely that the Arkansas church that appointed the two women as delegates allowed women broader participation than some other SBC congregations. Eagle and Early were surprised by the commotion their appointment caused in the convention. The Northern Baptists had debated the same issue eight years earlier; women had been delegates since that time.[81] The women's husbands defended their wives as the issue was debated on the floor. Early pointed out that the SBC Constitution did not exclude women and that the women's contributions gave them a right to representation: "The question before this Convention is, Shall the Baptist ladies of this country, who have sent more money into the vaults of this Convention than the men, be excluded from a part in its deliberations?"[82] A delegate from Alabama expressed the fear that women's participation would be an opening wedge by which they might take over the SBC: "If ladies are admitted

---

[80]Ibid., 34-36.
[81]McBeth, *Women in Baptist Life*, 108; and Allen, *Century to Celebrate*, 37.
[82]McBeth, *Women in Baptist Life*, 108.

as delegates, they will be qualified for any office. If one should aspire to be President of the Convention [no man] would allow his name to be used for that office. It is all wrong. We are not prepared for such a revolution. Our Southern women do not want it."[83]

The women withdrew their names, leaving the issue unresolved. Three days later a committee of seven men met to study the question. The committee recommended that the Constitution be amended to substitute the word "brethren" for the word "messenger," thereby excluding the women. The report was adopted and women were excluded from representation at the SBC until 1918.[84]

Meanwhile, the women held their own meetings. A male representative read the adopted resolution when it was sent to the SBC. It stated that the women did not intend to form an independent organization but wished to work directly through the local churches. Allen notes that the resolution was designed to be conciliatory, while others called it "a resolution of surrender."[85] After the annual meeting, Sallie Rochester Ford, who had presided over the women's meetings, publicly denied the two accusations directed toward the women: That they were planning a separate organization and that they were promoting women as public speakers.[86] Over the next two years Southern Baptist women would utilize their annual meetings, *The Heathen Helper*, and informal networks to formulate a unique plan of organization.

Formation of Woman's Missionary Union

Unlike the women's missionary organizations of other denominations, the Southern Baptist women kept their promise and did not create an independent entity. They devised a structure that would allow them to coordinate efforts for more efficiency but which conceded to the preference that they not organize a separate board.

---

[83] Allen, *Century to Celebrate*, 39.
[84] McBeth, *Women in Baptist Life*, 109.
[85] Allen, *Century to Celebrate*, 39-40.
[86] Ibid., 40.

The organization was formed in May 1888 during the SBC annual meeting in Richmond, Virginia. A group of women from Maryland came prepared with a constitution that had been carefully drafted by Annie Armstrong, Susan Pollard, and the FMB's Henry Allen Tupper. The preamble of the constitution reflects the women's desire to carry out their two chief purposes: fund-raising and dissemination of missions information but with assurances that their field of service was with women and children and that they did not intend to act independently:

> We, the women of the churches connected with the Southern Baptist Convention, desirous of stimulating the missionary spirit and the grace of giving among women and children of the churches, and aiding in collecting funds for missionary purposes, to be disbursed by the Boards of the Southern Baptist Convention, and disclaiming all intention of independent action, organize. . . . [87]

The organization was first named the Executive Committee of Woman's Mission Societies, Auxiliary to Southern Baptist Convention. Two years later the name was changed to Woman's Missionary Union, Auxiliary to the Southern Baptist Convention (WMU, SBC). Allen argues that the original name was chosen "in order to sound less threatening to the opposition."[88] Officers were elected: president, corresponding secretary, recording secretary, and treasurer, and Baltimore was chosen as the headquarters. Not all Southern Baptist states gave their women the freedom to join. The women of Virginia, North Carolina, and Alabama joined the WMU in later years.

The women did not appoint their own missionaries, nor did they actually spend the funds they raised. Instead they gave their money to the male-run mission boards that kept a separate tally of funds

---

[87]Ethleen Boone Cox, *Following in His Train* (Nashville: Broadman Press, 1938), 67.
[88]Allen, *Century to Celebrate*, 45-47.

raised by WMU. Funding was managed using a process known as "recalling," in which WMU officers would incur expenses to be recalled from the mission boards. In 1906 the WMU began selling literature to help with general operating costs. The women prided themselves on frugality; in 1912, WMU operating expenses equaled a mere 4.5 percent of the total amount raised for missions.[89] This emphasis on economizing was linked to the ideal of self-denial that permeated WMU literature.

The Evangelical Woman

In his description of Southern Womanhood in the nineteenth century, John Ruoff defines two primary images of upper- and upper-middle-class white women of the South: Evangelical Womanhood and Traditional Womanhood. The Traditional Woman was of a higher social class and a non-evangelical religion, was somewhat coquettish, and practiced submission to husbands, brothers, and fathers out of familial duty. In contrast, Evangelical Womanhood, as described by Barbara Welter, was basically a middle-class construct that embodied the virtues of "piety, purity, submissiveness and domesticity."[90] The ideal of the Evangelical Woman was not confined to the South; women's historians have described similar imagery used in other regions. Hardesty notes that the Evangelical Woman was required to be morally and spiritually superior to men. Women were "moral guardians" of the society, charged with the duty of guarding men and children from the evils that existed in society. The temperance movement, initiated by evangelical women, demonstrates the influence of the moral guardian image.[91] WMU women embraced the virtues of Evangelical Womanhood and saw themselves as responsible for the moral state of the globe. Through mission activity, they

---

[89]Ibid., 53.

[90]John Ruoff, *Southern Womanhood, 1865-1940: An Intellectual and Cultural Study* (Ann Arbor, Michigan: University Microfilms, 1976) 49.

[91]Nancy Hardesty, *Women Called to Witness: Evangelical Feminism in the 19th Century* (Nashville: Abingdon Press, 1984) 120-134.

intended to uplift others to a purer, more pious state. By formulating an organization that would maintain auxiliary status to the main SBC body, these women postured themselves as submissive to male Southern Baptist leaders as well as to God.

The Obligation of Self-Sacrifice

Catherine Allen points out that "the obligation of self-sacrifice as a Christian tenet was drilled into the [WMU] women's consciousness." Women were expected to make personal sacrifices for the missions cause. While a woman would never mention her own sacrifice, her friends would report it with admiration. WMU women noted that in Scripture the only offerings commended by Jesus were made by women: one a small offering brought into the temple by a poor widow and the other a gift brought into a home by a woman of means.[92] Women were encouraged to undertake "plainer dressing and plainer living." Superfluities were frowned upon. A woman in Missouri chided: "Think of the money spent for rings, earrings, kid gloves, dress trains—those trains that the women drag around in the dirt would support ten missionaries for the year."[93] The affluent WMU leader Fannie Heck said, "To have the privilege of giving is much; to have the privilege of giving up is more."[94]

Poor women were not excused from sacrificing for the missions cause. If they had no money, they were encouraged to set aside eggs or other agricultural products as contributions. When Annie Armstrong was criticized for asking poor frontier women to give to the missions cause she responded by citing Scripture: "The widow was called on to feed the prophet when she had only a little meal in the barrel and a little oil in the cruse. If we always took out the Lord's portion first, do you not think our experience would be the same? God would look after us."[95]

---

[92]Allen, *Century to Celebrate*, 117-118.
[93]Ibid., 118.
[94]Ibid.
[95]Ibid.

In addition to an ideal of self-sacrifice, WMU women were motivated by an obligation to lift women overseas out of oppression, while, ironically, not commenting on the oppression of women within their own denomination. Allen argues, "Woman's Missionary Union members have seldom uttered complaint about their own status in church or society." Instead, they believed that all Christian women were privileged:

> In the formative days of WMU a glance at their non-Christian sisters in the neighborhood, or a glimpse of the status of women in heathen lands convinced them to be grateful for the liberation they already enjoyed.[96]

Mission-minded women of other denominations took a similar stance, focusing on the oppression of others and turning their attention away from the movement in the United States that claimed women's political equality.[97]

Southern Baptist men also reinforced the idea that Christian women were fortunate to serve, as well as the ideal of self-sacrifice. In 1889 the president of the FMB told the women that it was their privilege "to tell these low ones of the gospel which makes all equal; to teach that Jesus is the truth; to lift up these women. . . . this work is purely unselfish."[98] Into the twentieth century, W. O. Carver, a popular professor among Training School students, praised Southern Baptist women for their spirit of humility and sacrifice:

> Women in this great [missions] enterprise have rarely asked for anything except the privilege of unselfish and unostentatious service. They will never forget to be handmaidens of the Lord. . . .[99]

---

[96]Ibid., 325.

[97]Brumberg, *Mission for Life*, 8.

[98]Allen, *Century to Celebrate*, 325.

[99]Allen, "Concerns Beyond Feminism," in *God's Glory in Missions*, edited by John Jonsson (Louisville, Kentucky: privately published, 1985) 52.

Woman's Domestic Role Was Primary

As noted by Gregory Vickers, most Southern Baptists of the late nineteenth and early twentieth centuries considered woman's primary role to be domestic. However, Southern Baptist men and women held differing beliefs concerning the scope of woman's domestic sphere. Vickers argues that while the men understood woman's chief roles to be wife, mother, and homemaker, WMU women claimed church worker as another primary role for themselves. They did not repudiate domestic roles but saw themselves as mothers and homemakers for all of society.

WMU was often called "the Great Mother Heart of the South," and its members claimed responsibility for women and children of all nations. Although a woman's "own call to service may begin in the home, and its chief duties lie there, it is too wide and compelling to remain there, her heart will yearn over the sons and daughters of the world."[100] Vickers argues further that the missionary endeavor was the force that led women to develop this alternative model to replace images used by Southern Baptist men to limit women's sphere of activity to the home. As Allen notes, Southern Baptist male leaders saw the maternal instinct as the driving motivation for women's involvement in missions.[101] Women took advantage of this view, claiming that precisely because they were mothers and homemakers they needed to move into the public realm.[102]

While some women used the missions cause to expand definitions of domestic responsibility, others did the reverse, defining their roles as mothers and homemakers as a form of missions activity. Mothers were responsible for the conversion of their own children. Lille

---

[100]Gregory Vickers, "Models of Womanhood and the Early Woman's Missionary Union," *Baptist History and Heritage* 24 (January 1989): 441-453.

[101]Allen, *Century to Celebrate*, 338.

[102]Vickers, "Models of Womanhood," 51; The rhetoric encouraging women to enlarge their domestic sphere to become world homemakers was used by nineteenth century leaders of the women's movement, most notably Frances Willard of the Woman's Christian Temperance Movement.

Barker, president of WMU from 1903 to 1906, believed that the home was preeminently a woman's sphere. Although she had no children herself, she told other women of WMU that the influence a mother has over her child's unformed character is a magnificent missions accomplishment.[103]

WMU and the Women's Movement

Southern Baptist historian Rufus Spain notes that nineteenth century Southern Baptists "opposed the organized feminist movement and all other efforts to effect any significant change in the traditional role of women in society." Although Baptists often held a variety of opinions, on this issue they spoke "almost with one voice."[104] Discussions appealed to biblical authority and most often centered on the issues of women speaking in mixed assemblies (those including both men and women) or preaching. Tennessee editor J. R. Graves articulated popular Southern Baptist opinion in 1879 when he wrote, "Paul forbids woman to occupy the position of public speaker or preacher, as being contrary to her womanly nature and at variance with the law of God."[105] Southern Baptist men pointed to northern women's public speaking as an "unscriptural and dangerous innovation," warning southern pastors not to allow women speakers to use their churches, even for a good cause.[106]

Many Southern Baptist women also opposed the women's rights movement. In 1889 Sarah Maverick chastised women who left their homes and children to attend woman's rights conventions and put themselves "in public notice." She warned that by stepping outside the domain "in which it is evident God himself placed her," such a woman was committing "a sin in his sight."[107]

---

[103]Allen, *Century to Celebrate*, 339.

[104]Spain, *At Ease in Zion*, 169-170; and McBeth, *Women in Baptist Life*, 112.

[105]McBeth, *Women in Baptist Life*, 113.

[106]Ibid.

[107]Betty A. DeBerg, *Ungodly Women: Gender and the First Wave of American Fundamentalism* (Minneapolis: Fortress Press, 1990) 51.

Women who engaged in the prohibited practice of speaking in public were denounced by the WMU. Mina Everett, WMU organizer for Texas, traveled around the state raising money for the missions cause. She became such a popular speaker among women that male audiences requested to hear her speak. She struggled over the decision about whether to speak before men:

> I wanted to do right. . . . I prayed. . . . I was awake much of the night. . . . The restful calm which came about noon on Sunday, I perceived as an answer to my prayer. . . . I said "Yes."[108]

In 1895, the mission boards censured Everett by cutting her pay. Texas women raised money for her support, but the next year Everett resigned, stating that she did not want to hinder the missions cause.[109] There is evidence that Southern Baptists in Texas were more lenient than the rest of the denomination concerning women's public speaking.[110] Not wishing to alienate other WMU members, the Baptist Women Mission Workers of Texas (antecedent of the Texas WMU) wrote to Annie Armstrong for advice. As was her custom, Armstrong consulted the male leaders of the mission boards who told her women would ruin their reputations by speaking to mixed audiences. Backed by the Executive Committee of WMU, Armstrong wrote to the Texas women advising them to keep silence if men were in the house.[111]

The issue of suffrage received a great deal of attention in Baptist publications. In the *Western Recorder*, the paper of Kentucky's Southern Baptists, suffragists were accused of being untrue women as

---

[108]L. Katherine Cook, "Texas Baptist Women and Missions, 1830-1900," *Texas Baptist History* 3 (1983): 40.

[109]Allen, *Century to Celebrate*, 329.

[110]Patricia S. Martin, " 'Keeping Silence': Texas Baptist Women's Role in Public Worship, 1880-1920," *Texas Baptist History*, 3 (1983): 20.

[111]Ibid., 330.

they were Christless and childless.[112] Southern Baptist men also used the arguments that "true women" did not want to vote. With a tone of chivalry, men claimed that their anti-suffragist arguments were sparing women of the shame of losing their "womanly modesty."[113]

According to Catherine Allen, very few Southern Baptist women advocated women's suffrage. Interestingly, while a minority of Southern Baptist leaders like J. B. Gambrell and Leslie L. Gwaltney supported women's suffrage, their wives never spoke out in favor of the vote. The Woman's Missionary Union officially took no notice of the struggle for woman suffrage. Fannie Heck, known as one of the most progressive WMU leaders, declined to comment when asked her views on the matter. She responded by saying that her only interest was in missions. Allen speculates that Heck and other WMU women may have been afraid of jeopardizing the missions cause by speaking up for the vote.[114] However, once the Nineteenth Amendment gave voting rights to women, WMU encouraged women to use the vote to bring about needed change. Minnie Kennedy James, president of WMU wrote:

> Whether she wanted the vote or not, the responsibility has been placed upon her and she must use this privilege in such a way that she will influence the life of the nation for good.[115]

Linked to the suffrage question was the temperance issue. John Ruoff argues that the temperance movement was an even more important factor than concern about the black vote in drawing women into the suffrage movement. He notes that many leaders in the southern woman suffrage movement like Lide Meriwether and

---

[112]Bill Sumners, "Southern Baptists and Women's Right to Vote, 1910-1920," *Baptist History and Heritage* 12 (January 1977): 48.

[113]DeBerg, *Ungodly Women*, 52.

[114]Allen, *Century to Celebrate*, 235-236.

[115]Ibid., 237.

Belle Kearney were also active in the Woman's Christian Temperance Movement (WCTU).[116]

Due to its general opposition to women speaking in public, the SBC did not endorse the WCTU until 1912, more than thirty years after the organization came to the South. Nevertheless, since temperance was an important issue for Southern Baptist women, a few became involved in WCTU before that time. In 1883, Mary Gambrell helped to organize a WCTU chapter in Corinth, Mississippi, where her husband served as pastor. Annie Armstrong kept a scrapbook on prohibition that contained WCTU literature, although she reserved her leadership activities for WMU. After 1912, WMU women began openly participating in WCTU, often advertising activities of the temperance organization at WMU meetings. The WCTU slogan, "For God and Home and Native Land" was borrowed and modified by WMU to read "For God and Home and Every Land." While WMU did not organize public demonstrations or marches, some WMU women found in WCTU opportunities for activism supporting the temperance cause.[117]

By the mid-twentieth century, Southern Baptist women were still being discouraged from becoming activists for the cause of women's rights. W. O. Carver preached against activism in his Training School Commencement address of 1941. While affirming that women had an important place in the work of the Lord, he also noted that women should not tell men about their rights; God would do so. Carver appealed to women students' sense of servanthood and Christian tradition, reminding them that:

> . . . the oppressed and suppressed elements of society were not taught or encouraged to go forth crusading for rights. Christianity calls upon its followers to serve, not to assert themselves. . . . Through the centuries women have witnessed and served and waited on God to enlighten Christian men

[116]Ruoff, *Southern Womanhood,* 178
[117]Allen, *Century to Celebrate,* 238-240.

concerning [women's] place and capacity in Christian institutions.[118]

Progressive or Conserving Influence?

Catherine Allen wrote in 1987 that within its 100 years of existence, WMU has never held any affiliation with women's rights movements. Recognizing that some women may have privately supported these ideas, Allen notes the low priority women's equality concerns have had for WMU officials: "These leaders had more important things to do, things of eternal significance." Yet Allen goes on to claim a victory for WMU arguing "change slowly came in the roles of all Southern Baptist women, as an indirect result of WMU."[119]

The victory claimed by Allen may not belong exclusively to WMU. Although early mission societies provided a vehicle for Southern Baptist women to practice leadership skills, WMU more likely was reflecting, rather than instigating changes in women's roles. Ideological shifts concerning appropriate roles for Southern Baptist women are due to a complex configuration of social progress. Leon McBeth gives a different interpretation of WMU's part in the slowly changing roles of Southern Baptist women. McBeth does not credit WMU with bringing about change but instead gives responsibility to the larger women's liberation movement for changing Southern Baptist women to the point that WMU had to adapt itself to accommodate "the more socially aware Southern Baptist woman and offer programs and activities to meet her needs." Nevertheless, notes McBeth, even the most progressive Southern Baptist women are appreciative of WMU for its role in preparing women for leadership.[120]

The story of WMU's formative years demonstrates a spirit that is both pioneering and conserving in terms of women's roles in Southern Baptist life. In spite of vehement opposition from many Southern

---

[118]"Christ's Gift to Woman and His Gift of Women to the Human Race," (address to the WMU Training School, May 8, 1941), TSC, SBTS.

[119]Allen, *Century to Celebrate*, 326.

[120]McBeth, *Women in Baptist Life*, 131.

Baptists, women forged ahead to create their own missions organization in 1888. They entered the public domain, practicing leadership
roles, raising and managing funds, and speaking in front of audiences,
although they limited public speaking to addressing other women and
children. On the other hand, WMU shielded itself against association
with the women's movements of the nineteenth and twentieth
centuries, sanctioned women like Mina Everett who wished to speak
to mixed audiences, and cautioned members to conform to SBC
prohibitions against women speaking out. Unlike women's missionary
societies of other denominations, WMU maintained an auxiliary,
rather than independent relationship with the SBC, turning over
funds to male-run SBC boards.

Training Women for Service

WMU leaders involved in establishing the Training School
brought this complex weave of pioneering and conserving influences
into the school's curriculum. Through the work of the Training
School, the traditional place of women in Southern Baptist life was
subtly challenged. Women were attending some classes that previously had been open only to men, which implies recognition of
women's right and ability to participate in theological study. The
vocations for which these women were preparing were nontraditional
as well. Whether she would sail overseas to the "Dark Continent,"
teach in an Appalachian mountain school, or serve in an inner city
ghetto, the Training School graduate was challenging the traditional
expectations that her mother and grandmother had been required to
follow. At the same time, however, the domestic curriculum for
women students served a conserving function by reminding students
that a woman's primary domain was in the home, even if her home
were located in Africa. The influence of WMU culture permeated not
only the school itself but would reach the women and children served
by graduates, both in the United States and overseas. W. O. Carver
noted that the Training School not only supplied the denomination

with women workers, but also set the standards in terms of culture and values for Baptist women worldwide.[121]

The story of the Training School's formation illustrates the tensions between the WMU leaders' progressive impulse to take women into places never before opened to them, tempered with an insistence that students would stay in their own feminine sphere of service. The Baptist Women Mission Workers of Texas first proposed the idea of a training school for Southern Baptist women in 1895. A few Southern Baptist women had been studying at training schools of the Northern Baptist denomination located in Chicago and Philadelphia.[122] However, Texas women wanted a school that was more centrally located in Southern Baptist territory.

The Texans requested that plans for a women's training school be discussed at the 1895 WMU, SBC Annual Meeting to be held in Louisville. They prepared a paper to be read at the meeting, but it was not included on the agenda. In a letter to the Texas women, WMU corresponding secretary Annie Armstrong wrote, "It is not time yet to discuss the subject."[123]

After the Louisville meeting, Texas women gathered more support for their proposal by presenting the idea of opening a training school at their own state meeting. Then the proposal was sent to the executive committee of the WMU, SBC in November 1895. The executive committee replied, "For the present we deem it wise not to undertake new work. We would recommend the Chicago and Philadelphia Training Schools."[124]

Four years later, a missionary to China, Dr. E. Z. Simmons returned to the United States on furlough to cultivate support for a training school for Southern Baptist women missionaries. During the years 1899 and 1900, Simmons campaigned all over the country talking about his impressions of women missionaries: "When they come to China, they readily learn the language but they do not know

---

[121]Allen, "Beyond Feminism," 59.
[122]Allen, *Century to Celebrate*, 263.
[123]Ibid., 263.
[124]Ibid., 265.

how to teach the Bible for they do not know it themselves. There should be a school for training women." He also capitalized upon on the fears of Southern Baptists that northern schools would encourage women preaching, insisting that training in the North was not suitable for southern ladies.[125] Simmons was successful in convincing many Southern Baptists that women missionaries should study the Bible in order to teach it overseas. Under his influence, the corner-stone for the training school curriculum was set: Southern Baptists became convinced that biblical and theological studies were impor-tant tools not only for male ministers but also for women missionaries.

Simmons's idea was that the Southern Baptist Theological Seminary would cooperate with the WMU, SBC to offer such training. The Seminary could open its classes to women while the WMU provided a home for women students and offered additional classes considered appropriate for women.[126]

Simmons presented his idea to the Seminary faculty in February of 1900. A committee was appointed to speak further with Simmons and to explore what relation the proposed school might have to the Seminary.[127] E. Y. Mullins, the Seminary's president, was a member of this committee and became one of the most vocal supporters of the plan. Perhaps he predicted that women students would continue to attend classes, presenting an awkward situation for the Seminary since Southern Baptists generally opposed ministerial training for women. Perhaps Mullins saw the formal creation of a women's school as a protection against anticipated accusations that the Seminary was training women preachers. He was also concerned about financial resources, stating repeatedly that the Seminary had no funds to

---

[125]Mullins, *House Beautiful*, 13; and Allen, *Century to Celebrate*, 264.

[126]Armstrong, "History of Movement to Establish a Training School," 1905, Historical Library, Sunday School Board of the Southern Baptist Convention, Nashville, TN (Hereafter cited as SSB); Bobbie Sorrill, *Annie Armstrong: Dreamer in Action*, (Nashville: Broadman Press, 1984) 115-117, 134-137.

[127]Faculty Minutes, Southern Baptist Theological Seminary, February 27, 1900, Louisville, Kentucky (Hereafter cited as SBTS).

support women students.[128] Simmons communicated with several key leaders in an attempt to gain support for his plan. R. J. Willingham, corresponding secretary of the Foreign Mission Board, believed that such a school ultimately would help the missions cause. J. M. Frost, corresponding secretary of the Sunday School Board, saw that the training of women workers would aid the Sunday school movement since most teachers were women.[129]

Simmons had campaigned for male support long before consulting WMU, the organization he hoped would sponsor a home for women students. He had already secured approval for his plan from the Seminary faculty and other key leaders such as the corresponding secretary of the Foreign Mission Board. When Simmons wrote to Armstrong asking her to recommend a matron and teacher, his confidence of widespread support was evident:

> I have talked with many brethren in Richmond, Louisville and other places. All agree as to the need of such an institution. All agree that the place for the school is Louisville in connection with our Seminary.[130]

Simmons was anxious to see the new school opened by the fall of 1900.[131] As Allen notes, "Simmons had his school fully planned and duly endorsed before he consulted Woman's Missionary Union just weeks before the 1900 [WMU] Annual Meeting."[132] This presumption infuriated Annie Armstrong, and while she had originally been open to the idea of a training school, she was now incensed that the cooperation of WMU had been taken for granted.[133] Out of her anger was born a determination to prevent WMU from becoming involved

---

[128]See "A Statement Regarding the Women's Training School" [1906?], Historical Scrapbook, microfilm reel 1, Southern Baptist Historical Library and Archives, Nashville, TN.

[129]Allen, *Century to Celebrate*, 264.

[130]Armstrong, "History of the Movement," SSB.

[131]Ibid.

[132]Allen, *Century to Celebrate*, 264.

[133]Ibid.

with the proposed training school. Armstrong would successfully undermine the implementation of Simmons's plan for the next seven years.

Armstrong's first step was to write to the WMU workers in Louisville to ask their opinions. None of them seemed to approve of a training school, according to Armstrong. Eliza Broadus, vice president of Kentucky's WMU, whose late father had been president of the Seminary, did not favor the training school plan at first. In a letter to Armstrong, she explained that the women of Kentucky's WMU were concerned that the plan was being rushed without sufficient time to think things through, that a Louisville home for women students would be too costly for the women's organizations to support, and that putting men and women together in classes would raise a difficult social question:

> [O]ur main reason for thinking Louisville not a good location, is that we deem it not advisable for the students and the young ladies to be thrown together in this way. . . . Many mothers would hesitate to send their daughters under such circumstances; and Mr. Simmons injured his cause here by intimating that the inevitable matchmaking would be a good thing. We do not feel that it is the business of the Woman's Missionary Union and our Committee to afford such facilities, or to have a Training School where there would be such temptations to neglect of study.[134]

Southern Baptist newspapers became involved in the campaign and generally supported a women's training school. However, many women, including Armstrong, were offended by those who joked in the press that a woman's school in Louisville would help the male students find wives to accompany them to the mission fields.[135]

---

[134]Armstrong, "History of the Movement," SSB.
[135]Allen, *Century to Celebrate*, 265.

In response to Simmons's request for support, Armstrong and the WMU Executive Committee officially opposed the idea of a training school in cooperation with the Seminary. The following motion was passed on April 10, 1900:

> That the Executive Committee, after careful consideration at two meetings, opposed the starting of a training school for women at any place at the present inopportune time. [The Committee] also stated that if there is to be a training school that Louisville, Kentucky was not the place.[136]

At the same time that WMU was documenting its opposition to the school, T. P. Bell and his wife Martha Bell suggested that Simmons write a letter to Baptist colleges to canvass for students. Simmons followed their suggestion, further alienating Armstrong. In fact, when others urged Armstrong to talk with Simmons directly, she resisted, saying, "the missionaries in Canton fully recognized that Dr. Simmons is a man of schemes."[137] In spite of initial reluctance, Armstrong did meet with Simmons in person at the 1900 Southern Baptist Convention in Hot Springs, Arkansas. Armstrong reported to J. M. Frost that she

> had a very plain talk with Dr. Simmons, and told him that unless he expected to carry on a training school himself, that it certainly was unwise for him to present the matter until those who had charge of the work had an opportunity to consider the advisability of same. I went over with Mr. Simmons point by point the ground he had taken, and I think he realized that he had not informed himself as thoroughly as he should have before presenting the subject.[138]

---

[136]Armstrong, "History of Movement." SSB. See also, Sorrill, *Dreamer in Action*, 215.
[137]Sorrill, *Dreamer in Action*, 216.
[138]Ibid., 217.

Simmons returned to China without accomplishing his goal of opening a training school in the fall of 1900. However, he had planted a seed that would later bear fruit. Two years later, the Seminary's board of trustees, realizing that they would not have the cooperation of WMU, decided to admit women officially to Seminary classes. Women could sit quietly in the classroom and take examinations, but they would not receive course credit at the Seminary. Nor would they have the privilege of reciting or speaking in class. In December 1903 the Seminary faculty recorded that they had:

no objection to ladies attending meetings in Room 2, New York Hall, but with the understanding that the Faculty distinctly desire that the ladies take no public part in any meetings nor have access to any other part of the building.[139]

The Seminary faculty, lacking the support of the national WMU organization, solicited local support from the Southern Baptist women in Louisville. Eliza Broadus, who had earlier opposed Simmons's plan to establish a training school, changed her opinion and began soliciting support from WMU women around Kentucky. She wrote to Armstrong on April 18, 1904:

You may remember that some years ago I opposed having a Training School for women located in Louisville, and I wish to say that in some respects my opinion has changed. In some important particulars the situation is different now. For one thing the expense will be less than I then anticipated. . . . As to the relations between the young men and young women, those problems can be worked out by matrons and directors if there is such a school here.[140]

---

[139]Mueller, *History of Southern Seminary*, 181-182; and Doris Devault, interview with Carrie Littlejohn, April 16, 1979, tape recording and transcript, Woman's Missionary Union Archives, Birmingham, Alabama, 14.

[140]Armstrong, "History of Movement," SSB.

Eliza Broadus organized a group of WMU women in Louisville to rent and furnish a home for women students. A matron was employed to chaperone the students and supervise the domestic duties each student was required to perform. In the typical spirit of self-sacrifice, WMU women donated their own furniture and pooled their money to pay household bills. This home was opened in November 1904, and was located a few blocks from the Seminary.

The WMU women of Kentucky, as well as many from other states, continued in the effort to convince the national WMU organization to offer financial support for a training school. Meanwhile, the national WMU organization began a separate movement to study the question of opening a training school for women. The committee's reasons for pursuing such a study are unclear. Perhaps Armstrong felt that an objective investigation would reveal that a training school would function best in a location other than Louisville. Perhaps she was ready to consider supporting the Louisville school if an investigation revealed that this was the best option. Some have speculated that she already had another location in mind: Baltimore, where she could have control over the new school. Perhaps those on the executive committee sincerely wished to study the matter and Armstrong agreed. Whatever the motivation, in May 1903 the executive committee convinced the SBC to appoint a committee of seven men to confer with seven women of the WMU "to consider the advisability of establishing a Missionary Training School for Women." The committee was expected to report at the SBC annual meeting in 1904 concerning location, methods of operation, and fund raising for the school.[141]

Annie Armstrong was asked to chair the subcommittee on curriculum. She spent a great deal of time and effort visiting training schools in the North and reviewing catalogs. The information she gathered perhaps would have been useful. However, neither her report, nor the reports of the other subcommittees, was given at the next year's meeting. Instead, at the 1904 meeting, Armstrong called

---

[141]"Attention! Southern Baptists!!" [1903?] Frost Papers, SSB.

for the dissolution of the committee before reports were read. The reason she gave was that the Seminary already had a training school in existence. One month prior to the Nashville meeting, E. Y. Mullins had written an article in the *Baptist Argus* noting the good work of the women students at the Seminary. Rather than clarifying that the Seminary did not financially support the women students, Mullins stated "We already have such a successful Training School in connection with our work at the Seminary."[142]

Armstrong seized the opportunity and quoted Mullins's public statement at the Nashville meeting. She argued that since the Seminary already had a Training School in place, there was no reason to consider creating another one. She moved that "no action be taken by the Committee, but that the whole subject be left with the Seminary for the present."[143] This gave Armstrong one more opportunity to disassociate the WMU from the women's school emerging in Louisville.

This was another setback for those who would have the WMU take financial responsibility for the enterprise. Mullins had made it clear from the beginning that the Seminary had no intention of offering financial support to the women's school. The women of Louisville were supporting the home for women students temporarily in an emergency situation. They needed WMU to take over the project and began working to build a support network of women in other states by writing about the home in Baptist newspapers. The goal was to get the subject of the Training School on the agenda of the 1905 SBC annual meeting at Kansas City. Since Armstrong had expressed such determined opposition, the Louisville women by-passed her and wrote directly to WMU vice-presidents in each state asking them to use their influence to ensure that the school was discussed at the meeting. This action outraged Armstrong who later accused the Louisville women of "political wire-pulling" and threat-

---

[142]E. Y. Mullins, "Training School for Women: Why Louisville is the Place," *Baptist Argus*, April 7, 1904.
[143]Armstrong, "History of Movement," SSB.

ened in a letter to Willingham that she would resign from WMU if the women adopted the training school at Louisville.[144]

In case she would need it in Kansas City, Armstrong prepared a paper giving the complete history of the training school movement from her point of view. While the true motivations for her actions throughout the controversy were muddled by comments from her critics, she clearly had taken offense from the beginning when Simmons did not consult her before formulating a plan. Her anger was further excited when Mullins and the women of Louisville bypassed her in gathering support for the cause. Her "History of the Movement" focuses upon her feeling that her Baptist brothers and sisters had mistreated her. She appealed to propriety and protocol emphasizing that this work was not done by "right methods." This personal injury, described in detail in letters to her friends and colleagues, seems to be the main cause of Armstrong's objection to the Training School's formation. Her public statements, however, masked her personal pique by emphasizing that the training school should not be near a seminary since a seminary teaches preaching and women are not expected to preach.

The situation was further complicated when T. P. Bell implied that Armstrong's main objection concerned the relations between Training School students who might court or marry. In his newspaper for Georgia Baptists, Bell taunted Armstrong:

> We have heard of its being charged against this Training School that it would prove a sort of matchmaking institution for the young women of the School and the young men of the Seminary. The great fear that this would be the case has always seemed to us an absurd one. It might well have risen in the fertile imagination of some maiden lady of uncertain age, who has come to look upon marriage as a dreadful thing, and

---

[144]Devault, Littlejohn interview, 24-25; and Armstrong, "History of Movement." SSB.

especially a marriage between two young Christians whose hearts are one in the service of the Master.[145]

Armstrong's writings, both private and public, mention the marriage question, but these issues are clearly not the central focus of her objections. In later years, however, W. O. Carver emphasized Armstrong's few statements about courtship and marriage, reinforcing the oral tradition that this was Armstrong's chief reason for opposing the school.

Thanks to the efforts of the women of Louisville, the idea of sponsoring the school did come up for discussion at the Kansas City meeting. President Mullins and W. W. Landrum, a leading pastor of the denomination, spoke in favor of the WMU adopting the school, noting that the majority of the women students planned to do mission work on home or foreign fields. Next, Annie Armstrong addressed the WMU, voicing her disapproval of the work itself and especially of the methods of the Louisville women in bringing the subject before the Kansas City meeting. When a vote was taken, the motion to adopt the home for women students lost by three votes. [146]

Although the motion had failed, Armstrong perhaps predicted that eventually she would be defeated. She had threatened earlier to resign from office if the school were to be adopted by WMU. At the Kansas City meeting, Armstrong and WMU President Mrs. J. A. Barker announced that they would serve one more year but would not stand for re-election. With this announcement, Armstrong severed a seventeen-year commitment to serving WMU without remuneration.[147]

In May 1906, WMU gathered in Chattanooga and again the motion to support the home for women students came before the body of women. Supporters were disappointed when the President

---

[145][T. P. Bell], "The Young Woman's Missionary Training School," *The Christian Index*, February 22, 1906.

[146]Carrie Littlejohn, *History of Carver School of Missions and Social Work* (Nashville: Broadman Press, 1958) 30.

[147]Ibid.

ruled that according to the constitution, any new endeavor could not be undertaken without three months prior notice to WMU unless the vote were unanimous. Although a strong majority voted to support the home, the vote was not unanimous, and the work was postponed another year. Fannie Heck, who supported the adoption of the home for women students, was elected WMU president and worked throughout the year making plans for the new school. In the May 1907 annual meeting at Richmond, WMU voted unanimously to establish the Woman's Missionary Union Training School at Louisville, Kentucky. The men of the SBC took up an offering equaling $4,700 to support the new school, while the women raised over $10,000 in their meeting.[148]

With this action, students would no longer be left to wander aimlessly through the various curricular offerings of the Seminary. Instead, they would be under the care and supervision of the Woman's Missionary Union who would pass on the WMU culture to the next generation of female denominational leadership. The leadership of the WMU often used the image of a maternal adoption to describe its relationship to the Training School. This sentiment is expressed in the following verse:

Thus the WMU has enshrined in her heart
Our School as the child of her prayers;
For she nurtures and tends it with true mother love,
Bearing always its burdens and cares.[149]

Like a mother, the WMU would teach Training School daughters the values and attitudes of WMU culture. In the next chapter, we meet the elite women of WMU who were the school's founders and administrators. These women embodied the values that would be passed on to teachers and students who came from the poorer classes.

---

[148]Ibid., 38-43.
[149]Maude McLure, "Lasting Foundations," [1917?], TSC, SBTS.

2

"SUCH NOBLE WOMEN THEY WERE"
Founders, Faculty, and Students
of the WMU Training School

The women of the Woman's Missionary Union Training School, both students and leaders, had much in common. They were a part of Southern Baptist culture characterized by white supremacy and resistance to change.[1] They shared a deep commitment to the Christian faith and to their denomination, which insisted that women work in their own domain of service, barring them from any position in which they might hold authority over men. These women felt called by God to take up the tasks in which they were engaged: founders and faculty were dedicated to educate young women; students responded to a call to the missionary cause and came to prepare for service. Yet one important factor distinguished the leaders who managed the affairs of the Training School from teachers and students who admired and followed them: economic privilege.

WMU Royalty

The hierarchy in operation at the Training School mirrored that of the denomination at large: Leaders were a part of the economic and religious elite, while the majority of Southern Baptists came from the poorer classes. Training School founders and administrators had been reared in families of privilege while teachers and students came

---

[1]Billy F. Sumners, "The Social Attitudes of Southern Baptists Toward Certain Issues, 1910-1920" (Masters thesis, University of Texas at Arlington, 1975) 6.

from households struggling against economic hardship. Ellen Rosenberg's analysis of economic conditions in the late nineteenth century South and its effects on the Southern Baptist denomination addresses these divisions.

Denominational leaders belonged to a religious elite; they were more affluent, better educated, and came from larger churches. The majority of Southern Baptists belonged to a "sub-church" that lay beneath the elite leadership in the denominational hierarchy. The sub-church was dominated by poor whites and led by uneducated preachers who farmed or worked in occupations similar to their parishioners.[2]

The elite women leaders were models of ideal Southern Baptist womanhood for the rest of the denomination. Southern Baptist writer Catherine Allen notes that early leaders of Woman's Missionary Union (WMU) were "a collection of denominational royalty;" WMU leadership did not typically include self-supporting career women until the late 1930s.[3] Students, on the other hand, generally came from poor families working as teachers to support themselves and save money for further education. These women students admired their leaders and embraced the values and priorities exemplified by them.

The example of the "denominational royalty" became solidified into a WMU culture that valued spiritual devotion, self-sacrifice, efficiency in organization, and education.[4] Allen states that early leaders "deliberately set out to include women from other walks of society." This invitation to membership initially included only white women and was open to women "of moderate and poor financial circumstances" who would typify the Training School student. WMU culture would be passed on to all Southern Baptist women and girls, primarily through WMU literature that was distributed widely after

---

[2]Ellen M. Rosenberg, *The Southern Baptists: A Subculture in Transition* (Knoxville: The University of Tennessee Press, 1989) 41.

[3]Catherine Allen, *A Century to Celebrate: History of Woman's Missionary Union* (Birmingham: Woman's Missionary Union, 1987) 60-61.

[4]Ibid., 47-56, 68.

1906 when a new Literature Department was formed.[5] Training School students who came to Louisville from rural areas of poverty met WMU leaders face to face. Jewell Legett felt privileged to be selected as a "serving girl" for a WMU luncheon held at the Training School in 1909. She was thrilled to serve the tables of WMU royalty

> They were beautiful to see. Most of them were wealthy and of course richly dressed. . . . As they were passing out, Jane and I were at the door and they all stopped to talk with us. I met women I've heard of always . . . such noble women they were, too.[6]

When the Woman's Missionary Union adopted the new school in 1907, these southern aristocratic leaders created its character, formed its traditions, and represented the ideal toward which women students would strive. Each had been reared as "a southern lady." Most were educated in colleges and finishing schools in an era when advanced education was a rare privilege for women of the South. Five women are celebrated as the Training School's founders. Two women represented the WMU organization: Eliza Broadus led Kentucky WMU to support Training School efforts, while Fannie Heck was president of the southwide WMU organization when the school was adopted. Two others represented the Southern Baptist women of Louisville who provided a home for the women students and served on its board of managers. These were Anna Eager and Emma Woody. Finally, Maude McLure, the first principal, played a key role in shaping the traditions and daily life that gave the school its unique character. Portraits of these women, remembered as Training School heroines, reveal commonly held images of the ideal Southern Baptist woman. Each one, whether she was involved in the school's daily life or was a frequent visitor, provided a model for Training School students.

---

[5]Ibid., 53.
[6]Legett, Diary, May 15, 1909.

The Five Founders

Eliza Broadus organized efforts to provide living quarters for women students at the Seminary. In 1904, she was asked by a Seminary professor to encourage local Baptist women to provide a home for female students attending Seminary classes.[7] Broadus's education, church experience, and family life had prepared her for leadership among Kentucky women. Eliza was born in 1851 into a family of Baptists, which "ranked high in Southern society."[8] Her father, John A. Broadus, was serving as a pastor in Charlottesville, Virginia, in addition to teaching Latin and Greek at the University of Virginia. In 1859, two years after the death of his wife (and Eliza's mother) Broadus remarried and moved the family to Greenville, South Carolina, where he joined the faculty of the newly founded Southern Baptist Theological Seminary teaching in the areas of New Testament and Homiletics. He became the Seminary's second president in 1889.[9] John Broadus personally educated his daughter at home in history, mathematics, literature, philosophy, French, German, "a little Greek and a great deal of Latin." He also encouraged her to read missionary magazines, and when she was older, he taught her how to speak in public, with the assumption that she would only speak before other women.[10]

Broadus was outspoken in his opinions about the proper place of women in the church and has been credited with helping to shape late nineteenth century Southern Baptist reaction and policy on the

---

[7]Carrie Littlejohn, *History of Carver School of Missions and Social Work* (Nashville: Broadman Press, 1958) 21.

[8]Rufus B. Spain, *At Ease in Zion: Social History of Southern Baptists, 1865-1900* (Nashville: Vanderbilt University Press, 1967) 11.

[9]B. L. Stanfield, "John Broadus," *Encyclopedia of Southern* Baptists, vol.1 (Nashville: Broadman Press, 1958); Mrs. George B. Eager, "Eliza Summerville Broadus," 1915, Training School/Carver Collection, Southern Baptist Theological Seminary, Louisville, KY, (Hereafter cited as TSC, SBTS); and "Tribute Paid to John Broadus", *The Tie*, (March/April 1993) 12.

[10]Ella B. Robertson, "Seeketh Not Her Own," *Baptist Courier*, December 10, 1936.

issue.[11] He believed that women were to remain in a subordinate position to men and therefore were not to teach men or "have dominion" over them. In vehement opposition to women speaking in "mixed assemblies," Broadus used biblical texts such as the Pauline letters to support his arguments. In his article, "Should Women Speak in Mixed Assemblies?" he stated that the Bible did not prohibit women from speaking publicly before one another, "Only keep the men out. And beware of some 'entering-wedge' in the shape of an editor or masculine reporter."[12] John Broadus never allowed his daughters to attend Seminary classes. Ten years after his death, as Eliza was seeking support for women students, Annie Armstrong used the noted professor's opinions to make her case against the Training School: "I know a change has come in the opinions of Dr. Broadus's daughters, but Dr. Broadus is in his grave and can no longer exercise his authority in the matter."[13] Growing up in the religious and academic community of the Seminary, Eliza was baptized at age fourteen and immediately began to offer Christian service, teaching a class in the colored Sunday school. In later years, after the family moved with the Seminary to Louisville, she taught mission Sunday schools and became a leader of women through local and state WMU organizations. The family had been accustomed to economic advantages, but had fallen on harder times since the Civil War. A family member described how Eliza dealt with the change: "It wasn't hard to wear calico to church, she used to tell the young ones, when everyone else did it too. . . ."[14]

When the WMU was first organized in 1888, Eliza Broadus served as the vice president from Kentucky. At the time she became involved with women students at the Seminary, she was fifty-three

---

[11]See Patricia S. Martin, "Keeping Silence: Texas Baptist Women's Role in Public Worship, 1880-1920," *Texas Baptist History* 3 (1983): 22.

[12]John A. Broadus, "Should Women Speak in Mixed Assemblies?" in *Feminism: Woman and Her Work*, ed. J. W. Porter (Louisville: Baptist Book Concern, 1923) 45-52.

[13]Annie Armstrong, "History of Movement to Establish a Training School," Sunday School Board of the Southern Baptist Convention, Nashville, TN. (Hereafter cited as SSB).

[14]Robertson, "Seeketh Not Her Own."

years old and living in the home of her sister who was married to a Seminary professor. She had become deaf in her middle years, using an otacousticon to aid her hearing as she continued to lead in women's groups. [15] Broadus, like many women leaders of her time, devoted herself to church work with a spirit of sacrifice, yet she found herself newly empowered by the experience. After Broadus's death, her sister observed that Eliza's work with women's groups had "aroused her interest, developed her powers, and increased her friendships, with never a thought on her part for any of this." Known for her wise judgment and self-sacrifice, she was described as a woman who "seeketh not her own," but provided "an example of ceaseless, persistent self-abnegating effort" in Christian service.[16] The life of Eliza Broadus is still celebrated by Southern Baptists of Kentucky who collect the state missions offering in her name.

Another WMU leader who is counted among the founders of the Training School is Fannie Exile Scudder Heck, president of the national WMU organization, which adopted the school in 1907. Heck was a strong supporter of higher education for women and worked diligently to raise funds to create Meredith College, a Southern Baptist women's college in her hometown of Raleigh, North Carolina. Heck was completing the last of her three terms as WMU president in the same year that Annie Armstrong, chief opponent of the Training School, resigned as corresponding secretary. Heck had resigned the presidency twice for reasons of ill health and conflict with Armstrong.[17] Heck took WMU's commitment to the new school seriously, visiting the school for extended periods and corresponding frequently with its principal, Maude McLure.

---

[15]"Anna Eager," Baptist Biography File, Southern Baptist Historical Library and Archives, Nashville, TN (Hereafter cited as SBHLA); and Robertson, "Seeketh Not Her Own."

[16]Robertson, "Seeketh Not Her Own"; and "Anna Eager," Baptist Biography File, SBHLA.

[17]Catherine Allen, *Laborers Together with God* (Birmingham: Woman's Missionary Union, 1987) 26-33.

Heck became a respected women's leader at a young age. At twenty-three she was elected chair of the Woman's Central Committee of North Carolina Baptists; she was president of the national WMU organization before her thirtieth birthday. Her family background, particularly the example of her mother, prepared her for such leadership. Fannie was born June 16, 1862, in Mecklenberg County, Virginia. The family followed her father from town to town in his wartime travels as a lieutenant colonel. Her mother gave her the name "Exile" to symbolize the family's status in Civil War years. After the war, the Heck family settled in Raleigh, North Carolina, where the father resumed his law practice and built the family mansion in one of Raleigh's best neighborhoods. Fannie attended Professor Hobgood's seminary for young women and later graduated from Hollins Institute near Roanoke, Virginia.[18]

Fannie's mother, Mattie Heck, was a leader among Baptist women. She had consented in 1876 to lead Southern Baptist women of North Carolina in the formation of a central missions committee, but male leadership vetoed the idea. Jonathan Heck also provided an example of denominational involvement for his daughter by entertaining Southern Baptist leaders in their home. Fannie grew up overhearing and learning from the discussions of her father and his Baptist friends.[19]

As she grew older, Heck was active in church and community work, teaching boys' Sunday school class and serving as vice president of the Southern Sociological Congress. In contrast to other WMU leaders, Heck did not reserve her energies for religious work alone but also exercised leadership in other arenas. She clearly favored social reform activities and identified herself with progressive efforts. She helped to establish Associated Charities of Raleigh and served as its chair. She was vice-president of the Wake County Betterment Association and helped develop North Carolina juvenile courts. Heck brought her social consciousness to WMU and pioneered in the area

---

[18]Ibid., 27-28.
[19]Ibid., 28-29.

of Christian social action by creating the "personal service" program in 1909.[20]

Women often admired Heck's fashionable style and physical beauty. A Training School graduate of 1915 recalled her "stately appearance and her lovely clothes."[21] An eloquent speaker and popular writer among Southern Baptist women, Heck wrote "The Woman's Hymn," official hymn of WMU, numerous articles and pamphlets, and four books, including *In Royal Service*, a history of Southern Baptist women's work, and several collections of inspirational stories and poems.

Throughout her long illness and until her death, Heck provided an example of strength and endurance for the women who admired her. Although her illness was never described, some have speculated it was cancer. On her deathbed she offered her resignation as WMU president, but it was not accepted. Although she was idolized throughout her life, Southern Baptist women thrust their leader "to an even higher pedestal" as she was dying.

> Heck turned her chamber into a legendary haven of happiness. She called it "The Room of the Blue Sky." She disciplined herself in pain so that no word of complaint left the room.[22]

During the months she was bedridden, Heck wrote two inspirational books and a farewell message to Southern Baptist women that would become the most quoted lines in WMU history. Heck died on August 25, 1915, at fifty-three years of age. As the Training School was planning a new building, the women decided to erect the Heck Memorial Chapel in memory of their beloved leader.[23] Fannie Heck was clearly a model for Southern Baptist women, and her particular

---

[20]Ibid., 31.

[21]Doris DeVault, interview with Carrie Littlejohn, tape recording, (WMUA, April 16, 1979) 16.

[22]Allen, *Laborers Together*, 33-34.; and Devault, Littlejohn interview.

[23]Allen, *Laborers Together*, 36.

devotion to the Training School ensured her example would influence students, even after her death. She was perhaps the most progressive of the five founders; in her words as well as by example, she stated clearly that Southern Baptist women should be concerned about social issues. However, the Training School leaders did not invest their energies in social improvement through structural reform as Heck had done. Instead, the Training School concentrated its efforts on changing society through the conversion of individuals using methods of "personal service."[24]

Heck and Broadus were already recognized leaders of the Woman's Missionary Union organization when the Training School was formed. Others found their place of leadership through service to the school. In September 1904, when Eliza Broadus called a meeting of Louisville Baptist Women to discuss a home for women students, two women emerged as leaders: Anna C. Eager, a newcomer to Louisville, and Emma McIver Woody, who had been asked to preside. By the end of the meeting, these two women had been elected chair and co-chair of the band that would lead the Southern Baptist women of Louisville to provide a home for women students. This group later became the local board of managers, of which Eager and Woody both served as chair and co-chair for the next twenty years. They were known as a remarkable team, each woman's background and experience having prepared her for leadership in the affairs of the Training School.

Emma McIver was born in 1863 and reared in Texas where her father was a lawyer. She was educated at a Baptist women's school, Baylor Female College. After marrying a young doctor named Samuel Woody, she came to Louisville and volunteered in church and community organizations.[25] Emma Woody lived a life of economic privilege, traveling in Europe several times and living in a "palatial

---

[24]For further discussion of personal service methods, see Chapter Five.
[25]"Emma McIver Woody," Baptist Biography File, SBHLA; and Littlejohn, *History of Carver*, 119.

home" that "breathed the spirit of refinement and culture."[26] Yet she shared her advantages with the Training School community, taking full financial responsibility for the rent and utilities of the first Training School home and leaving a four thousand-dollar endowment to the school after her death.[27]

Woody was about age forty-one when she became involved in the work of the Training School. Descriptions of her appearance and character portray her as "queenly" and "cultured." W. O. Carver said, "Culture is sometimes acquired by education, but not that culture which is acquired by heritage and inbreeding [sic]; Mrs. Woody was innately refined."[28] Adjectives such as "business-like" and "aggressive" were also used to describe Woody. "She was quickly ready to undertake anything." Her experience as a leader had taught her to be efficient and direct in her approach.[29]

Anna Eager, Woody's partner in management of Training School affairs, was also described as capable in business affairs. She was known as "a keen strategist" and "a tactful diplomat."Also, she was a gifted writer and published valuable information about Training School life in numerous pamphlets and articles.[30]

Eager came from a family that enjoyed economic privilege while the South was devastated by war. She was born in 1853 in Virginia. Her father was a physician who moved the family to Mississippi when Anna was ten years old. She attended public schools in her hometown of Jackson and pursued further education at Central Female Institution in the neighboring town of Clinton. She was described as "a lady of distinctive tastes and a woman of breeding."[31] She married George B. Eager, a promising biblical scholar, and the couple lived in

---

[26]Mr. C. V. Edwards, "Mrs. Emma McIver Woody," unclassified papers, TSC, SBTS.

[27]Carrie Littlejohn To Mrs. Townsend, July 16, 1933 unclassified papers, TSC, SBTS.

[28]W. O. Carver, "A Tribute to Mrs. S. E. Woody," [1933], unclassified papers, TSC, SBTS.

[29]Carrie Littlejohn, "A Magnificent Obsession," clipping, 1935, TSC WMUA; W. O. Carver, "A Book of Remembrance," TSC, SBTS, 13.

[30]Littlejohn, History of Carver, 118.

[31]W. A. Mueller, A History of the Southern Baptist Theological Seminary (Nashville: Broadman Press, 1959) 191.

Alabama where Anna Eager demonstrated her leadership skills and business sense through involvement in projects such as the establishment of an Industrial School for boys. Eager was fifty-one years old when her husband joined the faculty of Southern Seminary and the couple moved to Louisville. Within one year, she found her place of leadership among the advocates of a training school for women. Eager is celebrated as the key person responsible for convincing the WMU to adopt the young school. She was known for her relentless determination and ability to motivate others. When other leaders became discouraged, Eager's response was "Let us pray once more and try once more;" people "were fired by her enthusiasm."[32] One student remembered Anna Eager as "a choice spirit . . . one of those women who had all the Southern charm . . . you read about in books."[33]

Eager visited the school often, and in the 1920s, after her husband's retirement, the couple moved into the Training School's annex building, affording them daily contact with students. The couple became a part of the Training School family and was known as "Grandmother and Grandfather Eager."[34] In 1927, Eager resigned from the Training School's board of managers because of "family duties, the toll of years, and failing eyesight."[35] She continued to influence the lives of students, taking walks and sharing meals with them until she and her husband moved to Georgia, where she lived with relatives until her death in 1933.[36]

Each of these women visited the school often, creating and representing the ideals of Southern Baptist womanhood. However, one of the school's founders—the first principal, Maude Reynolds McLure—actually lived in the school providing a daily model for Training School students. Many believed McLure's example had the

---

[32]"Anna Eager," Baptist Biography File, SBHLA; Willie Jean Stewart, "The Founders," WMU Training School Bulletin, August 1947, 3; Juliette Mather, interview by Catherine Allen, tape recording, January 26, 1976, transcript, 19, WMUA.

[33]Mather Interview, 19.

[34]Littlejohn interview, 14.

[35]Anna Eager to Board of Managers, [1927], TSC, SBTS.

[36]DeVault, Littlejohn interview, 14.

power to transform students: "There was something about that good woman, her culture, her Christian ideals that got into the hearts of those girls. . . . after her coming they became beautified and less selfish. They were elevated."[37]

McLure's life experience prepared her to become a woman whom students admired. Born into the Reynolds family in 1863, Maude grew up on an Alabama plantation called "Mt. Ida." She was educated at home by private instructors and attended Judson College, a Southern Baptist women's school in Marion, Alabama. After leaving Judson, Maude went to a finishing school in Baltimore.

In 1886 Maude married Thomas E. McLure. The wedding was an enormous celebration. Friends and relatives came to the plantation to enjoy the wedding feast, which included the best hams and turkeys and rare fruits ordered from Florida. Maude wore the finest wedding gown money could buy.[38] The McLures moved to Chester, South Carolina, where Thomas practiced law. He died three years later of a dental infection, leaving Maude with an infant son. She moved back to Alabama and made her home with a sister until 1904 when she left with her teenage son to teach music at Cox College, in College Park, Georgia.

She had been teaching there three years when Anna Eager asked her to become the first principal of the Training School.[39] She turned down the offer several times, lacking confidence that she could perform the task. Early histories of the Training School credit her son for convincing McLure she was capable. Mullins writes that the son's "ardor, his high conception of her ability, made her heart leap to the call that she might not fail his faith in her."[40] McLure laughingly recalled later that as she went to bed on the night before she was to

---

[37]John Sampey, "Laying of the Cornerstone Ceremony" [1940], TSC, SBTS, 5.

[38]"Hannah Reynolds," Mrs. Maud[e] Reynolds McLure: A Brief Biography," [1940], TSC, WMUA; Allen, *Century to Celebrate*, 391, n.33.

[39]Reynolds, "Mrs. Maud[e] Reynolds McLure."

[40]Isla May Mullins, *House Beautiful* (Nashville: Sunday School Board of the Southern Baptist Convention, 1934) 27; DeVault, Littlejohn interview 47.

be inaugurated as the school's new principal she turned her face to the wall and prayed to die before morning.[41]

Although McLure had no formal training in mission work, she had one important asset: she was a southern lady. Her ability to model this image was valuable to the Training School board. One student who attended the school in 1909 comments:

> It was much later that I learned the Board had to choose between a trained worker from the north, or a cultured woman of the south who knew our traditions. How wisely did they choose![42]

Although she was reared in a home with servants, McLure was not averse to performing household tasks. One WMU leader seemed impressed that "with her own hands she helped to scrub wood work, clean wall paper, paint old furniture. . . ."[43] McLure was described as having "poise, charm, dignity, tact, practical common sense, an unfailing sense of humor, and a rich personal religious life." She took a keen interest in individual students, inviting them in the evening to do handiwork and crafts in the principal's apartment.[44] She was known at the Training School as "Mother McLure," a name that not only reflects her close relationship with students but also suggests her personal tendencies toward nurture and love. She was credited with giving the Training School a special ambiance: "It was more than a school—it was a home—because her love and faith and hope overshadowed us."[45]

---

[41]Littlejohn, *History of Carver*, 49.

[42]Elsie Gilliam to Kathleen Mallory [1938], unclassified papers, TSC, SBTS.

[43]Kathleen Mallory, "Mrs. Maude Reynolds McLure," (address to WMU Training School October 2, 1938), transcript, p. 5, TSC, WMUA.

[44]News Clipping, April, 1938, TSC, WMUA; Juliette Mather interview by Gertrude Tharpe and Ethalie Hamric, September 17-21, 1979, tape recording, transcript, p. 32, WMUA.

[45]Mallory, 5.

The experience of growing up on an antebellum southern plantation shaped McLure's racial attitudes. She sometimes upheld racist traditions that set her apart from more progressive students. On one occasion:

> . . . when a great Negro missionary and geographer came to the Training School to speak, we all wondered how she would introduce him, for she was an old-fashioned southerner in her race attitudes. Some of us suggested that "Doctor" as an earned title would be appropriate, but she vetoed it as well as "Mister," but held her peace about what she would do. And I shall never forget the little air with which she introduced "Missionary Shepherd". . . . [46]

The first principal was described as a strict disciplinarian, and several graduates commented on her quick temper: "Mrs. McLure's besetting sin was [her] ready and seething sarcasm. . . . How many times I have heard her plead in prayer for a guard upon her unruly tongue." [47] Yet these same students recalled that McLure possessed a remarkable sense of humor, often presenting practical jokes and games and bringing laughter to the school.[48]

More than any other person, Maude McLure is credited with giving the Training School its shape and form. In 1938, an alumna of the Class of 1911 observed, "She was the one who laid the foundations, who shaped the ideals, and worked out the methods which made the Training School what it is."[49] A leader with a powerful personality may greatly influence the culture of an institution, particularly in its early years. Mary Lyon gave such leadership to Mt. Holyoke, as did Bryn Mawr's M. Carey Thomas.[50] A Seminary

---

[46]Willie Jean Stewart to Kathleen Mallory, September 14, 1938, unclassified papers, TSC, SBTS.

[47]Ibid.

[48]Mallory, "Mrs. Maude Reynolds McLure," transcript, 2.

[49]Mrs. Marion Terrell Ball to Kathleen Mallory, [1938], unclassified papers, TSC, SBTS.

[50]Helen Horowitz, *Alma Mater: Design and Experience in the Women's Colleges from Their Nineteenth-Century Beginnings to the 1930's* (New York: Knopf, 1984) 9-27, 105-6.

professor commented in 1936, "Mrs. McLure came to the Training School in its formative period and impressed upon it a character which it has not lost, and I hope never will."[51]

Each of the five founders was dedicated to organizing women for church work. They loved mission work, valued education, and were willing to spend a great deal of energy to help young women receive missionary training. These five differed in their talents and styles of leadership. Eliza Broadus was a quiet, unobtrusive leader while Fannie Heck was more visible as an accomplished writer and public speaker. Woody used her business acumen in managing the affairs of the school, while Eager provided a spirit of encouragement and optimism. McLure provided the consistency of her daily presence in the school and a model of Christian womanhood by taking an interest in individual students. Although it is unlikely that these five women were acquainted before their involvement with the Training School, they were bound together by the common goal of creating a special place for women to prepare for missionary service.

The Principal and Faculty

Lynn Gordon notes an interesting contrast between college women of the North and South in their attitudes toward faculty. Northern women identified strongly with faculty, patterning their own lives after their teachers. Southern women students, on the other hand, respected women teachers but did not consider them personal role models.[52] In contrast to the pattern Gordon describes, many women at the Training School did want to emulate their principal. A graduate of 1921 says that she "just adored Mrs. McLure. I thought if we could just be like Mrs. McLure, the world could ask nothing more."[53]

---

[51]Mallory, "Mrs. Maude Reynolds McLure," transcript, 2.

[52]Lynn Gordon, *Gender and Higher Education in the Progressive Era* (New Haven: Yale University Press, 1990) 179, 39-40.

[53]Allen, Mather Interview, 19.

Gordon postulates that since "independent spinsterhood and women's communities" never became significant alternatives for women of the South, women students did not develop a strong identification with unmarried faculty members.[54] A 1920 graduate of Judson College in Marion, Alabama remembered her teachers:

> In later years I wondered what had happened to those invincible females to arouse in them such antipathy for the masculine sex and to convince them that the lowest emotion of womanhood was to be attracted to the male.[55]

Sally Brett notes that unmarried women faculty in the South found less acceptance than their northern counterparts since "the southern lady was by myth and tradition a belle or matron, not a spinster."[56] Perhaps since McLure had been married and was a mother, Training School students could more easily view her as a role-model for their lives.

Other teachers were respected and well liked, but students did not express an intense identification with them as they did with McLure. In contrast to the five founders, faculty and staff typically came from more modest backgrounds. They filled such positions as school nurse, housekeeper, elocution instructor, and music instructor. Since most Training School teachers were widowed or had never married, they lived with students in the school's building.[57]

Emma Leachman was an unmarried faculty member who began living with students before the school was adopted by the WMU.[58]

---

[54]Gordon, *Gender and Higher Education*, 39-40.

[55]Viola Goode Liddell, *With a Southern Accent* (Norman, Oklahoma: University of Oklahoma Press, 1948) 234, quoted in *Daughters of the Dream: Judson College, 1838-1988* by Frances Dew Hamilton and Elizabeth Crabtree Wells, (Marion, AL: Judson College, 1989) 132.

[56]Sally Brett, "A Different Kind of Being," in *Stepping off the Pedestal: Academic Women in the South*, eds. Patricia Stringer and Irene Thompson (New York: Modern Language Association of America, 1982) 17.

[57]"List of Faculty and Staff 1907-1958," unclassified papers, TSC, SBTS.

[58]DeVault, Littlejohn Interview, 23.

She instructed students in field work and directed the school's settlement house until 1921 when she became the first woman staff member employed by Southern Baptists' Home Mission Board. Leachman's background before coming to the school is similar to that of other Training School teachers.

Leachman was born in Washington County, Kentucky in 1868. She was educated in the local public schools and at Central Normal College in Evansville, Indiana. In 1898 she went to Louisville where she worked in the Louisville Baptist Orphans Home until 1900. In that year she began working with women and children at the Hope Rescue Mission, a Baptist mission that provided food, shelter, and "the Gospel of salvation" to Louisville's poor.[59]

In 1904 Leachman was appointed by Kentucky Baptists as a city missionary, continuing her association with the rescue mission and expanding her work into other areas of the city. At the rescue mission, Leachman met Alice Huey who had been attending lectures at the Seminary. Leachman soon began attending classes and asked if she might live with the students. At the age of thirty-six she moved into the rented home that would later become the Training School.[60]

Leachman was asked by the school's board of managers to direct the mission work done by Training School students in 1905. She did this in exchange for room and board until 1909 when she began receiving an honorarium of $100 per year.[61] She is listed in the 1907 school catalogue as teacher of "Applied Methods and City Missions."

When the Baptist Settlement House first opened in 1912 Leachman set up an office in the settlement, continuing her position as city missionary in addition to managing students' field work and teaching classes. Carrie Littlejohn, one of Leachman's students from 1913 to 1915, observed, "The girls either loved her or they were deathly afraid of her. Her criticism could be as biting as her praise was

---

[59]E. C. Routh,"Emma Leachman," Encyclopedia of Southern Baptists, vol. 2 (Nashville: Broadman Press, 1958) 781; *Baptist World*, May 6, 1909.

[60]Willie Jean Stewart, "The World in Her Heart," Woman's Missionary Union, 1938, Leachman Papers, WMUA.

[61]Stewart, "The World in Her Heart"; DeVault, Littlejohn Interview, 84.

genuine."[62] The students and faculty respected her for her knowledge and experience in helping needy individuals.

Who Were the Students?

With a few exceptions, students of the Training School, like their teachers, came from families of modest means. Although records providing demographic information about students are sketchy, it is possible to identify general demographic characteristics concerning students' ages, economic status, and geographic origins. Letters of application from the class of 1908, as well as brief biographical sketches of women attending in 1906 and 1907, provide information on the earliest students. Life sketches of former students who were employed by the Foreign Mission Board (FMB) in 1926 contain information about students who served overseas.[63] Foreign missionaries comprised about one third of alumnae and provide a sample of Training School students. Biographies of individual students also contribute to a portrait of the student body.

Historians of women's higher education have identified demographic patterns among the women students of the late nineteenth and early twentieth centuries. Generalizing about American women in higher education, these studies typically focus on women of the Northeast and Midwest, while the experiences of southern women students are relegated to tangential discussions and footnotes. While southern women certainly shared in the common experiences of other women at the turn of the century, they were a part of a distinctive culture. As the North was becoming heavily urbanized and industrial, the South was still largely agrarian. Financial difficulties in establishing colleges were often insurmountable for a region whose inhabitants

---

[62]Littlejohn *History of Carver*, 85; Juliette Mather to Una L. Roberts, April 6, 1950, U. L. Lawrence Papers, SBHLA.

[63]Information on 1906, 1907, and 1908 applicants is found in TSC, SBTS. Biographical sketches of missionaries on the foreign field in 1926 are taken from Foreign Mission Board, *Album of Southern Baptist Foreign Missionaries*, Richmond, VA: Foreign Mission Board of the Southern Baptist Convention, 1926.

often lived in poverty.[64] Segregation laws reinforced white supremacy and resistance to change characterized the region.[65] Samuel Hill, historian of religion in the South, claims that the South, being the most distinct regional subculture in the United States is "linked with the tightest bonds" to its religion and depends upon religion to legitimate its culture.[66] Therefore, it is not surprising that southern women in a religious institution formed a unique group and did not follow patterns described by historians of women's education. In spite of these differences, research concerning women in other areas of the nation provides a context in which to discuss the particularities of Training School students.

Education historians have drawn a distinction between a late-nineteenth-century pioneering generation of serious-minded "pauper scholars" and women students of the early twentieth century who came from the middle classes, desired more contact with college men, and aspired to a life of domesticity.[67] Studying student populations located primarily in the Northeast and Midwest, Barbara Solomon constructs a scheme of three generations of college women. The first generation (1860-1880) was composed of single-minded and serious students, while students of the second generation (1890-1900), although still pioneering, had a "more expansive spirit" and were "mentally and physically vigorous." The third generation (1910-1920) was composed of more sophisticated "new women" who desired the company of men and foreshadowed the 1920s flapper.[68]

Lynn Gordon notes that in the South the timetable for women's education was different, due to women's limited opportunities for

---

[64]Charles D. Johnson, *Higher Education of Southern Baptists: An Institutional History, 1826-1954.* (Waco, Texas: Baylor University Press, 1955) 6-7.

[65]Spain, *A Zion at Ease,* 210-211.

[66]Samuel Hill, "Epilogue" in, *Churches in Cultural Captivity: A History of the Social Attitudes of Southern Baptists* by John L. Eighmy (Knoxville: University of Tennessee, 1972) 200-202.

[67]Helen Horowitz, *Campus Life: Undergraduate Cultures From the End of the Eighteenth Century to the Present* (Chicago: University of Chicago Press, 1987) 193, 201.

[68]Barbara Miller Solomon, *In the Company of Educated Women: A History of Women and Higher Education in America* (New Haven: Yale University Press, 1985) 95.

good secondary education and the late development of women's colleges in that region. In the South, women entering college at the turn of the century constituted a pioneering first, rather than second, generation of students.[69] Helen Horowitz places pioneer collegiate women among a group of campus "outsiders" who did not participate in the college life of hedonism and uninterest in study that was popular. Typically from families of modest means who had made great sacrifices to pay for a college education, nineteenth century women and other outsiders took academic preparation seriously.[70] By the twentieth century, middle-class families began sending their daughters to college, and these women brought to the campus their own ideas about womanhood, marriage, and college fun.[71]

Education historians note a general diversification of women collegians occurring in the early twentieth century. Not only did students come from a broader range of economic backgrounds as the middle and elite classes began to educate their daughters, but student populations also became more diverse in terms of ethnicity as immigrant and black women gained admission to many colleges.[72]

The earliest Training School students did not follow the patterns described by these historians of Northeastern and Midwestern colleges, but rather maintained an image of piety and seriousness throughout the period of study. The Training School did not experience the growing ethnic or economic diversity, which was taking place in non-southern educational institutions for women. Immigrants and blacks were seen as populations to be proselytized and redeemed rather than included as students.[73] Student populations of the Training School continued to come from backgrounds of economic hardship through the 1930s with a shift toward the middle class occurring much later than in other populations described by historians of women's education. While remaining fairly homogeneous

---

[69]Gordon *Gender and Higher Education*, 49-50.
[70]Horowitz, *Campus Life* 17, 67.
[71]Ibid. 201; Gordon, *Gender and Higher Education*, 5-6.
[72]Solomon, *Company of Educated Women*, 75-77.
[73]Allen, *Century to Celebrate*, 81-83.

in terms of ethnicity, economic background, and community origins, Training School student populations showed variety in age, previous academic preparation, and vocational choice.

Most Training School students were from the rural South, having grown up in religious, yet low-income, families. Most had attended college or normal school previously. These women came to the Training School with an urgent desire, often expressed in terms of a call from God, to prepare for Christian service. The first generation of Training School students was intent on becoming foreign missionaries, whereas students who came later trained for many different types of Christian work considered appropriate for women.

Rural Southerners

While the first women students were from Louisville and surrounding areas of Kentucky, after the Training School was adopted by the WMU, students began coming from many different states in the South and Midwest. Then when Seminary classes were officially opened to the students in the 1902-1903 session, twenty-four women were listed in the catalogue as attending classes regularly. Of these students: Twenty were married women, assumed to be wives of male students; four single women, two from Louisville, and two from LaGrange, Kentucky. Forty-eight women were enrolled in one or more classes during the 1903-04 academic year. Again, most were Seminary wives, but six single women were in attendance, three hailing from Kentucky.[74] Although the vast majority of students continued to come from southern states, the number coming from northern and midwestern states grew as Southern Baptist territory increased.[75] A brief examination of WMU expansion into the West and North will suggest reasons why Training School students began to represent a larger geographical area.

---

[74]*Catalogue*, SBTS, 1901-06: Single women are counted in this analysis, following the assumption that they came to Louisville for the purpose of attending classes, whereas married women probably came to the Seminary with their student husbands.

[75]*Catalogue*, WMUTS, 1909-21.

When WMU was formed in 1888, women in four of the fourteen Southern Baptist states did not affiliate with the national organization. But by 1891, all four of these had joined and WMU was seeking to expand into new territory. Catherine Allen suggests three primary factors in geographic expansion of the WMU organization: first, the out-migration of Southern Baptists who did not break denominational ties, the splintering of Northern Baptists over theological disputes (some would align with Southern Baptists), and finally, evangelistic initiatives in new territories.[76]

Although the majority of students came from southern states, those from other regions were exposed to the hegemony of southern values and traditions operating at the Training School. Juliette Mather, born and reared in Chicago, was much impressed by a certain WMU executive: "She was sweet, gracious, and kind and good and polite. . . . I thought this was southern womanhood."[77] Mather recognizes a contrast between WMU leaders and women from the north stating that "we had lovely older women, but these were a little different. There was a gentleness about them."[78]

The Southern Baptist denomination flourished in the rural South, and biographical sketches of the earliest students reveal an overwhelming majority of students from rural areas. They came from towns like Pidcock, Georgia, Walter Hill, Tennessee, and Tecumseh, Oklahoma.[79] One pastor's description of a Training School student from his church could have described many others as well: "Her opportunities and chance for culture and practice has [sic] only been such as a country church can or will afford."[80] In the 1907-1908 session, only two of sixteen students were from urban areas.[81] After 1908, only the student's home state was recorded, thus rendering a determination of community origins impossible. However, an analysis

---

[76]Allen, *Century to Celebrate*, 70-73.
[77]Tharpe and Hamric, Mather Interview, 19.
[78]Ibid.
[79]Rosenberg 38; *Catalogue*, SBTS, 1906.
[80]Ida Wise Application File, 1908, TSC, SBTS.
[81]Student Biographies, 1907-1908; TSC, SBTS.

of biographical data published by the Foreign Mission Board indicates that the majority of students continued to come from rural areas into the 1920s. Out of the 106 former Training School students serving on the foreign field in 1926, fourteen were born in cities; the rest were from small towns and rural areas.[82]

Jane Hunter documented the rural origins of women missionaries in her study of American women missionaries in China. Hunter notes that while foreign missionaries were typically from small towns or rural areas, settlement workers were likely to have been city-dwellers.[83] In light of this important observation, it should be noted that in the case of community origins, the group that served in foreign missions may not be representative of the entire student body of the Training School. In other words, it is possible that a larger proportion of urban women who came to the Training School chose home missions, city missions, or settlement work rather than going to the foreign mission field. Nevertheless, the students from small towns and rural areas far outnumbered city dwellers in the Training School's earliest years and most likely remained in the majority reflecting the community origins of most Southern Baptists.

International Students

Whether from rural or urban settings, Training School students were not exclusively from the United States; international students began to appear at the Training School during its second decade of operation. The school had enrolled foreign-born students since its beginnings, but in early years these were missionaries' children who typically left their parents on the field and came to the United States to be educated. By the 1920s, however, a few foreign students whose parents were not American citizens began to attend. International students typically were supported by scholarships from churches or

---

[82]Foreign Mission Board, *Album of Southern Baptist Foreign Missionaries.*
[83]Jane Hunter, *The Gospel of Gentility: American Women Missionaries in Turn-of-the-Century China* (New Haven: Yale University Press, 1984) 28-29.

mission societies.[84] Women came from places such as Brazil, Hungary, and China.[85] This pattern reflected successful efforts of Southern Baptists in foreign missions. The missionaries who had converted them and desired to go to the United States to study inspired young women overseas. Ludovica Cristea heard Southern Seminary President E. Y. Mullins speak in her native Romania and was determined from that day to go to the United States. Three years later, a group of Southern Baptist tourists to that country pooled their resources to support Ludovica and another Romanian, Sofia Palyo, while they studied at the Training School.[86]

For Whites Only

International students did not change the homogeneous racial composition of the Training School; apart from two Chinese women, international students of this period were white women of European descent. Training School publicity assured readers that African students were Caucasian:

> Among the students enrolled at the Training School is Miss Frieda Woodford of Cape Town, Africa. She is almost twenty-one years old and was born in Essex, England. She wishes this to be known because a few weeks ago when it was stated that she was from South Africa some one inquired, "Is she black?" She is emphatically not. . . . [87]

Like the Training School, most other colleges in the South did not admit black students before the 1950s. In fact, in the state of Kentucky, the racial integration of colleges and schools was made

---

[84]"He Calleth His Own and Leadeth Them" [1909?], *Royal Service* "Florida's Scholarship Girl," clipping August 30,1917, TSC, SBTS.

[85]"List of Foreign Students who have Studied in the Training School"; unclassified papers, TSC, SBTS.

[86]Littlejohn, *History of Carver*, 93.

[87]"He Calleth His Own"

illegal by a statute known as the Day Law, which had been in effect since the nineteenth century. Students and instructors of institutions that illegally admitted both black and white students were subject to fines and penalties.[88] With the exception of a few Asian international students, the Training School enrolled only white women.

"Pauper Scholars"

Many Training School students depended on scholarships to help pay their expenses. Historians of higher education for women have observed that nineteenth-century pioneer female collegians came from modest backgrounds, whereas women students of the early twentieth century typically came from middle-class families.[89] Gordon observes that due to the high cost of tuition in Southern women's colleges, only upper middle class students attended. Fathers of these students were typically professionals and businessmen. Even in the less expensive state universities the majority of students' fathers were not farmers, clerks, or other lower middle class occupations. Rather, they were mainly professionals and entrepreneurs.[90]

The earliest students of the Training School did not come from middle-class families like their northeastern and midwestern counterparts. Most Southern Baptists of this period were "of humble birth and modest means" and, with few exceptions, students came from families struggling against economic hardship.[91] The school's effort to keep costs to a bare minimum suggests that it served a group that struggled against the economic burden of living expenses. A comparison of students' expenses at other women's schools will highlight the relatively low cost of the Training School. In 1908, students paid $350 per year to attend Mt. Holyoke.[92] A women's college of the

---

[88]Kentucky statute 4363-8, 1934, c65, Article I, 8.
[89]Horowitz, *Campus Life* 195.; Solomon, *Company of Educated Women*, 65.; Gordon, *Gender and Higher Education*, 5.
[90]Gordon, *Gender and Higher Education*, 5-6.
[91]Spain, *At Ease in Zion*, 10.
[92]Solomon, *Company of Educated Women*, 65.

South, Agnes Scott, charged students of the 1910-1911 session $325-
$350 per year for tuition, room and board.[93] The Training School,
charged no tuition, but students paid three dollars per week for board,
a furnished room, and utilities. The catalogue of 1910 recommended
that $175 per session would "comfortably maintain a student not
including clothing or traveling expenses." Parents and sponsors were
warned against extravagance and asked not to send more than $200.
for the year.[94] Students performed domestic duties, which kept
operating costs to a minimum. Churches and mission organizations
donated food items to the school regularly. Fruits, home-canned
goods, hams, peanuts, and other produce came from the farms of
Southern Baptists.[95]

The financial strain of students is demonstrated by the application
letters received in 1908, the second year of the school's operation.
When asked on the application form if they were able to pay three
dollars per week for living expenses, students often provided detailed
explanations about their financial situations. Dora Miller, "a daughter
of pious German Baptists" in Oklahoma explained that she earned a
small income from a farm but that her earnings were seasonal. She
asked if she might pay her expenses in three-month installments and
stated that since she cannot afford the train fare back home during
summer vacation she would like to remain in Louisville to work.[96]

Some women simply could not afford to attend but expressed their
sincere desire to do so. An applicant from Missouri wrote: "I think
that I have overcome every obstacle but the money question, and I
realize that this is no small one." Helen Stephens could not pay for a
full term at the Training School but expected divine intervention:
"[I] thought I would go while [the money] lasted and hope that God
will send me the rest."[97]

---

[93]Gordon, *Gender and Higher Education*, 171.
[94]*Catalogue*, WMUTS, 1910, 17.
[95]Allen, *Century to Celebrate*, 274.
[96]Dora Miller Application File, 1908 ,TSC, SBTS.
[97]Helen Stephens Application File, 1908, TSC, SBTS.

McLure and other WMU leaders attempted to help students find ways to finance a Training School education. The 1909 catalogue clearly stated that there is no students' aid fund and therefore the student or her friends must pay weekly expenses. State WMU organizations had begun to sponsor a few students, and it was hoped that women could find sponsors among family friends or members of their churches. McLure tactfully presented the sponsorship idea to the persons providing letters of reference for individual applicants. In the list of questions sent to the applicant's pastor and four church members, McLure asked "Would her pastor or people be likely to aid her in taking a course of training?" Although McLure did not ask directly about financial aid, respondents indicated that they understood her meaning by addressing the financial situations of both applicant and church. One church member drew a dismal picture of the applicant's situation: "She has no pastor now and her family is quite poor. I doubt the church members [will be] giving her help."[98] Yet in other cases, McLure's subtle prompting paid off. One pastor, who perhaps could not provide cash assistance, offered to lend the student his books.[99] Wallace W. Lawton, an attorney acquainted with applicant Viola Leasure wrote, "In regard to the expenses, as one of the deacons of our church, I propose to now be personally responsible for her expenses . . . [M]y wife and I wish to stand behind her in this matter of preparing herself for Christian work."[100]

Several applicants intended to work during the school term or summer vacation; one asked McLure about the possibility of teaching private music lessons in the city. Training School leaders, however, discouraged outside work, and from 1909 the catalogue declared it "impossible for a student to take employment as . . . the regular course requires all her time and strength."[101]

The students of 1908 were determined to come to the Training School in spite of financial strain. But what about students who came

---

[98]Nellie Brown Application File, 1908, TSC, SBTS.
[99]Mildred Buhlmaier Application File, 1908, TSC, SBTS.
[100]Viola Leasure Application File, 1908, TSC, SBTS.
[101]Helen Stephens Application File, 1908, TSC, SBTS; *Catalogue*, WMUTS, 1909, 18.

later? While it is likely that there were a few students from middle-class families, the majority continued to struggle financially into the 1920s, as evidenced by their dependence on scholarship support.[102] Scholarships were provided by state WMU organizations, which chose an applicant, usually a resident of the state, to sponsor financially. Not only did sponsorship include the amount needed for living expenses, but also usually clothing and other supplies were donated or purchased by the women of the state. When Beulah Stamps arrived from Florida without warm clothing for a Louisville winter, the Florida WMU expressed embarrassment and responded "willingly and gladly" to her need, although they did not want to set a precedent for providing a student's wardrobe.[103] When Kathleen McDowell received a scholarship from Alabama's WMU in 1926, she was also sent a check for ten dollars to buy a dress for commencement and other ceremonies. Alabama women wanted Kathleen to have "a white voile or some equally simple but pretty white frock. . . ."[104]

Southern Baptist women, often with little or no income of their own, made great sacrifices to help other women from their state receive an education. Women living on farms, if they had nothing else at all, usually had chickens. Missouri women began a scholarship fund for Training School students in 1917 by setting aside money earned from eggs laid on a certain day of the week.[105]

A student who received scholarship funds was expected to enter Christian work, either paid or unpaid. If she married a missionary or pastor, she was considered to be in Christian work as his helpmate. A woman who did not marry a pastor or who entered a vocation other than Christian work was expected to refund the money used for her education. Kathleen McDowell Timmerman completed one year at the Training School before leaving to marry a pastor and work with him in a mountain school. The Alabama WMU, indicating they

---

[102]Littlejohn, 109.
[103]Beulah Stamps Application File, 1908, TSC, SBTS.
[104]Kathleen McDowell Scrapbook, [1926-27], Timmerman Papers, WMUA.
[105]Allen, *Century to Celebrate*, 117, 286.

considered such "repayment" of a $200 scholarship a sufficient return on their educational investment, gave her a type of "receipt."[106]

Previous Educational Experience

Women students were resourceful in finding ways to pay for their education either by earning their own money or by applying for loans and scholarships. The same ingenuity women used to pay for Training School had been used to finance a college or normal school education in previous years. Ella Jeter financed tuition for a few months at the turn of the century:

> When [I was] fourteen years old my father gave me a little calf and my mother gave me a feather bed and some quilts. I had eight heads of cattle when the time came for me to go to college. I sold everything I had and struck out. I didn't get to stay the whole year for my money gave out and I had to go back home. . . .[107]

Jeter's short-term educational experience was not unusual among women in poverty who interrupted schooling to earn money.[108] This inconsistency in attendance is one of the factors that render students' prior educational experience difficult to determine. The other factor complicating this determination is that southern women's schools of this era often used the term "college" to designate schools with very different academic standards. Some southern institutions educating women established curricula similar to that of an academy or finishing school, offering training in subjects such as music, elocution, domestic skills, and etiquette. Others, like Judson College in Marion, Alabama, featured a preparatory division for young girls as well as a post-

---

[106]Kathleen McDowell Scrapbook, [1926-27], Timmerman Papers, WMUA.

[107]Ella Jeter Comerford, "The Training School Begins" (address given at WMU Training School, October 2, 1940) transcript, unclassified papers, TSC, SBTS.

[108]Solomon, *Company of Educated Women*, 69.

secondary department.[109] Therefore, when records of this period show college attendance, it is unclear whether the student was engaged in secondary or post-secondary learning.

Northern women's colleges began dealing with the issues of academic standards in the nineteenth century, but southern schools were still facing the question of standardization into the twentieth century. According to Gordon, this was because southern schools were established later and were handicapped by a shortage of solid secondary schools in the South. In 1903, Elizabeth Avery Colton founded the Southern Association of Colleges for Women (SACW), an organization that attempted to raise academic standards in southern women's colleges. In 1915, the SACW pointed out that although there were 140 institutions in the South calling themselves "colleges for women," only six were recognized as standard colleges. A report by Colton in 1916 classified women's schools into standard, approximate, normal and industrial, junior, unclassifiable, and imitation and nominal colleges. These classifications were based on factors such as whether or not the college had a preparatory department, number of special study students, library and laboratory facilities, salaries, and research and creative work of the faculty.[110]

Nevertheless, most students spent at least a few months engaged in higher education before coming to the Training School. A few women had earned undergraduate degrees. The foreign missions sample of 106 former Training School students contains only nine women who had not attended some type of institution of higher education. Schools that Training School students attended may be divided into two broad categories: non-Baptist affiliated schools, either private or state-supported, and Southern Baptist colleges. The former Training School students employed by the FMB in 1926 serve as a sample group. The ninety-seven students engaged in higher education prior to coming to the Training School are equally divided

---

[109]Elizabeth B. Young *A Study of the Curricula of Seven Selected Women's Colleges of the Southern States*, (1932; reprint, New York: Teacher's College Press, 1972) 22-44.

[110]Gordon, *Gender and Higher Education*, 48-49.; and Thomas Woody, *A History of Women's Education in the United States* vol. 2, (New York: The Science Press, 1929) 185-88.

between the two types of institutions with forty-eight having attended non-Baptist schools and forty-nine having attended Southern Baptist colleges.[111]

Training School students who were educated in non-Baptist affiliated schools attended three types of institutions: state universities (often coeducational), state-supported schools for women, and private colleges. While a few women attended state universities, the majority of women attending non-Baptist schools were enrolled in state normal and industrial schools for women offering practical training in teaching and other vocations. The South had a number of state-supported institutions for women, which resulted from a general reluctance of universities in southern states to offer coeducation. Eight institutions of this type were founded in the South within a relatively short period of time and attracted students from humbler backgrounds by offering low fees and reasonable living expenses. Winthrop Normal and Industrial College of South Carolina educated fourteen of the former Training School students in the sample group.[112]

Another South Carolina school that educated Training School students was Converse College, a private liberal arts school for women located in Spartanburg. Dexter Edgar Converse, a mill owner who believed that "the well-being of any country depends much upon the culture of her women," founded the school in 1889. Although Converse College was not affiliated with any denomination, it was "liberally and tolerantly Christian." Converse held high standards of academic excellence: it was one of only six women's colleges recognized as "standard colleges" by the Southern Association of College Women in 1915.[113]

---

[111]Foreign Mission Board, *Album of Southern Baptist Foreign Missionaries*. Richmond VA: Foreign Mission Board of the Southern Baptist Convention, 1926.

[112]B. H. Weaver, "Some Aspects of The Development of Liberal Arts Education for Women in the South," in *Trends in Liberal Arts Education for Women* (New Orleans: Newcomb College, 1954) 39-41; and "Winthrop College," in *American Universities and Colleges*, 12th ed. by American Council on Education, (New York: Walter deGruyter Publishers, 1983) 1730.

[113]Woody, *History of Women's Education*, 187; Converse College Catalogue, (1992) 6-12.

Single-gender institutions like Converse were popular in the South even into the 1920s and 1930s when coeducation was the norm for the rest of the nation.[114] The majority of Southern Baptist colleges attended by Training School students were also single-sex institutions. The first Baptist colleges originally had been created to educate young men for the ministry. While they wanted to educate their daughters, most Southern Baptists opposed coeducation. The Southern Baptist women's colleges began to appear in the 1830s and 1840s to provide the solution.[115] This type of institution educated the largest number of women in the sample group: thirty-four of the foreign mission sample attended Southern Baptist women's colleges. Meredith in North Carolina, Bessie Tift in Georgia, and Judson in Alabama were the colleges with the highest representation. Laura Cox earned a B.A. degree from Meredith College. She graduated in 1904 and came to the Training School in 1909 after working to pay college debts. At Meredith, she was required to study Latin, English, Mathematics, History, and Physiology; she could have elected to study other courses in the sciences, languages, logic, ethics, art, music, or pedagogy. Several courses available at Meredith may have helped Cox prepare for Training School studies; she could have elected to study Greek or perhaps taken a Bible course introduced in 1902.[116]

Although the majority of Southern Baptist colleges were gender-segregated, a few institutions began placing men and women in the same classroom in the late nineteenth century. Fifteen of the women in the foreign missions sample group attended coeducational Southern Baptist colleges. One of the earliest Baptist institutions to provide education for both men and women was Baylor University in Waco, Texas. Baylor became coeducational in 1886.[117] An earlier experi-

---

[114]Amy T. McCandless, Preserving the Pedestal: Restrictions on Social Life at Southern Colleges for Women, 1920-1940, *History of Higher Education Annual* vol. 7 (1987) 45-67.

[115]Leon McBeth, *Women in Baptist Life* (Nashville: Broadman Press, 1979) 106; and Charles D. Johnson, 5, 15.

[116]Laura Cox File, Foreign Mission Board Correspondence, SBHLA; M. L. Johnson, *A History of Meredith College* (Raleigh: Meredith College, 1956) 61,107.

[117]Eugene W. Baker, *To Light the Ways of Time: An Illustrated History of Baylor University, 1845-1986* (Waco: Baylor University, 1987) 57-58.

ment in coordinate education led to the formation of a separate women's school in 1866: Baylor Female College. Twenty years later, when Baylor moved from Independence, Texas to Waco, the school became coeducational. At first men and women followed different curricula, but by 1891 all degree programs were open to women.[118] Jewell Legett graduated from Baylor in 1907 and found that some of her male classmates at Baylor were also her classmates at the Seminary. Legett took courses in Baylor's department of Bible teaching, which was designed not only to train ministers, but also to equip both men and women in Christian work.[119]

The variety of southern institutions that called themselves colleges render the exact nature of a student's prior education difficult to determine. However, the school's entrance requirements ensured that all students had at least some formal education prior to enrollment in the Training School. Students were required to pass an entrance exam to exhibit competence equaling an eighth grade education in the public schools. Beginning in 1921, high school graduation was required for admission, but college attendance was not a prerequisite until the 1930s.[120]

Older Women

Since most students had been engaged in higher education prior to attending the Training School, they were often older than women at other education institutions. The school did not admit students less than twenty years of age nor more than thirty-nine.[121] Barbara Miller Solomon has observed that the earliest female collegians were generally more mature, usually in their twenties and thirties. Female students, and males as well, often interrupted their formal education with employment in order to support themselves.[122] Laura Cox

---

[118]Ibid., 67.
[119]Legett, Diary, 1909; Baker, *To Light the Ways*, 91.
[120]*Catalogue*, WMUTS, 1908, 1921, 1931.
[121]*Catalogue*, WMUTS, 1920.
[122]Solomon, *Company of Educated Women*, 69.; see also Horowitz, *Campus Life* 193.

wanted to serve as a foreign missionary from the time she was fifteen and accepted "any and all kinds of work," saving enough money to enter Meredith College at age twenty-four. After graduating, she taught school for six years to pay her debt for college and to save money to enter the Training School at age thirty-seven.[123]

Solomon notes that by the 1920s, colleges were enrolling younger students. For example, at Radcliffe graduates between 1890 and 1900 averaged twenty-nine years of age; the average age dropped to slightly over twenty-one and a half for graduates in the 1920s.[124] An analysis of the Foreign Mission Board biographical sketches indicates that this particular group of Training School students did not follow this trend. By calculating the median ages of students at the time they began Training School, we find that the median age of students enrolled between 1905 and 1915 was twenty-six, while those enrolled between 1916 and 1926 averaged twenty-five years of age. In other words, students who enrolled after 1916 were only slightly younger than the pioneer Training School students were.[125]

Many women in their thirties, either by personal choice or through the influence of others, did not consider the foreign missions vocational option. Letters of application from 1908 reveal that women in their thirties worried that they may be too old for service on the foreign field. Pearl Caldwell wanted for many years to be a foreign missionary but felt that at age thirty she had delayed missionary training too long: "I doubt the propriety of my going to China, really I doubt if I should attempt foreign work at all." The principal of Blue Mountain College concurred in her letter of support for Caldwell; "Pearl is too old I suppose to go as a foreign missionary. . . ." Perhaps the principal's influence contributed to Caldwell's uncertainty.[126]

---

[123]Laura Cox to R. J. Willingham, February 10, 1910, Laura Cox File, FMB Correspondence, SBHLA.

[124]Solomon, *Company of Educated Women*, 70.

[125]Subtracting two years from the Training School graduation date and then subtracting that figure from the birth date calculated students ages. However, ages are subject to one year variance, as students did not always attend the full two years.

[126]Pearl Caldwell, Application File, 1908, TSC, SBTS.

The Foreign Mission Board of the Southern Baptist Convention (FMB) seems to have discouraged women in their late thirties from going overseas. However, Laura Cox was quite certain that at age thirty-eight she was fit for foreign mission work. She wrote to the FMB from the Training School and prepared for possible disappointment:

> I am sending my application although I know you do not approve very much of a woman going out after she is thirty-five years of age. . . . Please allow me to ask that you pray very definitely . . . before you reject me. . . .[127]

The FMB wrote to Baptist leaders in Cox's home state of North Carolina to determine her fitness. She was appointed in 1910 and served as a missionary to Mexico for seventeen years.[128]

The Training School catalogue also discouraged mature women from choosing the foreign mission field. The maximum age of admission for students preparing for domestic missions was thirty-eight (raised to thirty-nine by the 1920s), while students preparing for the foreign field were not accepted into the school after age thirty-three.[129]

If older women felt compelled to choose vocations other than foreign missions, then the sample group used to calculate median ages of students may not be representative of the Training School student body. Apart from the Foreign Mission Board biographies, there are no written records indicating at what age students began their missionary training. However, there is evidence that Training School students may have conformed to the pattern described by Solomon in which younger students followed mature women in the 1920s. The annual report of 1919 notes students' enthusiasm for athletics and makes a comparison to earlier decades when students were "too mature to find

[127]Cox to Willingham. February 10, 1910.
[128]Laura Cox File, FMB Correspondence, SBHLA.
[129]Catalogue, WMUTS, 1910, 1926.

the exercise agreeable." The current students were different: "Now younger girls and college girls are crowding in, and they plead for athletics."[130] By 1919 the student body was composed of a younger group of women.

Called By God

Whether they came to the Training School in younger years or later in life, women students were responding to an urgent desire for vocations in Christian service. During the nineteenth century, as women's mission societies were collecting funds and stimulating missionary zeal in the churches, individual women began making commitments to go overseas as missionaries. In fact, woman's historian Jane Hunter reports a feminization of the missionary movement, with women composing sixty percent of the American mission force in 1890. At first, most students were missionary wives, but by the second half of the nineteenth century, single women were also dedicating their lives to foreign mission work.[131] The missionary enterprise opened a new career opportunity to women at a time when their options were limited. The missionary life offered women a sense of purpose, and a chance to demonstrate competence and strength.[132] It also provided a respectable route to notoriety, as the missionary became a heroic figure in her home church. For religious women of this era, options for adventure were limited, and exotic tales of missionary experiences were appealing.

The earliest Training School students were preparing for service as foreign missionaries. Some had very specific destinations, naming the country in which they planned to serve. Others were more indefinite in their aims, listing "miscellaneous mission work" or

---

[130]Annual Report of WMU Training School, May, 1919, 5, TSC, WMUA.

[131]Hunter, *The Gospel of Gentility*, xiii-xvi.

[132]Joan Jacobs Brumberg, *Mission for Life: The Story of the Family of Adoniram Judson* (New York: The Free Press. 1980) 79-80.

expressing flexibility in statements like: "My life is fully surrendered to God to be led by him."[133]

Like other American missionary women of their time, they spoke of their vocational choice in terms of a call from God, which sometimes came very early in life. Hunter notes that women missionaries often describe very dramatic experiences of conversion and calling.[134] The testimony of Eula Hensley, who came to the Training School in 1906, is typical. "When a child six years of age, sitting on her mother's knee she began to long to tell to the Chinese children [the story of] Jesus and his love." Hensley was baptized at age eleven and continued to think of foreign missions until "she came face to face with the question and gladly gave her life to the foreign work" during a revival meeting.[135] Many women like Hensley reported that in childhood they felt a general inclination toward mission work. From the late nineteenth century, Woman's Missionary Union sponsored organizations to promote missions education for young children called "Sunbeam Bands." Sunbeams raised money for missions, memorized Bible verses, and sang songs: "Over the ocean wave, far, far, away, There the poor heathen live, waiting for the day."[136]

Young people were often encouraged by pastors and church members to consider foreign missionary service. Joan Brumberg observes that adolescents living in a "culture of evangelicalism" might be moved to respond to the missions cause through a revival meeting, missionary stories, or college organizations for missionary volunteers.[137] Ella Jeter received a more personal prompting from her pastor who told her, "The Lord did not save you for nothing. He has a work for every Christian. I don't know what your place is, but you constantly pray that the Lord will show you what he wants you to do and I'm sure he will." Jeter followed the pastor's advice and began praying

[133]Pearl Fonteney and Jennie Allnutt, student enrollment records, 1906-08, TSC, SBTS.

[134]Hunter, 30-31.

[135]"Miss Hensley," *Foreign Mission Journal* (July 1908)10.

[136]Allen, *A Century to Celebrate*, 101-102.

[137]Brumberg, *Mission for Life* xi, 21-43; See also "Ethel Ray Stoermer Bailey," *Home and Foreign Fields* 8 (October 1924) 25.

about China. Finally she put her ideas to the test and made a bargain with God: "If you will save my Sunday School class, I will go to China." That night all of the boys in her Sunday School class were converted, and Jeter decided this was her answer.[138]

The search for a sign from God to affirm decisions is a common element in testimonies of Training School students. Jewell Legett was sure of her calling to be a missionary, but when she was asked to leave the Training School one year earlier than planned in response to a dire need in China, she was uncertain of her decision. One Sunday morning when she visited the Highland Baptist Church, she was surprised to find the preacher introducing a guest speaker. When she heard that the speaker was a missionary from China, she was sure this was a sign from God that she should go and do mission work in that country. [139]

Many women students kept their experience of God's calling a secret, perhaps fearing the reactions of family and friends. Cynthia Miller wrote an account of her own anxiety after announcing at church that she had been called to mission service:

> Cynthia was ashamed to go home and tell of her surrender to God, and afraid too, that it might break Mother's heart, and she was sure that her Father would ridicule and perhaps censure her too for making such a public demonstra-tion. . . .[140]

As service opportunities expanded for Southern Baptist women, students entered the Training School to prepare for other Christian vocations including home missions, WMU work, and social work. Like the foreign missionaries, these women sometimes articulated their vocational choice in terms of a call from God—often experi-enced during childhood or adolescence. Home missionaries and social

---

[138]Ella Jeter Comerford, "The Training School Begins."

[139]Legett, Diary, January 14, 1909.

[140][Cynthia Miller], "A Sketch of the Life of Cynthia Adaline Miller," Cynthia Miller File, FMB correspondence, SBHLA.

workers became interested in Christian service through the influence of family members, sermons, and stories of other women Christian workers.[141] Carrie Littlejohn, who left the Training School in 1915 to do Christian work in the mill towns of Georgia and South Carolina, recalled early influences:

> As a child, ten years old, I would read the articles that these women missionaries would write about their work in these mill towns. That was my first compelling desire to do similar things.[142]

Students like Littlejohn made great sacrifices to answer the call to service. Their Southern Baptist sisters of the WMU also made sacrifices to provide scholarships for needy women planning to dedicate their lives to Christian service. Young women were entrusted to WMU leaders and faculty who prepared them for Christian vocations considered appropriate for their gender.

Transmitting WMU Culture

The women associated with the Training School adopted the culture of Woman's Missionary Union, which was exemplified by the five founders, particularly Maude McLure. The founders, like other early leaders of WMU, were a part of the southern aristocratic elite transmitting their system of values to Training School students and teachers who came from humbler backgrounds. A hegemonic culture of Christian southern womanhood existed at the Training School, and its ideals applied to every student, including those from regions other than the South. Sometimes living up to the leaders' expectations could be wearisome; after a week of serving meals to women from the WMU and worrying about "unpardonable crimes committed

---

[141]"Mary Headen" and "Mildred Matthews," in *The Missionaries of the Home Mission Board* (Atlanta, GA: Southern Baptist Convention, 1936).

[142]DeVault, Littlejohn Interview, 2.

in the serving," Jewell Legett seemed tired of playing her part. With a hint of sarcasm, she describes a reception for WMU women:

> Everybody stood up. . . . and ate her cream and cake and drank her frappe in mortal terror lest some other grand lady would hit her elbow and spoil her wonderful dress. We waiters had to screw in and out among the crowd and be sweet and entertaining and interested."[143]

Women students like Legett were presented a standard of expected behavior for women through the examples of founders and faculty. These notions were then reinforced by what was learned at the Training School.

---

[143]Legett, Diary, May 12, 1909 and May 15,1909.

3

"ALL THAT FITS A WOMAN"
The Training School Curriculum

The first women students to attend lectures at Southern Seminary participated in a curriculum designed to train male ministers. Yet, as more women students came to the Seminary seeking theological education, administrators eventually designed a separate women's curriculum. Sally Schwager observes that such a pattern was typical of many coeducational institutions. For example Grinnell College, a midwestern liberal arts school, responded to an increase in women's enrollment by directing women students toward women's professions and segregating them into separate academic programs, housing units, and extra-curricular activities.[1] While such separation may superficially appear limiting, the freedom found within the setting of feminine communities of study and daily life ultimately worked to expand women's choices.

By opening its doors to women, the Seminary put itself squarely in the center of controversies over women's roles in Southern Baptist life. The curriculum for women that emerged from these debates reflects the views of one important sector of male denominational leadership: the Seminary professors. Although minor changes in curriculum were negotiated through the years, one thing remained constant: women and men were preparing for different spheres of service, and therefore separate curricula must be maintained. Describing the Training School, WMU president Fannie Heck wrote:

---

[1]Sally Schwager, "Education of Women in America," *Signs: Journal of Women in Culture and Society* 12 (Winter, 1987): 363.

To all who desire it the school offers the advantages of the highest and most thorough Theological Training, coupled with all that fits a woman for the practical, everyday life of a trained worker in her own home church, a missionary to any part of our country or to some far heathen land.[2]

A description and discussion of the women's curriculum will reveal what Southern Baptists intended to teach about women's proper place of service. Educators have noted that the concept of "curriculum" includes not only what is learned in the classroom but also through student activities, off-campus experiences, and associations with faculty and staff. While other portions of this work will examine additional avenues of learning, this chapter will focus on the classroom experience. In this context, the word "curriculum" refers to the formal plan of course work provided by the school.

Women had been attending lectures for many years prior to 1902 when the faculty officially allowed them access to the classroom. Wives of Seminary students and a few single women who desired a theological education listened quietly to lectures.[3] Mullins wrote of a stranger from Virginia who wore a drooping hat into the Seminary classroom in the 1884-85 session and listened to lectures "with demure attention."[4] The Seminary catalogue first mentions women in attendance in the 1901-1902 session, naming two single women preparing for the foreign mission field. After Seminary classes were officially opened to them in the 1902-1903 session, twenty-four women were listed in the catalogue as attending classes regularly. These women did not receive academic credit, but their names were recorded and their examinations were graded.[5]

---

[2]Fannie E. S. Heck, *In Royal Service* (Richmond: Foreign Mission Board of the Southern Baptist Convention, 1913) 205.

[3]Carrie Littlejohn, *History of Carver School of Missions and Social Work* (Nashville: Broadman Press, 1958) 8-9.

[4]Isla May Mullins, *House Beautiful* (Nashville: Sunday School Board of the Southern Baptist Convention, 1934) 11.

[5]*Catalogue*, Southern Baptist Theological Seminary, 1901-1902, 1902-1903; Littlejohn, 14.

In later years, a curriculum specifically for women would be established, but initially, as they silently audited courses, women had the freedom to explore any subjects they found interesting. The Seminary offered a typical theological curriculum, with courses in Old and New Testament, Homiletics, Systematic Theology, Comparative Religion and Missions, Sunday School Pedagogy, Church History, and Pastoral Duties. Southern Baptist theologians also studied ancient languages: Hebrew, Greek, and Latin.[6]

Women students showed interest in all areas of theological education including subjects that were later considered inappropriate for their gender. Mullins reported that the young woman from Virginia who attended classes in the 1880s studied biblical languages.[7] Most women attended the Old and New Testament courses, while a few were interested in Greek, Hebrew, Systematic Theology and Church History. The eyebrows of Training School opponents were raised when Mrs. Steinmetz took the Seminary's Homiletics course in 1903. Opponents used Mrs. Steinmetz's attendance of this course as evidence that the Training School and Seminary intended to train women as preachers. The only regular course that no woman attended was the course in Pastoral Duties.[8]

Asked to keep silent, women did not participate in classroom recitations or discussions. The attitudes of many Southern Baptists toward women speaking in mixed groups prompted the Seminary faculty to request in 1903 that women "take no public part" in classes.[9] In many coeducational colleges, women sat together in

---

[6]Robert Proctor, "The Classroom at Southern Seminary," *Review and Expositor* 81 (Fall 1984): 418-419.

[7]Mullins, *House Beautiful*, 11.

[8]Catalogue, SBTS, 1902-1903 and 1903-1904; W. O. Carver "The Origin of a New Era in Southern Baptist History" (address to WMU Training School, October 2, 1948), typescript p. 6, Training School Collection, Woman's Missionary Union Archives (Hereafter cited as TSC, WMUA).

[9]Faculty Minutes, Southern Baptist Theological Seminary, Louisville, KY, December 10, 1903.

groups, often at the front of the classroom.[10] By contrast, photographs of Seminary classrooms show women scattered about from the front to the back of the lecture hall. Married women presumably were sitting with their husbands, while single women sat together in groups. Alice Huey remembers meeting her friend Ella Jeter in the Seminary classroom, "She and I sat together as we were almost the only young ladies in the class."[11]

In the early years, women had no place on campus to study, rest, or take meals between classes. Seminary faculty restricted women to the lecture hall, so they had no access to the cafeteria or sitting rooms.[12] Classes began at 8 a.m. and the last class finished at 5:45 in the evening. Alice Huey lived in a boarding home so far away that she stayed at the Seminary between classes, returning home after dark. "One day I wandered into the Library," she remembered. "I felt very conspicuous, the only woman in there that day, but nobody told me to keep out."[13]

In some schools where women entered classrooms that previously had been male preserves, women were "as unwelcome as any uninvited guest."[14] When women came to the University of California at Berkeley, men expressed a desire for strict separatism, even in the classroom, and openly showed their contempt for the higher education of women.[15] In contrast, men at the Seminary did not seem bothered by the feminine presence, and even offered hospitable

----

[10]Photograph of classroom at Cornell, 1910 in Helen L. Horowitz *Campus Life: Undergraduate Cultures from the End of the Eighteenth Century to the Present* (Chicago: University of Chicago Press, 1987) 67.

[11]See Photographs featured in the 1903-1904 Catalogue, SBTS; Alice Huey, "Reminiscences of the Beginning of the Training School," (address to WMU Training School October 2, 1940) unclassified papers. WMU Training School Carver School Collection, Southern Baptist Theological Seminary, Louisville, Ky. (Hereafter cited as TSC, SBTS).

[12]Faculty Minutes, SBTS, December 10, 1903.

[13]*Catalogue*, SBTS, 1904-1905; Huey, "Reminiscences of the Beginning."

[14]Horowitz, *Campus Life* 68; Barbara Miller Solomon, *In the Company of Educated Women: A History of Women and Higher Education in America* (New Haven: Yale University Press, 1985) 58.

[15]Lynn D. Gordon, *Gender and Higher Education in the Progressive Era* (New Haven: Yale University Press, 1990) 190.

gestures to the female newcomers. One student recalled male reactions on her first day of class in 1904: "They saw we were so very scared and innocent, or something so they asked us into the hall." The ministerial students welcomed women with gifts of food; canned goods, chickens, and chestnuts were among the items brought from country churches where male students served as pastors.[16] When the first women students moved into the rented Training School home, the single men living in the dormitory presented them with a hat rack, signaling their intentions to call on the women.[17]

These gestures of hospitality toward women at the Seminary, in contrast to the open hostility of men in other coeducational colleges, may perhaps be attributed to the ministerial students' sense of Christian kindness or to a cultural imperative defining proper behavior of a "southern gentleman." In addition, seminarians often courted Training School women, perhaps initiating courtship with gestures such as bringing food from the churches they pastored, or inviting women to hear them preach.[18]

Several unique features that distinguished campus life of the Seminary from other colleges may be contributing factors in the unusually welcoming attitude of male students. First, wives of Seminary students had been attending classes for years, and students were accustomed to a female presence.

Second, the Seminary was different from other campuses in that it did not have a well-developed male "college life." A "college life" focused on disagreements with faculty, a devaluation of academics, and contempt for those outside its circle.[19] In contrast to other colleges, the Seminary community placed academics, church, and family life at its center. Many students traveled into the country each weekend to preach, leaving little time for social outings. Instead of the tightly knit and exclusive male communities existing at other schools,

---

[16]Rena Groover Shepard, "The Great Adventure," (address to WMU Training School, October 2, 1940), unclassified papers, TSC, SBTS

[17]Mullins, *House Beautiful*, 16.

[18]See Legett Diary, 1909.

[19]Horowitz, *Campus Life*, 13.

the Seminary community included married students and their families, suggesting less rigid boundaries for newcomers to break through.[20] Helen Horowitz suggests that coeducational colleges without a strong element of "college men" may have been less hostile to female classmates.[21]

Third, women students at the Seminary had been requested by the faculty to keep silent in the classroom. One of the arguments used by opponents of coeducation was that women would take over the classroom and otherwise interfere with male academic performance.[22] The women of the Seminary classroom were seen and not heard. Their inconspicuous presence could hardly bring complaint from male students.

Fourth, those in favor of women attending Seminary classes, as well as the women students themselves, had stated clearly that they did not intend to become preachers but were preparing for women's work. Unlike students in other colleges who took classes with women interested in becoming doctors or scientists, Southern Baptist ministerial students would not be competing against female classmates for ministry positions.[23]

Finally, Seminary men courted and often married Training School women, as the school's early opponents had predicted. Jewell Legett was impressed by a gesture of affection offered by Seminary men toward the Training School women who were their classmates. In her diary she described the processional of Seminary students and Training School women during a special service at the 1909 annual meeting of the SBC held in Louisville. Her writing reveals her awareness of early debates between the school's supporters and those who feared impropriety among courting students:

---

[20]Bill J. Leonard, "Student Life at Southern Seminary," *Review and Expositor* 81 (Fall 1984): 450.

[21]Horowitz, *Campus Life* 13, 200.

[22]Solomon, *Company of Educated Women*, 58.

[23]"A Statement Regarding the Women's Training School," [1906?], Historical Scrapbook, microfilm reel No. 1, Southern Baptist Historical Library and Archives, Nashville, TN (Hereafter cited as SBHLA).

As we marched down the aisle they, the Seminary boys, rose and with their faces wreathed in mischievous smiles (they knew what some of the old fogies there were thinking) gave us the salute and remained standing until we were seated. A pretty little compliment it was and one that we appreciated.[24]

Jewell would later marry one of her classmates from the Seminary.

Historians of higher education note another source of tension between male students and female classmates—problems occurred when women surpassed men academically. In addition to jealousies among students, faculty members of coeducational colleges blamed women for the lower scores of males, claiming women hindered the academic performance of men.[25] On the other hand, women were under pressure to demonstrate their intellectual capabilities since early objections to coeducation were based on arguments that women were intellectually inferior to men. Women were caught in a double bind. If they performed well in the classroom they might face male resentment, but if they did not perform well they would fulfill predictions of failure. Although collegiate women of the late nineteenth century did prove their intellectual worth, early twentieth century women were still under pressure to perform well in the classroom.[26]

It is not clear whether Seminary men resented women who excelled academically. In spite of their reticence in the classroom, women proved their intellectual abilities by performing well on examinations. In 1903 Mrs. R. A. Lansdell passed with high credit in the Biblical Introduction and English Old Testament courses and passed satisfactorily in Junior Church History. As Robert Proctor points out, she would have received "diplomas" in each of the three areas if she had been a male student. Instead, her accomplishments were acknowledged in a footnote in the commencement program.[27]

---

[24]Legett Diary, May 15, 1909, TSC, WMUA
[25]Solomon, *Company of Educated Women,* 58.
[26]Ibid., 56.
[27]Proctor, 422.

The next year several women's names were listed as passing examinations, but the classification "with honors" was dropped. Mrs. Lansdell is listed as simply passing the exam in Comparative Religions and Missions, but the professor later noted that while she was the first woman to ever stand for the exam, Lansdell made the highest grade in the class.[28]

A New "Curriculum for Ladies"

In 1904 a Baptist woman in Louisville named Elsie Fuller provided an honorarium for missions professor W. O. Carver to teach a course especially for women. In this course, called "Practical Work," women learned basic methods of evangelism and other forms of missionary service. Twenty-five women were enrolled in the course; fourteen were married women and eleven were single.[29] In the minds of Southern Baptists of this era, feminine methods of evangelism differed from masculine forms in several ways. First, men had the option of using preaching as a part of evangelistic efforts, whereas preaching was prohibited practice for Southern Baptist women. Secondly, for women the field of prospective converts was narrowed; women were expected to evangelize other women and children exclusively. Women's mission societies expressed this idea in the slogan "woman's mission to woman."[30] Finally, women adopted an approach to evangelism that provided social services to individuals while men primarily dealt with groups, evangelizing others by preaching. The Woman's Missionary Union eventually adopted the term "Personal Service" to describe their own method of evangelism, which carried feminine distinctive and yielded results:

---

[28]Commencement Program, SBTS, 1904; Littlejohn, 169.

[29]George A. Carver, "Carver School of Missions and Social Work," *Encyclopedia of Southern Baptists* vol. 1. (1958) 8.

[30]For a discussion of Woman's Mission to Woman see Allen, *Century to Celebrate* 23-27.

You can shut your door in the face of a priest or preacher, but you can not shut it in the face of a woman who comes with love in her heart and flowers in her hand to nurse your sick child. . . .[31]

Teaching women methods of mission work different from those available to men led the Seminary to formulate a separate women's curriculum. This provided some advantages to women, although some privileges were lost. In coeducational courses at the Seminary, women had been warned that they were guests in the classroom and therefore were not to distract the professors or draw attention to themselves by asking questions.[32] Now, in a new course designed especially for them, women had the freedom to inquire openly about topics that were considered relevant to their sphere of work. Along with this new freedom, however, came a corresponding loss of privilege. As a woman's curriculum was developed, women could no longer choose the studies that would comprise their theological education. From this point forward, the women's curriculum designed by the Seminary professors, with minimal changes through the years, would be the only option for women students during the next half-century.

The idea of maintaining different curricula for men and women was not unusual in this era. Colleges like Oberlin, which were called "coeducational," often maintained gender-segregated curricula, channeling men and women into different courses. Separating the curricula reinforced popular ideas concerning the separate fields of work for men and women.[33] In addition, separate curricula for men and women ensured Southern Baptist educators that males and females would serve in the domain considered appropriate for their respective genders. The separation was formally instituted at the

---

[31]Maude McLure, "Is it Worthwhile?" (Baltimore: Woman's Missionary Union, 1908) 6. For a discussion of the personal service program of WMU see Allen, *Century to Celebrate*, 211-218.

[32]Littlejohn, *History of Carver School*, 9.

[33]Florence Howe, *Myths of Coeducation: Selected Essays, 1964-1983* (Bloomington: Indiana University Press, 1984) 215-216.

Seminary with the first course designed especially for women students. Soon a coordinating women's school would become the place in which women learned to "meet the problems of women's lives in a woman's way."[34]

The Seminary faculty formulated the basic curriculum reflecting their choice of topics considered appropriate for Southern Baptist women. In 1904, a committee on "curriculum for ladies," headed by the Seminary's president, E. Y. Mullins, reported that this special curriculum would include the following: Old Testament English, New Testament English, the first half of Biblical Introduction, Systematic Theology, Junior Church History, Comparative Religion and Missions, and the last half of Ecclesiology and Hymnology. These were mainly survey courses that introduced the student to broad topics. Language courses, specialized topics, or any courses intended to prepare preachers (Homiletics and Pastoral Duties) were reserved for men only. The committee recommended additional courses for women in Personal Work, lectures for nurses, and a "course under matron of Women's Training School if located here."[35] The Training School was indeed located in Louisville and adopted by the Woman's Missionary Union in 1907. In that year, courses in music, domestic science, and elocution were added to complete a curriculum that changed very little during the next twenty years. Seminary faculty continued to advise the women on matters of curriculum for the rest of the Training School's existence [36]

A Coordinate Arrangement

The new school would operate as a coordinate of the Seminary, taking advantage of selected Seminary classes, while managing its own daily operations in a separate building five blocks away. Historians of women's higher education observe that coordinate colleges provided

---

[34]Allen, *A Century to Celebrate*, 211.

[35]Faculty Minutes, SBTS, April 25, 1904.

[36]See Faculty Minutes, SBTS, May 27, 1907, December 15, 1925; "In Gratitude for the Seminary," *Home and Foreign Fields* 9 (May 1925): 14.

a means for institutions to avoid coeducation. Reaction against coeducation had prompted the formation of women's colleges within universities, offering a compromise between single-sex education and coeducation. Coordinate colleges such as Barnard in the North and Sophie Newcomb in the South provided prototypes. A wide variety of arrangements existed among coordinating colleges. For example, Barnard and Sophie Newcomb maintained a great deal of independence, with their own faculties, endowments and campuses while other coordinates such as the Women's College at the University of Rochester simply provided separate activities and classes for women without any separate resources.[37]

Southern Baptists had shown a preference for educating men and women separately, forming colleges such as Mercer Institute (1833) and Wake Forest Institute (1834) to prepare men for the ministry and women's schools, such as Judson Female Institute (1838) and Blue Mountain Female Institute (1873) to educate Southern Baptist daughters.[38] A 1910 Baptist editorial responded to objections against "grinding the woman through the same curriculum as the man though she will, in all probability, occupy a different sphere in life from that which he is to fill."[39] A few Baptist colleges, however, had experimented with coeducation and coordination. For example, Baylor University was founded in Independence, Texas, as a coeducational institution in 1845, but within six years had formed a coordination arrangement in which women lived in their own building one mile away from the main campus. Women students followed a separate curriculum and received their diplomas from the Female Department of Baylor University. The coordinating women's department eventually broke ties, moved to the town of Belton, and was chartered as Baylor Female College in 1866.[40] Twenty years later, when the all-

---

[37]Solomon, *Company of Educated Women*, 55; Gordon, *Gender and Higher Education*, 45-46.

[38]See Charles D. Johnson, *Higher Education of Southern Baptists: An Institutional History, 1826-1954* (Waco: Baylor University Press, 1955).

[39]"On the Education of the Girl," *Baptist World*, September 1, 1910, 17.

[40]Charles Johnson, *Higher Education*, 28-29.

male Baylor moved from Independence to Waco, Texas, coeducation was resumed with strict rules limiting interaction between the sexes. At first, women and men followed different curricula, but by 1891 all courses of study were open to women, and a few ventured into courses such as business that previously had been male preserves.[41] Such arrangements of coordination and coeducation were unusual for Southern Baptist colleges; institutions supported by the denomination, like most other private schools in the South, typically remained gender-segregated well into the twentieth century.[42]

Although the WMU Training School functioned as a coordinate institution to the Seminary, the women's school maintained a high degree of independence, managing their own building, classes, and student activities. Lynn Gordon notes that this type of separatism at coeducational institutions helped women cultivate communities of support in which they could develop leadership skills and discuss career opportunities. Women faculty and administrators of this era encouraged such separation, which created a place for women's values on campus.[43] A separate, but coordinating school to train women missionaries would provide the best of both worlds: an excellent theological education complemented by a women's curriculum and student experience designed to reinforce Southern Baptist notions of ideal Christian womanhood.

A Structured Curriculum

After the incorporation of the new Woman's Missionary Union Training School in 1907, women students could matriculate officially in their own school and work toward a degree. Students could choose between a Bachelor of Missionary Training, a two-year degree, and a Master of Missionary Training, which took three years to complete.

---

[41]Baker, *To Light the Ways of Time*, 56-63.

[42]Leon McBeth, *Women in Baptist Life* 106; Amy T. McCandless, "Preserving the Pedestal: Restrictions on Social Life at Southern Colleges for Women, 1920-1940," *History of Higher Education Annual* 7 (1987): 45.

[43]Gordon, *Gender and Higher Education*, 41-42.

Single women lived in the Training School building while married women, typically wives of Seminary students, were registered as day students.[44] It is clear that single women living in residence at the Training School had a very different experience from married women who spent evenings with their families. Similarly, the unmarried man living in the dormitory would have engaged in different activities from his married classmate. The variety of lifestyles represented gave texture to this learning community. Questions concerning differences in classroom and extra-curricular experiences for married and unmarried students deserve attention. However, the primary focus of this discussion is the unmarried boarding students, who constituted the majority of Training School students.

A student entering the Training School spent her first year in classes gaining a basic understanding of the Bible as well as skills she would need as a Christian worker. Six days a week she would walk a few blocks to the Seminary to take classes with male students in Old Testament, New Testament, and Sunday School Pedagogy. She would also attend the class for women called "Personal Work" which taught methods of evangelism and "friendly visiting" involving service visits to the homes of those in need. At her own Training School home she would study domestic science, music, elocution, and attend lectures on basic nursing. The second year student followed a similar schedule, studying Systematic Theology, Church History, Biblical Introduction, and Missions at the Seminary, and advanced level courses of domestic science, music, and personal work at the Training School. Very few students continued into the third year. The third year included advanced courses in selected topics at the Seminary as well as music lessons at the Training School.[45] All students did field work in local churches, and agencies. Descriptions of selected courses will provide a more complete picture of the curriculum.

---

[44]Allen, *Century to Celebrate*, 271.
[45]"Scheme of Lectures," Catalogue SBTS, 1907-1908, 56; [Fannie Heck],"Purpose and Preparation" (Baltimore: Woman's Missionary Union [1910?]).

Seminary classes in topics such as Biblical Introduction, Old and New Testament, and Systematic Theology were typically taught using the lecture method.[46] Classes were large and men were in the majority. For example, in the Old Testament course taught by John Sampey in 1908, there were fourteen women and 108 men. In the late 1910s, an increase in enrollment brought a higher proportion of women, but men continued to constitute a clear majority.[47] One student was overwhelmed on her first day in class:

> I had never seen so many men in my life—literally hundreds of them. . . . We were glad to simply sit in classes and listen. We studied our lessons hard just as if we were going to recite.[48]

In early years, only men were allowed to recite or ask questions. Alice Huey, who attended classes in 1904-1905, reported that Dr. Cree, an "assistant in Theology" was the first to ask women to recite in class. "And poor little me had to be the first one to face the ordeal!" she wrote. Evidently the recitation of a woman in the classroom was quite controversial. "My, such a storm of protest as was raised!" recalled Huey. "Weren't 'theologues' funny in those days?"[49] Carrie Littlejohn, a 1915 graduate of the Training School pointed out that students were socialized to keep quiet: "It was impressed upon Training School students that they were guests in the Seminary classes, and so they must not take up the time of the professors or make themselves conspicuous by asking questions." Littlejohn noted that the shy student may have preferred this practice, but the prohibition frustrated more aggressive students. The time came when she would no longer accept the assumption that she was a second-rate member of the classes.[50] It is not clear exactly when the women's

---

[46]Proctor, 424.
[47]McLure, "Is it Worthwhile?" 4; See *Catalogue*, SBTS, 1918.
[48]Rena Groover Shepard, "The Great Adventure."
[49]Huey, Reminiscences of the Beginning."
[50]Littlejohn, *History of Carver*, 9.

practice of quiet listening changed, but by 1915, women were regularly reciting in classes. A visitor to the Training School in that year accompanied the women to the Seminary classes "where they sat in constant fear of having to recite but where they were so faithfully prepared to do so. . . ."[51]

B. H. DeMent first taught the class in Sunday School Pedagogy at the Seminary in 1906. While this class was also of interest to the men, it was a very comfortable spot for women. Southern Baptist historian Leon McBeth notes the paradox of women's place as Sunday School teachers. While many Southern Baptists spoke out against women teaching in the church, Sunday School teaching was, from its nineteenth century beginnings, mostly the work of women. It was viewed as an acceptable role for women so long as they did not teach men or mixed classes.[52] In the Sunday School Pedagogy course students were required to prepare two theses (minimum 2000 words) in the areas of "genetic psychology" and "some practical Sunday School problem." After 1915, new instructors in the course added a section called "Out of Class Work" in which students became familiar with Sunday School supplies and did "clinical laboratory" work in local churches.[53]

After a morning at the Seminary, the Training School student walked back to her own school for lunch in the dining room and resume classes in the afternoon. While second and third year students returned to the Seminary for afternoon classes, first year students would remain at the school for classes in Domestic Science and Performing Arts. Evenings and Saturdays were also times for learning. Special lectures on missions topics were often given in the evening. Saturdays and some weekday afternoons were spent doing field work in area churches, charity organizations, and settlement houses. Sunday was a day of worship and rest.[54]

---

[51]K. Mallory "Report of Corresponding Secretary to W.M.U. Executive Committee," March 3, 1915, WMUA.

[52]McBeth, *Women in Baptist Life*, 105

[53]Proctor, 423-424.

[54][Heck],"Purpose and Preparation"; *Catalogue*, WMUTS, 1914.

Training For Denominational Work

Southern Baptist leaders intended for students associated with the Seminary, both male and female, to be instructed in the particularities of the denomination. Since women students were not destined to enter the male domain of ministry, their clearest path to service was through the WMU organization. Even those who left the United States to serve overseas would take WMU culture and organizational methods with them.[55] Lessons of professional propriety, reinforced by the subtle text of the principal's or teacher's example, were supplemented by lectures relating content of WMU principles and methods.

The WMU had developed its own methodology of missions education and organization to be used in churches and these ideas were taught to students as a part of the Training School curriculum. WMU leaders were invited to give evening lectures, which taught WMU methodology; Maude McLure taught lessons from the book *In Royal Service*, written by WMU's president Fannie Heck. Students also created pageants and playlets featuring WMU study topics to be used by Southern Baptist churches.[56] Local board member Anna Eager taught a required course in mission study using WMU materials until 1924 when Wilma Bucy joined the faculty to teach a course called WMU methods. Many graduates would use this training as employees of WMU or as volunteers in their churches. Juliette Mather (class of 1921), describes her growing attraction for WMU and its leaders as a "conversion" which took place while she was at the Training School: "I came to see the organization as a group of women dedicated . . . to something that was big and wonderful!" Mather went to work for the WMU immediately after graduation. Mather's employment by the organization lasted for thirty-six years.[57]

---

[55]Allen, *Century to Celebrate*, 173-179.

[56]Catherine Allen, Juliette Mather Interview, January 26, 1976, tape recording, transcript 173-179, WMUA; "Report of Corresponding Secretary," WMU Executive Minutes, March 1913, TSC, WMUA.

[57]Allen, Mather Interview, 20 ; Allen, *Century to Celebrate*, 452-453.

Catherine Allen, in her history of WMU, suggests that a hidden curriculum of commitment to the Woman's Missionary Union existed at the Training School:

> Students were expected to graduate with intense loyalty to WMU and ability to operate in church, state, or national roles of WMU leadership. The school was expected to be a distillation of WMU values. Worship, prayer, mission study, social action, sacrificial giving, commitment to mission service—all these features were stressed.[58]

Practical Skills

The WMU culture permeated other courses at the Training School. Classes designed to teach skills in social work carried an emphasis on evangelism mixed with McLure's style of *noblesse oblige*. The lessons were designed to create in students a sense of their own "spiritual duty to the poor, neglected and outcast of their own neighborhood."[59]

After 1907, Maude McLure taught the course called Practical Work. This course had been taught by W. O. Carver in the earliest years.[60] The terminology surrounding the concepts of evangelism and social work changed throughout the years. "Personal Service" was the term used by Woman's Missionary Union to describe the type of mission work that employs social work as a means to share the gospel.[61] The Training School's course called "Personal Work" taught soul-winning as well as social work methods. The first-year students studied "Christ's Methods in Winning Souls," while the second year they focused on "Relief Problems, Settlement and Welfare Work." Texts included *How to Work for Christ*, by the evangelist R. A. Torrey, and *Principles of Relief* by social work educator Edward T. Devine. By

---

[58]Ibid., 273.
[59]Ibid., 215.
[60]Mullins, *House Beautiful*, 30.
[61]Allen, *Century to Celebrate*, 215.

the early 1920s, Personal Work was divided into two separate courses. McLure continued to teach the class called Personal Work, which now focused exclusively on soul-winning. The other course was called "Christian Social Service" (changed to "Social Work" by the late 1920s) and was taught by graduate Carrie Littlejohn.[62]

Students also took a course in "Applied Methods in City Missions" until 1921 when the instructor, city missionary Emma Leachman, resigned. Thereafter, this content merged with the course in Christian Social Service and expanded to include town and rural communities.[63] These courses functioned as a theoretical component offered in conjunction with the practical experience students gained from field work in agencies and churches in Louisville, and after 1912, in their own settlement house. Some of the organizations in which students did field work were:

> King's Daughters Home for Incurables
> Masonic Orphans Home
> City Alms House
> Union Gospel Mission
> Local Churches[64]

WMU leaders believed that in addition to sharing the Gospel with those in poverty, Christian women should educate other women and girls to be "economical and healthful" homemakers. With Training School students as models and instructors, poverty-stricken women met at the school's settlement house and were given lessons in the niceties of WMU culture. "Teas, chats, and lectures" were used to teach poor women preferred methods of managing a home.[65] In order to teach domestic skills to women in poverty, Training School students learned to cook and clean, care for the sick, and maintain their own health through physical fitness. Domestic skills were a part

---

[62]See *Catalogue*, WMTUS, 1914-1915, 1922-1923, 1926-1927.
[63]See *Catalogue*, WMUTS, 1914-1915, 1922-1923.
[64]See *Catalogue*, WMUTS, 1914-1915 for sampling.
[65]Allen, *Century to Celebrate*, 219-220.

of the informal curriculum even before an actual domestic science course was established.

From their first years in the Training School home, students entered into the housekeeping routine and were required to keep their rooms "in perfect order."[66] After the domestic science course became an official piece of the curriculum in 1907, the housemother traditionally served as instructor. The course featured lectures and a practical element. Students were given lessons in sewing, cooking, and laying the table. The daily routine reinforced the lessons, as students were required to serve in the kitchen and dining room as well as clean their rooms and public areas.[67] This is in contrast to the men's Seminary where a janitor performed household chores.[68]

Domestic training was structured so that students might use these skills in mission work. McLure stated that the purpose of sewing lessons is not only for the benefit of the student herself, but so she may "learn the best method for teaching children and ignorant mothers how to sew." Cooking lessons taught the preparation of an invalid diet so the missionary might properly care for the sick.[69] Training School women were not only being prepared to manage their own households, but were also being taught that their special ministry was to be nurturing caretakers of others.

Skills in basic nursing were considered a necessary part of training for missionaries. In 1905, the Volunteer Band, a group of Seminary students preparing for mission work, asked the faculty for permission to study basic medical techniques under Cynthia Miller, a nurse who was taking Seminary courses. The faculty decided that Miller should not teach mixed classes or men, but only the ladies.[70] After the school was incorporated and a more structured curriculum was established, Dr. Julia Ingram of the University of Louisville was employed to give

[66]Mullins, *House Beautiful*, 19.
[67][Fannie Heck], "Purpose and Preparation," Woman's Missionary Union, [1912?].
[68]Inman Johnson, *Of Parsons and Profs* (Nashville: Broadman Press, 1959) 11.
[69]McLure, "Is it Worthwhile?" 2-3.
[70]Faculty Minutes, SBTS, January 31, 1905.

medical lectures to Training School students.[71] In 1921, the school began offering a program to train nurses in religious work so they might also serve as missionaries. Students took a three-year course at an accredited hospital and spent one year at the Training School completing a curriculum similar to that of the first year student.

Physical fitness was considered an important piece of the curriculum since a missionary must be in good health. In early years, the School arranged to have instruction in "physical culture" using the teachers and building of the local Young Woman's Christian Association (YWCA). However, it was later said that this course did not appeal to the students, By the 1920s, as the school attracted younger students coming from colleges with athletic programs, a new emphasis was placed on physical fitness, but rather than maintaining a required course, athletic activities became voluntary. Budget reports reflect that tennis courts were maintained for student use.[72]

Performance Skills

Skills in domestic science, nursing, and physical culture were considered a vital portion of missionary training. Yet it was also desirable for women to achieve performance skills in areas such as music and public speaking. While eighteenth and nineteenth century female academies taught these "ornamental" subjects so that women could "please, charm, and entertain at home among their friends," the Training School saw these performance skills as necessary elements in sharing the gospel.[73]

Music has traditionally been an important part of worship for Southern Baptists, and women were encouraged to praise the Lord in song. At the Training School, music lessons were given in two areas:

---

[71]Report of Annual Session, WMU, 1912, WMUA; "Gift of $20,500 to the Woman's Missionary Union," *Baptist Argus*, October 10, 1907.

[72]"Report of Treasurer of WMUTS," September 1920, September 1921, TSC, SBTS.

[73]Ann Gordon, "The Young Ladies Academy of Philadelphia," in *Women in America: A History* edited by Carol R. Berkin and Mary B. Norton (Boston: Houghton: Mifflin Co. 1979) 75.

sight-singing and piano. McLure was a skilled musician and had been teaching music in Cox College, Georgia before coming to the Training School. She taught vocal music at the Training School, while another teacher gave lessons in piano.[74] Students practiced their music skills in the daily chapel services by playing and singing hymns. Musically talented students wrote hymns and songs that became a part of Training School tradition.[75] Songs by Training School students were a featured part of each commencement ceremony. In 1919 the WMU executive board discussed creating a more elaborate music department, but decided that the aim of the school was not to train musicians but to provide women with enough skill in music to carry out their mission work.[76]

Public speaking was another arena in which women had class instruction supplemented by practical experience. Classes in elocution were taught in the afternoon, and students used their skills to lead the daily chapel services.[77] Most students had no experience in speaking before an audience and many tell of how frightened they were on their first occasion. Carrie Littlejohn recalled: ". . . the leading of chapel was certainly a great day for me . . . I had done very little speaking before I went there and I was scared to death."[78] Juliette Mather remembered that McLure sat in the back of the chapel insisting that timid students speak louder. "And sometimes the girls were so scared they couldn't speak any louder and she would say it again."[79]

McLure assured Southern Baptists through Training School literature that women students were taught to make speeches exclusively before other women.[80] In the early years this notion was

---

[74]Allen, *Century to Celebrate*, 270; Mullins, 60.

[75]For examples of songs written by students see Gwynn McClendon, "House Beautiful," TSC, WMUA and Rose Goodwin Pool, "Alma Mater Hymn," TSC, WMUA.

[76]Annual Report, WMU, 1919, 5.

[77]"Purpose and Preparation."

[78]Doris DeVault, Carrie Littlejohn Interview , 25.

[79]Gertrude Tharpe and Ethalee Hamric, Juliette Mather Interview, September 17-21, 1979, tape recording, transcript 34.

[80]McLure, "Is it Worthwhile?" 3.

reinforced by the model of Training School faculty who arranged for male Seminary faculty to deliver addresses at commencement ceremonies that took place in local churches. However, beginning in 1918, the women used their own recently completed chapel for commencement services to which they invited women speakers.[81]

In its formative years, the Training School had defended its existence by reminding opponents that it did not intend to teach women to preach.[82] Students were instructed to draw this distinction in their public speech. A graduate of the 1920s recalls that students were "always reminded to step to the side of the pulpit when we spoke publicly, for no lady would stand behind the sacred desk."[83]

In later years, the principal of the Training School gave a different message to the students concerning women and public speech. In 1916, Maude McLure and WMU Secretary Kathleen Mallory became the first women to address the all-male Southern Baptist Convention to raise funds for a new building for the School. The story became a favorite among Training School students and everyone seemed very proud of their principal. McLure recalls the incident, speaking of herself in third person:

> The lights were switched off and under a cover of darkness the principal mounted a goods box . . . not presuming to stand on the platform. With shaking knees and pounding heart she very simply explained the rather crude, wholly innocent, slides as they were pictured on the screen, then sank into a chair to revive again. . . .[84]

McLure's description of her anxiety calls to mind the words of students who expressed their own fears about speaking in chapel for

---

[81]Littlejohn, *History of Carver School*, 77.

[82]"A Statement Regarding the Women's Training School," 7-8.

[83]Mrs. G. R. Ferguson, "A Tribute to Mrs. James H. Anderson," *Address to Carver School of Missions and Social Work*, October 2, 1959, 1, TSC, SBTS.

[84]McLure, "Highlights of Twenty Years," Birmingham WMU, [1927], 7; Littlejohn, 70-71.

the first time. She believed that her message was important enough that she would find the courage to proceed in spite of anticipated controversy. Practices did not change overnight; McLure did not launch a campaign for a woman's right to address mixed audiences, nor did she arrange for students to speak before men. When Baptist editorials chastised her for her action, she did not respond but quietly waited for the male leaders to defend her. Her courage in addressing the audience of Baptist men surely would leave a lasting impression in the minds of Training School students.[85]

In addition to the required core curriculum, the Training School cooperated with other schools in Louisville to offer a few electives. In 1911, the Training School arranged for a small group of students to attend classes in Spanish and Italian at the University of Louisville. Laura Cox took the Spanish course and was relieved to have some familiarity with the language when she reported to her mission field in Mexico.[86] Training School catalogues indicate this arrangement was discontinued within a few years. The Training School also cooperated with the Louisville Kindergarten Training School beginning in 1909 offering a course of study called "Child Culture" in which students studied one year at each institution. Faith Snuggs participated in this joint program and used her knowledge and experience to teach children in Luichau, China. Graduates of this program were few, and it was discontinued in 1922.[87]

Other Missionary Training Schools

With its emphasis on preparation of women for particular forms of evangelistic work, the curriculum of the Woman's Missionary Union Training School was remarkably similar to other Baptist

---

[85]"Dr. Gambrell's Message," *Baptist Standard*, June 15,1916, 10; and W. B. Crumpton, "Our Alabama Women at Asheville," June 1915 news clippings, TSC, SBTS.

[86]Laura Cox to R. J. Willingham, February 10, 1910 and October 29, 1911, Laura Cox File, Foreign Mission Board Correspondence, SBHLA.

[87]*Catalogue*, WMUTS, 1922-1923; "Faith Snuggs" in *Album of Southern Baptist Foreign Missionaries* (Richmond,VA: Foreign Mission Board, Southern Baptist Convention, 1926.

Schools designed for the same purpose. Most notable among these was the Baptist Missionary Training School of Chicago, which was sponsored by Northern Baptists, and the Women's Department of the Southwestern Baptist Seminary, a sister Southern Baptist institution. The Chicago training school was definitely a model for the WMU school. The Seminary faculty corresponded with this and other missionary training schools in 1903 when designing its "curriculum for ladies." Maude McLure was sent to the training school in Chicago to observe for one month before beginning her work at the Louisville school.[88]

The Women's Baptist Mission Society of the Northern Baptist Convention founded the Baptist Missionary Training School of Chicago in 1881. The school began with eighteen students enrolled in a short course lasting three to six months, which was soon expanded into a ten-month term, and by 1892 had become a two-year course.[89] The main elements of the curriculum were biblical, medical, and domestic training. Chicago pastors who volunteered their time taught many courses. Most teachers were men, but there were a few women teachers including Miss Elizabeth Church, who taught biblical courses from 1886 until she became preceptress in 1904. Professors from the University of Chicago also crossed the city to lecture on such topics as church history or Old Testament history. Two women from the Columbia School of Oratory taught a course called "Voice Culture," in which women learned Bible reading and speech delivery. The Chicago School also used the term "practical work" to describe the work done by students who visited in homes, led women's meetings, and taught Sunday school. A large part of students' practical work took place in industrial schools scattered across Chicago. These "schools" were sponsored by local churches and designed to provide programs in recreation, story-telling, worship, and crafts for children, many who were immigrants. Students were

---

[88]Faculty Minutes, SBTS, September 28, 1903; Littlejohn, 48.

[89]Faith C. Bailey, *Two Directions* (Rochester, NY: Baptist Missionary Training School, 1964) 2, 13-14, 19.

required to keep journals of their experiences. These were discussed weekly with the principal.[90]

The purpose of the Baptist Missionary Training School of Chicago was similar to that of the Louisville school. Baptist women of the North were also being prepared for special women's work. Mary Burdette, first preceptress of the Chicago school, lists the responsibilities of a trained missionary: "She must know how to cook, to clean, to keep a house with neatness and economy . . . to sew, to mend . . . to feed the hungry, clothe the ragged . . . to teach manners and morals; to profess sanctified tact, self-control, and the spirit of the Master. . . ." Students were required to spend five hours per week on such domestic tasks as serving meals, ironing, cooking, and washing dishes. These activities were supervised by a matron and listed in the catalogue as "daily practice in house work." Elizabeth Church, insisted that students always address one another as Miss or Mrs. One young woman who was caught using first names while playing games in the courtyard was called into the office of the preceptress and reprimanded.[91]

Another school, which offered missionary training to Southern Baptist Women, was the Southwestern Baptist Theological Seminary in Fort Worth, Texas. Originating as a theological department of Baylor University in Waco, Texas, Southwestern moved to Fort Worth in 1910. While original buildings were reserved for men's dormitories and classrooms, Texas Baptist women promised to provide funds for a special building for women students.[92] Southwestern Seminary was considered coeducational since it enrolled women as Seminary students, providing a coordinate arrangement like the one existing between the Seminary at Louisville and the Training School. At Southwestern, the women did not have their own board of trustees nor did they grant separate degrees. However, they did live in a separate building where they studied a women's curriculum.

---

[90]Ibid 1-15, 21-23, 32.
[91]Ibid. 13-14, 33.
[92]Allen, *Century to Celebrate*, 282

Barbara Solomon notes that at many coeducational colleges such as Oberlin, women did not take the same curriculum provided for men but were assigned to a separate female department.[93]

In their own building, women students at Southwestern Seminary took courses in domestic science, religious education, typewriting, and home nursing. Similar to the Louisville Training School, the Fort Worth women's building was designed as a home with strict rules and regimented daily life controlled by a superintendent and women teachers.[94]

A nursery and kindergarten was provided so that married women could study with their husbands and "become efficient partners with them in the service of the Savior."[95] Yet it was clear that women were preparing for "women's work" and thus had a separate curriculum. The school observed the Southern Baptist sanction against women entering professions reserved for males, including preaching. In his Inaugural Address of 1915, L. R. Scarborough, Southwestern's president, made clear that women and men were preparing for separate professions:

> Our purpose is to do for women in their work what we are doing for men in theirs—give them trained workers, thus reaching the fields opening to Christian womanhood for service. Our aim is not to turn out women preachers, but to give the world trained women in all the teaching, missionary and soul-winning activities of Christ's coming kingdom.[96]

Although the Texas seminary was coeducational in its organization, the expectations for women students at Southwestern were similar to those at the Seminary and Training School at Louisville. Both seminaries provided a place where women could receive

---

[93]Solomon, *Company of Educated Women*, 50.

[94]Allen, *Century to Celebrate*, 283.

[95]L. R. Scarborough, *A Modern School of The Prophets* (Nashville: Broadman Press, 1939) 134.

[96]Ibid., 183.

orthodox training in vocations considered appropriate to their gender under the careful supervision of Southern Baptist men. Some found assurance in knowing that men were in charge of the women's education. One Baptist expressed confidence in the Louisville situation: "Our Seminary will prevent the young women from becoming preachers, granting that any of them should so far miss their aim."[97]

African-American women also received training for the mission field. The Baptist Missionary Training School of Chicago served as a model for missionary training programs established in schools for African-American women.[98] Northern Baptist women assisted in the establishment of several programs in southern schools including those at Spelman Seminary, Shaw University, and Bishop College in the early 1890s.[99] Spelman Seminary, a school for women located in Atlanta, Georgia, founded a missionary training department in 1891 featuring a two-year course with five months of field experience. Graduates of the Spelman program worked in Alabama, Tennessee, and Georgia addressing churches, organizing Sunday Schools, distributing Bibles, and performing other missionary activities.[100]

In the twentieth century, The National Training School for Women and Girls was launched in 1909 under the leadership of Nannie Helen Burroughs. Burroughs inspired members of the Woman's Convention, Auxiliary to the National Baptist Convention, U.S.A., to provide training for African-American women in domestic service, teaching, and missionary work. In its first year the school enrolled thirty-one students, ranging in age from twelve to forty-three. Unlike the training schools at Louisville and Fort Worth, the

---

[97]*Biblical Recorder*, March 14, 1906.

[98]Evelyn Brooks [Higginbotham], *The Women's Movement in the Black Baptist Church 1800-1920*, (Ph.D. diss., Ann Arbor, MI: University Microfilms International, 1984) 264-265. This dissertation includes analysis that was not included in the revision that became the author's later book, *Righteous Discontent: The Woman's Movement in the Black Baptist Church, 1880-1920* (Cambridge, MA: Harvard University Press, 1993). By use of brackets, I also note the author's name change.

[99]Ibid., 265.

[100]Higginbotham, *Righteous Discontent*, 35.

National Training School offered training in vocations that were secular as well as religious.[101]

Like other schools for women of this era, the National Training School focused on developing moral character through strict behavioral codes. It was called the "School of the 3 B's," emphasizing the Bible, bath, and broom as tools to advance the African-American race. At 6:00 each morning, the neatness and personal cleanliness of each student was inspected. Those who had been untidy or careless in attire did not receive diplomas. Students provided hard labor to help control the school's expenses. While women at other schools were involved in extra-curricular recreation, the women of the National Training School cleared weeds, planted trees, and built concrete walkways. They gardened, raised pigs, milked cows, and churned butter.[102]

Due to the emphasis on racial self-help, no contributions from white donors were accepted until after the school was operating. However, in 1912, northern white women of the Woman's American Baptist Home Mission Society supplied a model home in which domestic science lessons could be taught. Evelyn Brooks [Higginbotham] noted an important difference between domestic science courses in the National Training School and in schools for white students. Courses in domestic science in schools for white students were designed to train women to become better wives and mothers. On the other hand, domestic science courses in schools for African-American women trained women for paid domestic service.[103]

The school's program of missionary training began with fifteen students in 1909. Five were preparing for the foreign field and the remainder planned to serve in home missions. The curriculum of the missionary department included field work in a settlement house in Washington, DC known as The Centre. The Centre provided social

---

[101]Ibid., 257, 263.
[102]Ibid., 284-285; 292
[103]Ibid., 279, 276.

services including a soup kitchen, academic tutoring, sewing, kindergarten, and other services of the typical settlement house.[104]

Brooks concluded that the middle-class orientation of the Woman's Convention sometimes led them to take a conservative view. The notion of racial self-help occasionally drew attention to negative values and unintentionally supported racist discrimination and stereotyping. However, the emphasis of self-help and self-reform was consistent with the dominant theories held by most African-Americans in the late nineteenth and early twentieth centuries and was expressed in the National Training School's slogan "Work, support thyself, to thine own powers appeal."[105]

Although the Chicago School served as a model to the other three schools described in this discussion, each school developed its own unique features. There were many similarities of curricular content and all four schools relied upon field work as an important means of instruction. In each of the training schools described, women were preparing for vocations considered appropriate to their gender, race, and class.

Curricular Changes

For the first two decades of its existence, the WMU Training School followed the basic "curriculum for ladies" suggested by the Seminary professors in 1904.[106] However, in 1924, a new specialization called "Course for Church and Educational Secretaries" would take a few women in a different direction. The Training School cooperated with a Louisville business school to offer classes in stenography, supplementing the core women's curriculum. In addition, two new courses were offered: Christian Education and Church Organization and Administration.[107]

---

[104]Ibid., 316.
[105]Ibid.
[106]Seminary Faculty Minutes, SBTS, April 25, 1904.
[107]Catalogue, WMUTS, 1924-1925, 1927-28.

The course in church administration, taught by Seminary professor Gaines S. Dobbins, allowed women to explore territory that had previously been reserved for men. The program's title suggested the traditionally feminine role of secretary, and women did study subjects such as care of an office and desk, handling correspondence, and organizing a library. Yet they also ventured into topics like church structure, denominational polity, and church planning. Although the course initially emphasized a secretarial role, it became the foundation for a degree program that would inspire women to take a bolder step into the male domain.[108] Dobbin's class in church administration was the first Training School course, which did not suggest a strict separation of gender roles in the church but allowed an overlapping of fields traditionally assigned to men and women. In 1930, the course's title would be changed to "Religious Education," the name of a developing field that would accommodate both male and female church workers, leading women of later decades to begin using the title "minister" as they pursued careers as Ministers of Education in local churches.

---

[108]*Catalogue*, WMUTS, 1923-1924.

4

The Lessons of House Beautiful
Daily Life and Learning

Wen the Southern Baptist Theological Seminary officially opened its doors to women, Louisville was a rapidly growing river city with a population of 204,000.[1] Single women traveled to Louisville in pursuit of their dreams to become missionaries in foreign lands. They found themselves in situations similar to working women living on their own in the city. They were far away from their families and struggling to live on the meager savings they brought with them. Joanne Meyerwitz uses the term "women adrift" to describe single women who came to urban areas to work. In her study of independent wage-earning women in Chicago between 1880 and 1930, Meyerwitz found that the most popular image of a woman alone in the city was that of "the endangered orphan." Charity organizations such as the Salvation Army and the Young Women's Christian Association (YWCA) used this image to describe a pure woman needing protection from the evils of the city. The YWCA, fearing female victimization, organized dormitory housing for women tenants. Attempting to reproduce the family environment, the organized homes of the YWCA provided companionship and moral guidance plus protection from urban threats.[2]

Women adrift were sometimes under suspicion of immoral sexual behavior while men who lived alone enjoyed independence without

---

[1]George H. Yater, *Two Hundred Years at the Falls of the Ohio: A History of Louisville and Jefferson County* (Louisville, KY: Heritage Corporation, 1979) 144.

[2]Joanne J. Meyerowitz, *Women Adrift: Independent Wage Earners in Chicago, 1880-1930* (Chicago and London: The University of Chicago Press, 1988) 50.

being stigmatized.[3] Before 1930, women adrift typically lived with surrogate families in boarding houses or under the protective care of organizations like the YWCA. However, the growing desire of working women for independence drove many to head their own households or share a home with roommates.[4]

The founders of the WMU Training School shared the concerns of the YWCA for single women living in the city. They viewed the women who had come to the Seminary as orphans needing protection. Those interested in starting a school also believed they could attract more women to the Seminary classroom if they provided living quarters. Motivated by these goals, women of Kentucky's WMU devised a plan, which culminated in the creation of a new school for women missionaries.

The Big Four

In 1904, two years after the Seminary officially had opened its classrooms to women, a group of twenty-five students were enrolled in a new Practical Missions course taught by Seminary professor W. O. Carver. Four of the single women were Rena Groover from Pidcock, Georgia; Clemmie Ford, from Knoxville, Tennessee; Alice Huey from Bessemer, Alabama; and Ella Jeter from Walter, Oklahoma.[5] The four were boarding in Louisville homes until they became acquainted at the Seminary and decide to become roommates. They rented one small room from a married couple they met in Seminary classes. The women enjoyed their independence, cooking their own meals, studying theology, and dating men from the Seminary.

We made a bedroom out of one corner, kitchen out of another, and wardrobe out of the other. Out in the center we

---

[3]Ibid., 24.

[4]Ibid., 70.

[5]*Catalogue*, Southern Baptist Theological Seminary, 1904-05; and Catherine Allen, *A Century to Celebrate: History of Woman's Missionary Union* (Birmingham: Woman's Missionary Union, 1987) 267.

had the dining room, living room, and study. Thus we began
housekeeping. . . . This student friend where we lived would
let us have his study when we had dates.[6]

Meanwhile, Carver became concerned about the living situation
of the women. Although the four students had not requested housing
assistance, Carver enlisted Eliza Broadus, leader of the Kentucky
WMU, to provide it. Broadus assembled a group of local Southern
Baptist women who made plans to rent a house for the women
students. This group became known as the "Board of Managers,"
responsible for providing housing and "proper chaperonage" for
women students.[7] Everyone but the four students seemed to have
fears about women living alone and unsupervised. One Board member
spoke of "The cry . . . of four lonely girls that they might have a
decent place to live . . . in comfort and safety."[8] The faculty of the
Seminary also showed concern, stating that the women students must
be "surrounded by a suitable Christian atmosphere" during their stay
in Louisville.[9]

Later that year Carver invited the women students to move into
a house near the Seminary that had been rented for them by the
board of managers. At first they declined the offer because they could
live more frugally in their present situation. Perhaps they also enjoyed
the freedom of living on their own. Carver persisted, however, arguing
that such a move would benefit others:

He did not give up. He talked on and explained to us that
perhaps if we didn't take advantage of this opportunity we
would stand in the way of other girls in the future who might

---

[6]Rena Groover Shepard, "The Great Adventure," (address to WMU Training School
October 2, 1940), unclassified papers, WMU Training School/Carver School Collection,
Southern Baptist Theological Seminary, Louisville, Ky. (Hereafter cited as TSC, SBTS).

[7]Allen, *Century to Celebrate*, 266.

[8]Mrs. Trevor Whayne, "I Remember, I Remember, "*The Window of YWA* 10 (September
1938): 1-2.

[9]Minutes, Board of Trustees, Southern Baptist Theological Seminary, Louisville KY,
May 12, 1904.

want to come for study. This might be the beginning of a larger school.[10]

After initial reluctance, the four women accepted the offer and moved into the rented quarters. These women students became the legendary figures in the Training School's history known as "The Big Four." Traditionally, they have been known as the first four students; actually they were among many other women in the Seminary classes. However, they were the first women to move into the rented house on November 26, 1904. Others soon joined them and the house was filled to the limit by February.[11] A housemother was employed and another chaperone, city missionary Emma Leachman, moved in as well.

The initial idea was to provide protection and supervised living for these "women adrift." After Seminary professors designed a formal women's curriculum, however, and the school was adopted by WMU in 1907, Maude McLure came to Louisville to create a social curriculum. Operating in conjunction with the formal curriculum of the classroom, this social curriculum was composed of the daily routine and student activities created by the principal and other WMU leaders. The social curriculum was designed to teach students the roles and behaviors that the majority of Southern Baptists considered appropriate for women.

Nineteenth Century Models

The home provided for the "Big Four" would be a place of protection and comfort as well as a laboratory in which they would learn lessons of domesticity. The building functioned as both home and school, similar to the buildings of nineteenth century female seminaries. Predecessor of the modern women's college, the female seminary prepared women as teachers and mothers. There was

---

[10]Shepard, "The Great Adventure."

[11]Carrie Littlejohn, *History of Carver School of Missions and Social Work* (Nashville: Broadman Press, 1958) 22.

enormous variety in the curriculum. Some seminaries emphasized polite accomplishments such as music and art while others offered skills in housekeeping. History, philosophy, modern languages, and natural sciences were sometimes offered to prepare women as teachers. According to Helen Horowitz, Mt. Holyoke Seminary became the model for women's colleges emerging in the nineteenth century. In 1837, when Mary Lyon created Mt. Holyoke at South Hadley, Massachusetts, she produced a plan that would affect generations of women students. Women's colleges of the Northeast like Vassar and Wellesley, as well as female departments of coeducational colleges like Oberlin and Knox, were originally patterned after Mt. Holyoke.[12] Horowitz describes the key elements of the Mt. Holyoke model, including:

> academic subjects to train the mind as an instrument of reason; domestic work and a carefully regulated day to meet material needs and to protect health; a known, clear sequence of each day to lend order and predictability; a corps of transformed teachers who provided proper models for imita-tion; and a building shaped like a dwelling house as the proper setting for study, prayer, work, and rest.[13]

Although the Training School was created nearly seventy years after Mary Lyon's school, it shows some similarity to the Mt. Holyoke pattern. By the time the Training School was founded, northeastern women's colleges had already abandoned the female seminary model used at Mt. Holyoke. Students were no longer confined to a strict schedule or required to perform domestic duties. Women students in the Northeast, like their male counterparts, had developed an independent student culture. Architecturally, these women's colleges had begun to imitate schools for men, leaving behind the tradition of placing students and faculty in one home-like building and favoring

---

[12]Helen L. Horowitz, *Alma Mater: Design and Experience in the Women's Colleges from their Nineteenth-Century Beginnings to the 1930's.* (New York: Alfred A. Knopf, 1984) 11.
[13]Ibid., 12.

a system of several buildings arranged in a group. Smith developed the "cottage system" in which students resided in smaller homes arranged to resemble a New England town. Others, like Bryn Mawr, were designed in imitation of men's colleges with a central quadrangle surrounded by gothic-style buildings. Even Mt. Holyoke itself had restructured its design to conform to the newer styles. These new architectural arrangements allowed students more freedom to create their own social groups, contributing to the emergence of a separate student culture.[14]

The turn of the century showed many women's colleges of the South following the trends set by the northeastern schools. Rather than enlarging existing buildings, many Southern colleges for women chose to create campuses composed of several buildings. The campus of Hollins Institute in Virginia was made up of five large brick buildings situated on five hundred acres.[15] Newcomb College, the women's coordinate of Tulane University in New Orleans, brought a variation of the cottage idea to an urban location, with several buildings in a city block composing a campus group. Students and faculty were divided among several residential buildings that were formerly family mansions.[16]

In contrast to newer styles, the Training School continued to use the older architectural models, which offered protection and supervision for students while preparing them for future domestic roles. The result of this pattern of living was the same for the Training School of the twentieth century as it had been for Mt. Holyoke many years earlier: "Neither space, time, nor will allowed a separate student culture to emerge."[17] Instead, students conformed to the culture prescribed by faculty and administration. An examination of the Training School building, daily schedule, domestic duties, and regulations will demonstrate how the use of the older female seminary

---

[14]Ibid., 70-71, 117-121, 223-236.
[15]Mary Caroline Crawford, *The College Girl of America* (Boston: L.C. Page, 1905) 235.
[16]Ibid.
[17]Horowitz, *Alma Mater*, 24.

style of operation reinforced Southern Baptist notions about women's roles while inhibiting the development of a separate student culture.

When Maude McLure came to Louisville in 1907 to give shape and form to the new WMU Training School she envisioned a school that would "give to the world a sensible spiritual uplift, and will girdle the earth with an influence that cannot be measured."[18] Most importantly, McLure wanted the Training School to be a home. For the first ten years of its existence the school used a rented or purchased family residence as a place for living and learning. When a new building was built in 1917, the family home was used as a model.

Training School Homes

A housemother supervised the first Training School home. "Mother Wiegal" ensured that women students were properly chaperoned. In the fall of 1905, seven more women came to sit in on Seminary classes and a larger house in the same neighborhood was rented to accommodate them. It was described as "a beautiful old mansion . . . a home of dignity and charm."[19] These rented buildings were not furnished in an elaborate manner. Most of the furniture was donated by local Southern Baptists to create a mixture of many different styles, more practical than beautifully coordinated. Mrs. Whayne of the board of managers recalled, "how we sent out an S.O.S. call for furniture and what a hopeless mess some of it was, but enough was salvaged to make living possible." To cover the old house's rough and splintered floors, local women brought rags for the weaving of carpets.[20]

When the school was adopted by WMU in 1907, the Sunday School Board of the Southern Baptist Convention donated $20,500 toward the purchase of a building to serve as both school and home for the women. A three story brick house located at 334 East

---

[18]Maude McLure, "Is it Worthwhile?" Baltimore: Woman's Missionary Union, 1908.
[19]Isla May Mullins, *House Beautiful*, (Nashville: Sunday School Board of the Southern Baptist Convention 1934) 16-18.
[20]Whayne, "I Remember, I Remember."

Broadway near the men's Seminary was purchased right away.[21] For the next ten years, Training School students and faculty lived together under the direction of their new principal, Maude McLure. Both the exterior and interior of the new building retained the appearance of a home. Interior spaces were arranged like a typical family dwelling with common areas on the first floor. A staircase separated public areas from private living quarters located upstairs. Students' rooms generally accommodated two persons, while faculty members and the principal had small private rooms.[22] The home-like interior provided a setting in which women were preparing to care for their own homes after graduation.

The Southern Seminary Campus

In contrast to the idea of having one home-like building for women students, the men of the Seminary enjoyed a campus composed of four buildings: a dormitory, library, academic building, and gymnasium. In 1877, the Seminary moved to its Louisville location from Greenville, South Carolina due to the war devastation and poor economic conditions in the area. Like the first Training School students, the men of the Seminary lived in rented buildings until money could be raised for construction. However, while residential homes were considered appropriate rental property for female students, two floors of the Public Library, and rented rooms at the Waverly hotel were used as classroom and living quarters for Seminary men. The first building of the new Seminary campus was completed in 1888, thirty years before women students were admitted officially to the Seminary classroom. New York Hall was a student dormitory built at Fifth and Broadway in downtown Louisville. It was named in honor of John D. Rockefeller and other New York benefactors who donated generously for the construction.[23]

---

[21]Littlejohn, *History of Carver School*, 46.

[22]Mullins, *House Beautiful*, 28. See also Horowitz, *Alma Mater*, 20-21.

[23]Badgett Dillard, "The Campus of Southern Seminary," *Review and Expositor* 81 (Fall 1984): 428.

Although the first building was not completed until eleven years after the Seminary moved to Louisville, the rest of the campus was built rather quickly. The library, built with contributions of a Louisville benefactor, Mrs. J. Lawrence Smith, was completed in 1891. Two years later, Norton Hall, the academic building that housed classrooms, faculty offices, and a chapel, were erected. Named after two members of the family that provided funds for its completion, Norton Hall was built in the German renaissance style and became the focal point of the campus. The building that completed the Seminary campus was the Joshua Levering Gymnasium, finished in 1897. It was named for the Maryland Baptist layman who was a member of the Seminary's board of trustees.[24] Each building of the Seminary campus served a different purpose, in contrast to the Training School building, which was both home and school.

A Larger Training School

The Training School thrived in its purchased home until 1914 when the WMU decided that the building, "bursting at the seams," would need to be enlarged. While money was being raised for the enlargement, it was decided in 1916 to tear down the existing building and create a completely new structure.[25] For the first time in the school's nine-year history the women could make some real choices about their building. The choice they made was a hybrid of new and old. The exterior was designed in the Gothic style following the trend of other women's colleges. M. Carey Thomas pioneered in the last decade of the nineteenth century by designing Bryn Mawr in the Gothic style previously reserved for men's colleges. The academic seriousness that the form suggested made it popular with other women's colleges of the Northeast.[26] At first glance the Training School was designed to look like other women's colleges of its day,

---

[24]Ibid., 429-430.
[25]Littlejohn, *History of Carver School*, 68-70.
[26]Horowitz, *Alma Mater*, 201.

dressed in collegiate Gothic. However, the interior retained the form of a domestic dwelling. Beyond its front door, the school did not resemble a college, but a home in which students completed "many womanly tasks in a sweet homely way."[27]

Excavation for the new building was begun in November 1916. Students took temporary residence in three rented houses across the street from the building site. By the following April, just three days after the United States entered the First World War, the ceremony for the laying of the cornerstone took place. Mullins reported that the construction "went forward during the summer with even more than normal speed, since it was a time when nothing and no one stood still."[28] By October, the new building, though not complete, was livable and the students and faculty moved in to begin the fall session. The school contributed to the war effort by renting its west wing to the YWCA. These rooms were used to accommodate mothers, sisters, and other women visiting soldiers at Louisville's Camp Zachary Taylor. By the spring of 1918, the new Training School building was finished and a dedication service on May 22, 1918 celebrated its completion.[29]

Many visitors, particularly women associated with the WMU, came to admire the new Training School building. The interior of the three-story structure, like a traditional family dwelling, had workrooms in the basement, public rooms on the first floor, and private rooms on the top floors. However one public area, the chapel, occupied a portion of the second and third floors. The basement was the place where many domestic chores were performed. The kitchen, laundry room, storage rooms, and heating plant were located in the basement. The first floor held the library, dining room, classrooms, music practice rooms, and a parlor. The new quarters were more spacious. The principal, who had previously occupied only a single room, now had an entire suite with bedroom, living room, and office

[27]Maude McLure, "Lasting Foundations," [1917?], TSC, SBTS.
[28]Mullins, *House Beautiful*, 49.
[29]Littlejohn, *History of Carver School*, 73-75.

on the first floor. In the old building there had been no place for guests, so they often shared the principal's single room. Now there were six guest bedrooms, as well as more spacious quarters for faculty who lived on the first floor. Student rooms, which held two occupants, were located on the second floor along with the chapel. On the third floor was the chapel's balcony, a few bedrooms, and an infirmary complete with living quarters for the resident nurse.[30]

The pride and joy of the Training School women was the Heck Memorial Chapel. Fannie Heck, the beloved WMU president, died while plans for the school's enlargement were under way. It was decided to make the chapel, which became the centerpiece of the school, a memorial to her. The chapel was "a spacious room with lovely stained glass windows . . . the central thing of sacred beauty in the whole building."[31] The construction of this larger chapel carried great significance. The previous chapel had been too small to accommodate visitors and therefore commencement ceremonies had been held in Louisville churches. Since women did not typically address mixed audiences or stand behind a pulpit, male seminary professors had given commencement addresses and presented the diplomas. With the creation of the new chapel, the women could preside over their own commencement ceremonies for the first time in the school's history.[32]

One drastic change came with the new building: an emphasis on beauty. While the earlier buildings had been furnished with cast off items from local Baptist families, the new school was much more lavish, with all new furnishings made to order.[33] Many visitors admired the beautiful marble staircase that, as in the traditional family home, separated common areas from private quarters.[34]

---

[30]"Training Baptist Women for Service," [1916?], Training School Collection, Woman's Missionary Union Archives, Birmingham, AL (Hereafter cited as TSC, WMUA).

[31]Mullins, *House Beautiful*, 50-51.

[32]Littlejohn, *History of Carver School*, 77.

[33]Mullins, *House Beautiful*, 50.

[34]"Training Baptist Women for Service."

A great deal of energy and expense ensured that the new building was aesthetically pleasing. Mrs. J. W. Druien of the board of managers described the new school.

> If you have the impression when you go in that I always do, you will feel as if you have entered the Holy of Holies. Its marble floors and stairway, solid columns and beautiful arches, library, reception room, office, literature room, class and music rooms made of the first floor so lovely and harmonious a whole that one is tempted to linger there indefinitely.[35]

The opulence of the new Training School building was a stark contrast to the more humble quarters occupied by male students at the Seminary. Inman Johnson, who began theological study in 1916, described his room in the dormitory called New York Hall.

> It was not inviting. The floor was splintery, the walls dirty, a single forty-watt clear light bulb hung from the ceiling; and the room was furnished with a small ancient table covered with carvings of Greek and Hebrew words, a decrepit washstand with a cracked china bowl and pitcher, one straight chair, and an iron bed with sagging springs and a faded mattress.[36]

"Ain't This a Palace?"

The emphasis on elegance also created a more obvious difference between the living conditions of the students and those of the neighbors served by the school's settlement house. The women's accommodations were no longer modestly simple. Now the students lived in an elegant building. A young visitor who came with a group

---

[35]Mrs. W. J. Druien, "History of the WMU Baptist Training School," [1932?], TSC, SBTS.

[36]Inman Johnson, *Of Parsons and Profs* (Nashville: Broadman Press, 1959) 11.

of boys from the settlement to see the new building noted the difference:

As they entered the lobby and looked toward the marble stairway bathed in old light from the beautiful stained glass windows behind it, he said in awed tones, "say fellers, ain't this a palace?"[37]

The school had come a long way in ten years: from a dwelling with rag-covered floors to a structure as exquisite as a palace.

Creating a residential building, which was extravagantly designed and elegantly furnished, was not an unusual choice for women's colleges of this period. Mabel Newcomer, in her classic work *A Century of Higher Education for American Women*, argues women's colleges typically provided more luxurious surroundings for their students "partly because women are assumed to appreciate the refinements of life more than men" and "partly because they are more protected."[38] When Read Hall was built at the University of Missouri to accommodate women students, "the greatest pains were taken to have it the best possible building of the kind," complete with natural wood furnishings and Oriental rugs.[39]

The women of the Training School wanted to have a beautiful building as well. Literature used in fund-raising for the building emphasized that other schools for missionaries, including the Southwestern Baptist Theological Seminary in Texas, had built new buildings for their students. Training School students deserved no less.[40] Before the building was completed in 1917, it took on a name that reflected new priorities: "House Beautiful." The name was an allusion to Bunyan's *Pilgrim's Progress* in which House Beautiful was the house of learning for the daughters. Fannie Heck had allegedly

---

[37]Littlejohn, *History of Carver School*, 75.

[38]Mabel Newcomer, *A Century of Higher Education for American Women* (New York: Harper, 1959) 113.

[39]Crawford, *The College Girl*, 233.

[40]"Training Baptist Women for Service."

used the phrase in earlier years to describe the school's beautiful spirit. However, with the completion of a new, truly elegant building, "House Beautiful" became the universally used nickname for the Training School.[41]

Daily Life at House Beautiful

The Training School building, like the original design of Mt. Holyoke, was made to replicate a typical home. In addition, the Mt. Holyoke model required domestic work and a very rigorous schedule with little free time. Helen Horowitz draws an interesting parallel between the methods of the newly reformed asylums of the day and the structured daily routine of Mt. Holyoke. Health reformers believed that psychic distress was caused by disorder. Not only did the asylum take the dwelling house as its architectural form, using domestic rhetoric to describe its system, but it also used "the rule of the clock" to bring order into the lives of its patients.[42] Many women's schools imitated the Mt. Holyoke's use of a system of bells, which held students accountable to a daily regime with little free time. In fact, the system of bells became so important that when Wellesley was opened in 1875 without the necessary bell in place, a woman in the town allegedly loaned the school her dinner bell so that a schedule could be maintained.[43]

By the turn of the century, the northeastern women's colleges had abandoned the regimented routine and strict regulations. This allowed more freedom for women students to develop their own student culture. Women organized activities and clubs that paralleled the college life of men. Once the confining building and strict schedule of the Mt. Holyoke model had been rejected, organizations, clubs, sporting events, dramatics, and rituals all became a part of the college experience.[44] In contrast, many women's schools of the South

---

[41]Littlejohn, *History of Carver School*, 76; and Mullins, *House Beautiful*, 49.
[42]Horowitz, *Alma Mater*, 14-21.
[43]Ibid., 54.
[44]Ibid., 147-178.

still maintained a strict schedule that was observed by all. This inhibited the development of an independent student life in southern women's schools. In 1904 Mary Crawford described the daily routine of Randolph-Macon Woman's College in Virginia. The rising-gong sounded at 7:00 A.M. and the students prepared for breakfast, chapel services, and morning recitations. Lunch was at noon, followed by afternoon recitations, and physical exercise. An evening meal, a second chapel service, and a half-hour of independent leisure kept students occupied until 7:30 P.M. At that time, a study-bell called for quiet until 10:30 when all must go to bed.[45]

The Training School followed a similar routine with variations to accommodate domestic work and classes at the men's Seminary. Although Training School students were older than most college women (all were between the ages of 21 and 38), there was no corresponding increase of freedom. The following schedule was published in the Training School's 1909-1910 catalogue:

General Programme

6:00 AM: Rising Bell

6:45 AM: Silence Bell

7:00 AM: Breakfast. Beds and rooms thoroughly aired.

7:30 AM: Prayer Service, conducted by students in regular rotation, as directed by Principal, except on Sunday morning.

8:00 AM: Domestic occupations.
[classes]

---

[45]Crawford, The College Girl, 157.

1:30 PM: Dinner. Students are expected to be in their seats at all meals, in time for grace, and to remain until the signal for rising is given by the Principal.
[classes and field work]

6:00 PM: Supper.

6:30 PM: Evening Devotions, led by students, except on Sundays.

10:00 PM: Retiring Bell.

10:30 PM: Lights out. It is expected that this will be faithfully observed.[46]

Although the day was tightly structured, there was some variety among students' schedules before and after the 1:30 meal. While all students walked to the Seminary for morning lectures, first and second year students took different classes. In the afternoons, first-year students stayed at the Training School for music lessons while second year students returned to the Seminary for additional lectures. At the 6:00 supper, all students were united into a common routine for the rest of the evening.[47]

The practice of requiring women students to perform daily domestic tasks was used successfully by Mary Lyon at Mt. Holyoke and imitated by other women's schools. However, founders and administrators were not always in agreement about the purpose of domestic work. Mt. Holyoke focused on the economic necessity of student labor while Wellesley argued that domestic work was a necessary part of the curriculum to train women for their future roles as wives and mothers. The Training School put forth both arguments

---

[46]*Catalogue*, Woman's Missionary Union Training School, 1910-1911, TSC, SBTS.

[47][Fannie Heck],"Purpose and Preparation" (Baltimore: Woman's Missionary Union, [1912?]); and *Catalogue*, WMUTS, 1910, 1911.

in its literature, claiming that the sharing of domestic work made the school more affordable as well as teaching women how to supervise a household. The principal also argued that students who were well-trained in household chores could teach immigrants and other women in poverty to maintain their homes in a manner that was considered acceptable.[48]

The cook and janitor performed the more difficult tasks such as the preparation of food and building maintenance while students served at meals, washed dishes, and cleaned parlors, library, and bathrooms.[49] A matron who lived in the school was responsible for "the making of a comfortable and well ordered home." She assigned specific tasks and graded students on their ability to perform their duties successfully. After 1921 the title of "matron" was changed to "Director of Home Economics" emphasizing the learning component of domestic work. The daily domestic chores performed at the Training School served as object lessons for students learning to operate their own households.[50] This daily routine remained in effect at the Training School throughout the 1920s with only a few minor changes. After 1916, morning prayer services were held before, rather than after breakfast and the fifteen minutes of morning silence was discontinued. Beginning in 1921, students were required to turn lights out one half-hour earlier; the reason for this change is not known.[51]

Such rigid scheduling of women students' lives reinforced the protective nature of home living. Faculty and administration could more easily control activities and ensure safety and proper behavior. In contrast, many colleges for men published schedules for classes only, leaving the time outside of class to be managed by each individual. Apart from the classroom and chapel, Seminary men's lives were generally unsupervised. A separate student's culture

---

[48]McLure, "Is it Worthwhile?"

[49]Three Training School Students, "A Week in the WMU Training School," [1909], Historical Scrapbook, TSC, SBTS.

[50]*Catalogue*, WMUTS, 1917 and 1921.

[51]*Catalogue*, WMUTS; 1916, 1921.

emerged from men's activities, both organized and spontaneous, which occurred outside of the classroom.[52]

The single men of the Seminary developed their own student culture centered on daily life at the dormitory. There was no schedule mandating study times and no bell signaling "lights out." Meals were offered in the dining hall but were not mandatory. Students often held part-time jobs off campus. Male students were not confined to campus in the evenings, but they often enjoyed recreational activities together. One favorite pastime of the 1920s was playing the game of Rook in the dormitory "almost all hours of the day and night. Midnight was usually the deadline, but at times the game continued until morning hours." The ministerial students were not immune to dormitory pranks. Students were known to throw one another in the showers, use cornbread from the dining room as a weapon in skirmishes, and tie several doorknobs together with rope, trapping fellow students inside.[53] More constructive recreation was found in sports. Although physical exercise was not a required part of the curriculum, the gymnasium was well utilized. The Southern Baptist male students also played competitive sports with Presbyterian ministerial students in the city.[54]

The women of the Training School had fun too. However, in contrast to the independent leisure that male students enjoyed, the women's recreation was scheduled into the daily routine. In this way students enjoyed most recreational pleasures as a chaperoned group rather than as individuals. For example, in October 1923 the principal reported social activities taking place at the Training School and off campus:

> The girls observed Hallowe'en in the dining room on the evening of the thirty-first of October with a pleasing and

---

[52]Helen L. Horowitz, *Campus Life: Undergraduate Cultures from the End of the Eighteenth Century to the Present* (Chicago: University of Chicago Press, 1987) 42.

[53]Johnson, *Of Parsons*, 18, 8-22.

[54]Bill J. Leonard "Student Life at Southern Seminary," *Review and Expositor* 81 (Fall 1984): 451.

attractive program. Other social affairs were receptions at Broadway Baptist Church and Norton Hall, which the entire student body attended. . . .[55]

During holidays, students typically did not return home but remained at the Training School. The following is a description of a typical Thanksgiving celebration:

The seniors had charge of the chapel service, giving again the Thanksgiving pageant that was given last year. With an abundant and delightful dinner and a treat in the evening of ice cream and Tennessee cake, the day was made most enjoyable and home like for the Training School family.[56]

Women of the Training School enjoyed both writing and acting in pageants, particularly on occasions of celebration. David Glassberg describes the "pageantry craze" of the early twentieth century when historical pageants, using local citizens as actors, were organized "as a form of boosterism, patriotic morality, and public entertainment." Glassberg argues that residents of a town attempted to act out "the right version of their past" and thereby influence social and political events of the future.[57] Holiday pageants, staged by social workers, recounted events in American history for immigrants and children in an effort to promote patriotism. Historical pageants often depicted an idealized past, present, and future without racial, ethnic, or class conflict.[58]

Dramatic events were popular in women's colleges of this era and the pageant, featuring symbolic imagery depicting historical events, was a less controversial form of dramatic expression in an era when Southern Baptists generally frowned upon the theater. In the spring

---

[55]"Principal's Report," October 1923, unclassified papers. TSC, SBTS.

[56]"Principals Report," December 10, 1923, TSC, SBTS.

[57]David Glassberg, *American Historical Pageantry* (Chapel Hill: University of North Carolina Press, 1990) 1-4.

[58]Ibid., 60, 126.

of 1912 the student body of the Training School traveled on the Ohio by riverboat to see "The Pageant of Darkness and Light" performed at a missionary conference in Cincinnati. A few weeks later, McLure started a graduation tradition by adding to the commencement program the processional "Take the Light," from the Cincinnati pageant.[59]

Two years later, Training School students traveled to the WMU annual meeting in Nashville to perform their first pageant, "An Episode in Training School Life." Pageants performed by Training School students were based on religious themes and often portrayed the lives of missionary heroines. One student was inspired to dedicate her life to be a missionary in Africa when she played the part of missionary Ann Hasseltine Judson in a Training School pageant.[60] The production of pageants served both entertainment and educational functions.

Another type of recreation scheduled by the school was courting. One night each week women students could receive "gentleman callers," typically Seminary students, in the Training School parlors.[61] These visits were chaperoned by faculty until the 1920s when a student served as monitor. If a male visitor lingered past the 10:00 bell, he risked the stern admonition of the chaperone. One night as the warning bell rang a young man made a hasty exit:

> In his hurry he failed to button his overcoat and the heavy door closed on the corner of it. What should he do? The solemn nurse, Miss Coombs, was on duty that evening. He remembered the look she gave him as he hurried out and didn't have the nerve to ring the bell and face her again! He took out his knife, cut off the corner of his coat, and hurried down Broadway.[62]

[59]Littlejohn, *History of Carver School*, 63.
[60]Maude R. McLure, "Highlights of Twenty Years," [1927], TSC, WMUA, 5.
[61]Three Training School Students, "A Week in the WMU Training School."
[62]Littlejohn, *History of Carver School*, 59.

Occasionally the Seminary students brought their dormitory pranks to the Training School. Juliette Mather recalled an incident that occurred while she was the student in charge of visitation night. A group of young men brought in two baby mice:

> and turned them loose when all the girls and their suitors were having their tête-à-têtes in the parlors of the Training School. And the girls did just what [the men] thought they would; they screamed, they got up on chairs. . . . I was perfectly furious. . . . I said to the two men, "Pick these up and get them out!" and they would go and put their hands down just behind the poor little things and make them jump a little further.[63]

Historian Beth Bailey describes how American patterns of courtship changed from the system of "calling" to "dating":

> Keeping company in the family parlor was replaced by dining and dancing, Coke dates, movies, parking. In the twentieth century, youth increasingly moved their courtship from the private to the public sphere.[64]

Bailey argues that the shift from the practice of calling, in which women controlled who was invited to visit while parents chaperoned, to a system of dating, in which men invited women out of the house away from chaperones was economical. The newer dating system, in which men spent money to entertain women, brought a change in men's and women's roles in courtship, with the power being attached to the man's wallet.[65]

---

[63]Gertrude Tharpe and Ethalee Hamric, Juliette Mather interview September 17-21, 1979, tape recording, transcript 33, WMUA.

[64]Beth Bailey, *From Front Porch to Back Seat: Courtship in Twentieth Century America* (Baltimore: Johns Hopkins University Press, 1988) 3.

[65]Ibid., 19-24.

Until the 1920s, courtship at the Training School was chiefly a group activity with all students entertaining guests in the same parlor. Over time, however, students gained the privilege of having a few "times out" when they could enjoy dating alone or in smaller groups. In 1926 students were allowed six nights out per academic year.[66]

Learning While Having Fun

Recreational events were not always just for fun; sometimes they were learning experiences. Occasionally students were taken on chaperoned excursions out of Louisville. In 1914, students attended the annual WMU meeting in Nashville where they presented a pageant called "The Beginning of a New Session." While women of the WMU learned about the Training School, students were experiencing WMU culture first hand. One student found the excitement of her first meeting nearly unbearable: "I was thrilled to death to be there and see what went on in this big organization."[67] In 1920, while attending the WMU annual meeting in Washington DC, students were invited to the White House to meet First Lady Edith Wilson.[68] Excursions to WMU meetings gave students first-hand knowledge of the organization and reinforced their loyalty to it.

Students also encountered women of the WMU within the walls of their own Training School. Many guests such as WMU officers, returning missionaries, and Training School alumnae came for overnight visits. Students felt honored to meet the women they had been taught to revere. When Kathleen Mallory, WMU's corresponding secretary, visited the school in 1921, the student social chairman was thrilled to have the assignment of accompanying her to a revival meeting. A few weeks later the student was offered employment at

---

[66]*Student Handbook*, WMUTS, 1926, 14.

[67]Doris, DeVault, *Carrie Littlejohn Interview* April 16, 1979, tape recording, transcript 17, WMUA; and Littlejohn, *History of Carver School*, 69.

[68]Littlejohn, *History of Carver School*, 62-63; Ralph Wayne to Mrs. Chipman, May 8, 1920, unclassified papers, TSC, SBTS; Juliette Mather interview by Catherine Allen, January 26, 1976, tape recording, transcript 60, WMUA.

WMU headquarters. The student was convinced that McLure had arranged the outing to help her get the job.[69] Visitors also provided a model of Southern Baptist ideals. When Mrs. W. C. James, president of WMU, was a guest at the school, McLure commented, "To have her in the house with her whole-hearted interest, her helpfulness, and her cultured Christian womanhood is to present to our students a character which will stimulate them to higher ideals and wider service."[70]

Even while entertaining dignified guests, the women still made time for fun and games. McLure was known for her keen sense of humor and she loved to make the students laugh. When her cousin Kathleen Mallory visited the school on official WMU business, the two women performed a skit mocking the hairstyles and fashions worn by Training School students.[71] Students also had a good laugh when Fannie Heck visited the school on April Fool's day. She arranged for a special box of "candy" which was secretly spiced with hot peppers to be served to McLure after dinner. A graduate recalled McLure's response after the first bite:

> It never occurred to her that Miss Heck would do a thing like that and she thought that some of us girls had done it. I know that she could have killed us every one right there. Then before we left the table Miss Heck let her know it was her joke so it turned out all right".[72]

When visitors came to the school, students had an opportunity to observe the principal and teachers as hostesses. Students were also encouraged to develop their own skills in hospitality by planning parties. The tea for married couples of the Seminary became an annual event, as well as a party for single men living in the

---

[69]Allen, Mather Interview, 14-15.

[70]Maude McLure, newspaper clipping, [1918?], Historical Scrapbook, TSC, SBTS.

[71]Tharpe and Hamric, *Mather Interview*, 20.

[72]Littlejohn interview, 17.; Mrs. W. C. James, *Fannie E. S. Heck: A Study of Hidden Springs of a Rarely Useful and Victorious Life* (Nashville: Broadman Press, 1939) 108-109.

dormitory.[73] The ability to organize and host such entertainment was considered an important part of the Training School's social curriculum:

> Any girl who has lived here a year must have learned . . . how to have a pretty "party" without extravagance. . . . To serve afternoon tea charmingly is no small accomplishment, and to have everything delicious and up-to-date, yet inexpensive, is invaluable knowledge for any social or religious worker.[74]

In addition to preparing women as hostesses, the Training School supported student organizations that provided opportunities to cultivate leadership skills. Like other college women of their time, Training School students learned to organize and direct their own projects, trying out new responsibilities. While the students of most women's schools created a wide array of student organizations, Training School students organized only two types of organizations: mission societies and the student government.

Mission Societies

Students of the Training School operated a mission society for its own students as well as cooperating with Seminary men in joint mission organizations. In their own Young Women's Auxiliary, students prepared for future responsibilities as members of WMU. As they attempted to gain entrance into the men's groups, women students were socialized into roles expected of women in the male-led Southern Baptist Convention.

Many women's historians recognize the role of mission societies in providing an opportunity for women to be leaders, make speeches,

---

[73]Littlejohn, *History of Carver School*, 57-58.
[74]Mrs. Robertson, clipping, [*Royal Service*, 1912], Historical Scrapbook, TSC, SBTS.

and create organizations.[75] Through the Young Women's Auxiliary (YWA) Training School women developed leadership skills within the context of a WMU organization. A group of students describing the organization noted that YWA provided an opportunity "to display our knowledge of parliamentary practice," and "develop inventiveness in programme making."[76] The group of students attending Seminary classes organized the first mission society in 1906. The organization adopted the constitution of WMU and took the name "Young Ladies Missionary Society of the Baptist Missionary Training School." Monthly meetings opened with a song, prayer, and Scripture reading followed by a lesson on missions. Lessons typically centered on cultural information about foreign countries or reports of mission work done by Southern Baptists. Occasionally, visiting missionaries presented information about their work. The society also collected offerings for home and foreign mission efforts.[77]

In 1907, the WMU established the YWA as a missions organization for young women aged sixteen to twenty-five. Fannie Heck spearheaded the movement aimed to "develop a symmetrical Christian young womanhood and to bind together the young women of the church for worldwide service for Christ."[78] Heck was interested in preparing young women to serve in WMU as well as "to keep them in the Baptist fold as potential missionaries." Non-denominational student movements such as the Young Women's Christian Association (YWCA) and the Student Volunteer Movement threatened a young woman's loyalty to Southern Baptist missions. As one WMU member expressed it "We must train the girls for denominationalism."[79]

---

[75]See Anne F. Scott, *Making the Invisible Woman Visible* (Urbana, IL: University of Illinois Press, 1984); Patricia Hill, *The World Their Household: The American Woman's Foreign Mission Movement and Cultural Transformation, 1870-1920*, (Ann Arbor: University of Michigan Press, 1985); and Joan J. Brumberg, *Mission For Life*, (New York: The Free Press, 1980).

[76]Three Training School Students, "A Week in the Life of the Training School."

[77]See Minutes, Young Ladies Missionary Society, TSC, SBTS.

[78]Allen, *Century to Celebrate*, 104.

[79]Willie Turner Dawson, quoted in Allen, *Century to Celebrate* , 104.

After the southwide YWA organization was established, the mission society of the Training School changed its name to the Anne Hasseltine Young Woman's Auxiliary. The name, used to designate YWA organizations established in colleges and universities, was chosen in memory of Anne Hasseltine Judson, the first Baptist woman missionary. Although membership in YWA was voluntary, a majority of the Training School student body participated.[80] Solomon notes that similar religious organizations, including the YWCA and Bible study groups, flourished both at evangelical colleges and at secular schools during this period.[81] Many Training School students who attended Southern Baptist colleges perhaps were involved in YWA in their college years. Judson College in Marion, Alabama formed the first Anne Hasseltine YWA, which became a model for similar groups in other colleges.[82] By incorporating YWA into the student experience, Training School officials could impart WMU values and methods using the mission society as a learning laboratory. The YWA president of 1921 stated this function: "Our aim has been to gain information, inspiration, and power for promoting the work of the [Woman's Missionary] Union"[83]

In addition to the mission society of the Training School, a few women were involved in organizations at the men's Seminary. On November 1, 1910, the Virginia Society of the Southern Baptist Theological Seminary voted to permit women students from Virginia to attend the next meeting. Wives of seminary students also began attending the monthly meetings; the Virginia Society membership list of 1912-1913 includes thirteen men and nine women. Monthly meetings were similar to those of other mission societies: a song and a prayer were followed by a lesson on missionary efforts.

---

[80]"Training School Report," n.d., Historical Scrapbook, TSC, SBTS.

[81]Barbara M. Solomon, *In the Company of Educated Women: A History of Women and Higher Education in America*, (New Haven: Yale University Press, 1985) 107.

[82]Ethlene Boone Cox, *Following His Train*, (Nashville: Broadman Press, 1938) 161.

[83]Clifford Barrat, "Report of Training School YWA," May, 1921 clipping from WMU Annual Report, Historical Scrapbook, TSC, SBTS.

Training School students and wives of Seminary students became more integrated into the Virginia Society over time, though they continued to play secondary roles. In the fall of 1912, women began to participate in committees and to hold the office of secretary. Secretary was the only office to which women were elected. For example, the position of Secretary/Treasurer, previously held by a male member, was divided into two offices and a Seminary man was elected to the position of Treasurer while a Training School student was elected Secretary. Women also began to participate in the monthly programs, although not as often as "the brethren." In 1913, two wives of Seminary students sang a duet, and in February 1915, Training School students presented the lesson. This was a controversial practice, as many Southern Baptists of this era did not approve of a woman addressing mixed audiences. By 1917, women were participating in every part of the Virginia Society meetings except for the public prayer, which was always led by a male student. However, the name of the organization was never changed to reflect Training School student involvement.[84]

Another missions organization involving a few Training School students was the City Volunteer Union, a group of mission volunteers from the Louisville Presbyterian Theological Seminary and the Southern Baptist Theological Seminary. The group was chartered in 1907 with Training School women listed as associate members. It functioned as a chapter of the national Student's Volunteer Union, which was begun in 1886 for the purpose of inspiring and encouraging college men and women who had dedicated their lives to foreign mission service. Women students may have participated in the student volunteer movement in their college years.[85]

In November 1907 the small group of Training School women attending the City Volunteers Union meeting was presented for membership at the suggestion of a male student. In the fall of 1908,

---

[84]See Minutes of the Virginia Society of the Southern Baptist Theological Seminary, November 1, 1910, November 1, 1912, April 2, 1913, February 3, 1915.

[85]Dorothy Garrett, "The Student Volunteer Movement, the Training School, and the Carver Family, 1981," TSC, WMUA. See also Hill, *The World Their Household*, 65, 128.

Miss Irene Haire was elected secretary, and women continued to hold that office through the years. The inclusion of women in the monthly meetings progressed at a pace similar to that of the Virginia Society. In earlier years, women were hardly mentioned in the records, but over time they began to take a more public part in the meetings. In December 1918, Louise Tucker, a Training School alumna, addressed the group concerning her mission work in China. In April 1919 a woman led the devotional message, although instead of saying a prayer after the devotion, as was the usual practice, the woman yielded the floor to a male student who led the prayer.[86]

Women students who participated with Seminary men in mission societies learned organizational roles, which paralleled those of women in the Southern Baptist Convention. Interestingly, Training School women began speaking to mixed audiences in the local student societies at about the same time their principal made a speech at the Southern Baptist Convention in 1916. Two years later women became voting delegates to the SBC.

Through the mission societies at the Training School and Seminary, students were socialized into their future roles as women in the Southern Baptist Convention. In contrast to students at many other schools, Training School women could participate in organizations that were strictly for women as well as in coeducational groups. Helen Horowitz notes that at women's colleges students did not have to compete with men for leadership opportunities. At coeducational schools, women were often barred from activities such as student government, the newspaper, and athletics, inspiring them to create their own parallel women's organizations.[87] Training School women participated in both single-sex and co-educational activities although with a significantly different level of involvement in each group. The experiences of organizing and leading their own YWA mission society were intended to prepare women as leaders of WMU. Meanwhile, the

---

[86]See Minutes of the City Volunteer Union, 1907-1919, unclassified papers, TSC, SBTS.

[87]Horowitz, *Campus Life*, 202.

circumscribed roles of Training School students in the coeducational mission societies prepared them for the limited influence they would have as women in the Southern Baptist Convention.

Student Government

Another organization in which students developed leadership skills was the Student Government Association. In the eighteenth century, the University of Virginia was one of the first American colleges to institute a system of student government. Thomas Jefferson believed that the experience of self-government in college would contribute to the training of statesmen for a democracy. Among women's colleges, Bryn Mawr pioneered in this area. Women's colleges had traditionally used the honor system to enforce regulations created by the administration. The students of Bryn Mawr asked to have a voice in making the rules. In 1892 students were granted rule-making as well as rule-enforcing power.[88] The first women's colleges of the South to adopt a system of student government were Randolph-Macon and Limestone in 1899. Converse College was not far behind, organizing its student government association in 1905. As Amy McCandless points out, the purpose of student government organizations was more social than political. They stressed group interests and were concerned with maintaining order. Leaders in student government freed faculty from enforcement of minor regulations such as "lights out" rules.[89]

Student government came to the Training School in 1911. The first constitution defined the purpose and procedures. An elected Student Committee represented the student body ". . . in whom authority shall be vested as to the discipline for the protection, reputation, and welfare of the student body." The Student Committee granted "requests, privileges, and permissions." The Chairman alone

---

[88]Newcomer, *A Century of Higher Education*, 117-118.
[89]Amy McCandless, "Preserving the Pedestal: Restrictions on Social Life at Southern Colleges for Women, 1920-1940," *History of Higher Education Annual*, 7 (1987): 54.

granted ordinary permissions[90] while "more important and doubtful ones shall be referred to the Student Committee in session." The Chairman granted permission to women who wished to attend any social function that did not involve all students. The student body met once each month when "suggestions and discussions for the good of the school may be presented."[91] One such suggestion was to secure an ironing board for student use. Many discussions involved regulations concerning interaction with male students. In the December meeting of 1912, the students decided to allow themselves the privilege of accepting invitations to meals two evenings per month. They agreed to leave the hostess' address with the principal. They also agreed not to make arrangements to meet Seminary students at social functions. However the minutes also stated "if one should accidentally meet a Seminary student . . . no embarrassment need be felt and certainly none expressed."[92]

By the 1920s, the SGA Constitution had been revised to include a statement of purpose emphasizing "cooperation in a spirit of loyalty to the school and to Christ in all our relationships." The Student Committee was also reorganized to include five officers, each holding responsibility for one aspect of student life. The General Chairman presided over meetings and granted all permissions not reserved for the principal; the Chairman of Religious Life assigned chapel talks to students and served as President of the YWA mission society. The Chairman of Social Life planned entertainment in consultation with the Principal and worked to "foster the spirit of sisterhood." The Chairman of Physical Culture organized athletic activities and the Chairman of General Culture encouraged interest in current events and served as Librarian.[93] By reorganizing and expanding the responsibilities of officers, student government became more than a

---

[90]The term "Chairman," employed by the Training School, will be retained here, although it is noted that women students held the office.

[91]Constitution of Student Government Association (SGA), 1911, TSC, SBTS.

[92]Minutes of the SGA, December 7, 1912, TSC, SBTS.

[93]See Constitution of SGA in *Student Handbook*, WMUTS, and Minutes of SGA, 1926-1929, TSC, SBTS.

system of enforcing regulations. It became the core organization around which student activities were organized. However, as SGA's role in the school's social life was expanded, its legislative powers were gradually curtailed. As the decade of the twenties brought new challenges to time-honored social regulations, the administration of the Training School limited the freedom of students to make their own rules.

Student Life in the 1920s

The decade of the twenties brought a host of new rules to the Training School. These changes suggest that women students were pushing the limits previously accepted without question. Another possible reason for additional rules was the uneasiness concerning behavior that was felt among administrators of women's colleges across the nation. According to Paula Fass, "Youth suddenly became a social problem in the 1920s." Fass describes the youth problem as "part myth, part reality" as young people came to represent "the strains of a culture running headlong into the twentieth century."[94] Fass notes that, although the behavior of all youth was scrutinized, the behavior of women was a cause of particular concern as it underlined a change in women's roles. No longer was she the "special stabilizer" of nineteenth century culture; now she was reaching toward a new definition of equality in the era of the flapper.[95] These changes were a cause of concern for college faculty and administrators who struggled to conserve the old order. On other campuses, smoking, drinking, and dancing became symbols of liberation for women students.[96] Although these activities were not likely to be temptations for the missionary-minded women of the Training School, two other indulgences: dating and fashion became a source of contention between students and faculty.

---

[94]Paula Fass, *The Damned and the Beautiful: American Youth in the 1920's* (New York: Oxford University Press, 1977) 13-15.

[95]Ibid., 23.

[96]Ibid., 292.

At the Training School, a student handbook that clarified additional rules was published starting in 1921. The handbook described the honor system in operation as well as the disciplinary function of student government. Regulations addressed such behavior as promptness, quiet periods, class absences, and appropriate dress. Most of the rules, however, were designed to ensure proper interaction between women and men. In the early years of the Training School, rules concerning appropriate social interaction with men were given brief mention in the school catalog under the headline "Social Life." Women were allowed to receive gentlemen callers on Monday evenings and to accept an escort to church on Sunday evenings. Going out on any other occasion required permission from the SGA Student Committee. Students were instructed to sit as a group in Seminary classes and not to linger in hallways or in classrooms where they might encounter male students.[97] The 1921 regulations still required that students sit as a group in Seminary classes and, women could only accept escorts and callers on designated evenings. However, the prohibition of other activities indicates that the new decade had ushered in additional temptations:

> Students will not accept invitations to meals in which young men are invited, except on evenings before Missionary Days. On these evenings escorts maybe accepted. Students must not visit restaurants, ice cream parlors, concert halls, nor other public places with young men friends.[98]

New regulations concerning dress appeared during the decade of the twenties. The 1922 student handbook declared, "We believe the Christian duty of every woman called to definite service is to be an example in modest dress. This being our conviction we discourage all extreme styles." Students' skirts were to be no more than nine inches above the floor. The "bobbed" hairstyle, which had recently come

---

[97]*Catalogue*, WMUTS, 1913.
[98]*Student Handbook*, WMUTS, 1921, TSC, SBTS.

into vogue, was strictly forbidden. In the fall of 1923 the board of managers voted not to admit any students wearing bobbed hair, and students who had already cut their hair short were required to "allow it to grow and wear nets until it has attained proper length."[99]

The desire of Training School students to create an image through fashion, and the Board's corresponding prohibition of that expression, exemplified the nationwide preoccupation with the behavior of 1920s youth. According to Solomon, the emancipated flapper who bobbed her hair, powdered her nose, and wore lipstick and short skirts captured the image. The reactions of college administrators to these changes in appearance and behavior suggested a profound anxiety toward the changing roles of American women.[100] Professor Willystine Goodsell wrote of her frustration with the "insurgent young wom[a]n of the 1920s who "turns her back with entire self-assurance on the mid-Victorian standards of her grandmother and asserts her inalienable right to frame her own ideals of conduct and abide by their consequences."[101] Gordon describes a generation gap created by the very different childhood experiences between young women students and older faculty. Women born later in the nineteenth century grew up with more personal freedom and more activities with boys, including coeducational schools. This generation, more than the previous generations of college women, wanted heterosexual companionship in college:

> Whereas in the late nineteenth century female collegians had been fulfilled by their relationships with "girls, girls, girls," it was boys, boys, boys who most appealed to the college women of the new generation. . . . They were beneficiaries not only of

---

[99]*Student Handbook*; WMUTS, 1922; Minutes, Board of Managers of WMUTS, September 24, 1923.

[100]Solomon, *Company of Educated Women*, 158-59.

[101]Willystine Goodsell, *The Education of Women: Its Social Background and its Problems* (New York: The Macmillan Co., 1924) 262.

the earlier women's movement, but also of the sexual revolution that had overturned Victorian patterns of courtship.[102]

Another indication of changes in student behavior is found in the reaction of the principal to the students of the new decade. McLure found it increasingly difficult to maintain control over the student body. When McLure learned that a group of students had been meeting Seminary men at the cinema, at married students' homes, and in the Seminary halls and classrooms she came close to resigning in frustration. A graduate later recalled the incident: "Mrs. McLure had very high ideals for her girls and nothing disappointed her so much as to have one fall below her standards."[103]

When McLure resigned in 1923, the public believed it was because she wanted to make a home for her son who had been injured in the war. Isla May Mullins, wife of Seminary president E. Y. Mullins, wrote "all friends of the School stood in silent awe before the call of motherhood to its first duty."[104] However, those closest to her knew that tension between herself and the students of a new generation was an additional motive for McLure's leaving the Training School. Carrie Littlejohn, who was serving as director of the school's settlement house when McLure resigned, observed:

Transitions are never easy for those most vitally affected. This one was not easy for the students, products of their day and generation. It was difficult for Mrs. McLure. She belonged to the old school, and she could not accept happily the changes that the new day was bringing."[105]

---

[102]Lynn D. Gordon, *Gender and Higher Education in the Progressive Era*, (New Haven: Yale University Press, 1990) 161.

[103]Willie Jean Stewart to Kathleen Mallory, September 14, 1938, unclassified papers, TSC, SBTS.

[104]Mullins, *House Beautiful*, 57.

[105]Littlejohn, *History of Carver School*, 88.

McLure felt that, at age sixty, she had become too old to lead a new generation, and a younger woman should serve as principal. A WMU employee and graduate of the Training School expressed her respect for McLure's decision: "She was not old, but her standards were a part of her. How we old girls should have hated to have her compromise them!"[106] As the women of the 1920s responded to a national shift in courting patterns, McLure found their behavior unacceptable. Her disillusionment was similar to that of other college faculty and administrators who felt betrayed by students of the 1920s. As Helen Horowitz noted, "Only a few years earlier they had been objects of student admiration. Now they were cast in the role of upholders of the Victorian moral order that had lost its hold over the young."[107]

A New Principal

After McLure's resignation, Carrie Littlejohn served for one year as acting principal while the board of managers searched for a new leader for the school. They selected Janie Cree Bose who, like McLure, was widowed with one son. Bose was in her forties when she began her term as principal in 1925 and before long students were calling her "Little Mother." Ironically, this younger woman did not create a more lenient atmosphere. The new principal did not change the regulations published in the student handbook during McLure's administration. Instead, additional regulations were printed and distributed to students. Bose struggled, as McLure had, to hold women students accountable to regulations that seemed outmoded.[108]

In the first year of Bose's administration, the Seminary moved from downtown Louisville to a suburban location known as "The Beeches." During the final weeks of the term, Training School students traveled by bus to lectures at the Seminary. However, due to

---

[106]Stewart to Mallory, September 14, 1938.

[107]Horowitz, *Alma Mater*, 293.

[108]*Student Handbook*, 1925-1929; "Janie Cree Bose," Baptist Biography File, Southern Baptist Historical Library and Archives, Nashville, TN.

the inconvenience of this arrangement, in 1926 the Training School discontinued the tradition of joint classes with Seminary students. A new professor was employed to teach Bible courses and a few Seminary professors traveled to the Training School to deliver lectures.[109]

Under the new arrangement, women students no longer had daily interaction with Seminary men in the classroom. There is no indication that dating between Seminary students and Training School women diminished, although opportunities for interaction were limited. Kathleen McDowell, a student from Alabama, managed a courtship with Seminary student J. A. Timmerman. The couple met when they were students at Howard College, a coeducational Southern Baptist school in Alabama. In Louisville, Sunday evenings became prime time for McDowell and Timmermann to date, as Training School regulations permitted women to accept an escort to evening church services. Student organizations of the Seminary often included women in their meetings. McDowell and Timmerman were both members of the organization for Alabama students. Teas and receptions given by local churches provided opportunities for Training School and Seminary students to socialize.[110]

The tradition of Missionary Day presented another chance for students of the two schools to interact. Missionary Day was a monthly event at the Seminary when classes were suspended and the entire campus focused on "the cultivation of the missionary spirit." Students gathered to hear reports of the work being done in various mission fields. Women had been participating in the Missionary Day tradition since they first began attending classes at the turn of the century. After the relocation of the Seminary, it was decided that women students would travel to the Beeches once each month to continue the tradition. However, women were not allowed to sit with male students in the chapel but were required to sit together as a group.

---

[109]Littlejohn, *History of Carver School*, 97-99.
[110]Kathleen McDowell Scrapbook, [1926-1927] Timmerman Papers, WMUA.

New rules concerning Missionary Day were created to ensure that interactions between the sexes were appropriate.[111]

Negotiating the Rules

As the rules of the Training School multiplied, the Student Committee charged with enforcing regulations found their task more difficult. Mabel Newcomer notes that student government organizations of the 1920s demanded more legislative power and more freedom. For example, in the northeastern women's colleges such as Vassar and Bryn Mawr, pressure applied by student government won permission for students to smoke on campus. Students also campaigned for more relaxed rules regarding chaperonage and curfews. When Wellesley students voted to allow themselves the privilege of going to the cinema unchaperoned, angry faculty resigned from the joint faculty-student College Government. The students immediately modified other rules regarding chaperonage until the college eventually affirmed students' rights to make their own rules.[112]

There is some indication that Training School students attempted to use their system of student government to change school regulations. Prior to 1925, the SGA Constitution instructed students who wished to amend regulations or add new ones to submit a written proposal. If the Student Committee approved the proposed change, the student body would vote on it.[113] However, the 1925 handbook contains an added paragraph under the Constitution's Legislation section. This statement gave final authority regarding rules to an Advisory Board composed of the Principal, Associate Principal, and Chairman of the board of managers. In violation of proper procedure for amending the Constitution, the student body never voted on this paragraph as an amendment to the Constitution. It simply appeared in the student handbook, probably inserted by the administration. It

---

[111]Minutes of Board of Trustees, SBTS, May 7, 1903; *Student Handbook*, WMUTS, 1926-1927, TSC, SBTS.

[112]Horowitz, *Campus Life*, 288.

[113]*Student Handbook*, WMUTS, 1921, TSC, SBTS.

is not clear if the clause was added in response to student attempts to change regulations. Perhaps Bose suggested the addition as a preventive measure, since it appeared in the first year of her administration. Whatever the statement's origin, the result was clear: students' rights to amend or create rules on their own were curtailed.[114]

In the 1926-1927 session, a "Findings Committee" composed of students was assembled to investigate recent appeals of students for less regulations and more privileges. The women requested that student government be given the power to make rules as well as enforce them. They asked that "unwritten rules be incorporated in the handbook or abolished," that students be allowed to use the telephone, and that several changes be made to household rules. The majority of suggested changes related to outings away from campus and interactions with men. Students wanted to have more evenings designated for outings with escorts. They requested the privilege of eating in ice cream parlors and restaurants. Students also suggested that there be "no artificial segregation" between Seminary students and Training School students during Missionary Day services.[115]

Students of the Training School were not as successful as northern college women were in negotiating changes. The administration of the Training School did not yield to any of the students' requests. Outings to ice cream parlors continued to be forbidden, sitting with men in chapel on Missionary Day was still taboo, and additional rules not stated in the handbook were enforced.[116] According to Amy McCandless, women in colleges of the South were much less likely to be successful in negotiating with tradition-bound administrators for more lenient rules.[117] Change in social regulations occurred much later in the South than in other parts of the nation. For example, while chaperonage had nearly disappeared in northern colleges in the 1920s and 1930s, it was still a requirement in Southern

[114]*Student Handbook*, WMUTS, 1925, TSC, SBTS.
[115]"Report of The Findings Committee," McDowell Scrapbook.
[116]*Student Handbook*, WMUTS; Minutes of SGA September 30, 1929, TSC, SBTS.
[117]McCandless, "Preserving the Pedestal," 55.

women's schools. While college women of the North were experi-
menting with sexual expression described by the new term "petting,"
the strict regulations of Southern colleges inhibited unsupervised
contact with the opposite sex. Southern women's colleges also
retained, longer than their northern counterparts, rules forbidding
smoking, drinking, card playing, and dancing with men.[118]

Although Training School students' efforts to gain more personal
freedom in the 1920s were not successful, their attempt to negotiate
regulations indicated a new confidence not demonstrated by students
in previous years. New political involvement, which came with the
right to vote, taught women of the 1920s that their voices could make
a difference. Perhaps women students had practiced negotiation with
administrators of colleges they had attended prior to the Training
School. Some came from state universities and other colleges with
more relaxed regulations, creating a sharp contrast to strict Training
School rules.

Since women of the Training School were unable to change
school rules, they resisted. One mild demonstration of protest took
the form of sarcasm. The following "regulations" for dating were listed
in a student's version of the handbook:

> *Times Out*
> Not less than ten each month and more than thirty. Anyone
> failing to comply with this will be brought before the Student
> Committee.
>
> *Sunday Night Dates*
> Sunday night when having a date please make the gentleman
> stop at a convenient Drug Store and have a good Banan[a]
> Split and Sandwich before coming in, thereby, eliminating
> Sunday Supper. Please have your *date-man* leave promptly at
> the 12:00 o'clock bell.

---

[118]Ibid. 48-49; Horowitz, *Campus Life*, 208.

Missionary Day
In Norton Hall girls are requested to sit with as many preachers as possible—Linger after service for a good social hour—not lasting later than three o'clock. Be sure to have a good chat with everybody.[119]

Students sometimes resisted efforts of the WMU to enforce outmoded social practices. When a member of the Board of Trustees requested in 1924 that students address one another with the title "Miss," students politely refused. They explained that the "sister spirit" engendered by the use of first names was more important than traditions of formality.[120]

Perhaps the most frequently used form of protest to regulations was the passive resistance of disobedience. The minutes of the Student Government Association of the late 1920s indicate widespread negligence of Training School rules. Each meeting featured a long list of reminders about rules that students had broken:

Music which is played on Sunday shall not be jazz.
Hats are always to be worn on streetcars.
Your men friends are not to go to the car with you after parties.[121]

In spite of student resistance, the principal, supported by the WMU through its governing boards, was always the winner in the battle over regulations. Women who disobeyed regulations lost their dating privileges.[122] Those who continued to break regulations were interviewed by the principal and board of managers and often placed on probation or asked not to return the following session.[123]

---

[119]*Student Handbook*, WMUTS, 1926, TSC, SBTS.
[120]Lydia Greene to Mrs. Davis, October 6, 1924, TSC, SBTS.
[121]See SGA Minutes, WMUTS, September 30, 1929, October 6, 1929, November 4, 1929, TSC, SBTS.
[122]"Report of the Findings Committee," McDowell Scrapbook.
[123]"Qualified Notifications, 1925," TSC, SBTS.

Disobedience to the rules was interpreted as a sign of disloyalty to the school, to the WMU, and ultimately to Christ. In a letter that explained the prohibition of the bobbed hairstyle, the board of managers reminded students that they were indebted to the WMU and should meet its expectations concerning appropriate physical appearance. Students were asked not to "do anything to detract from the beauty and dignity of your beloved House Beautiful, made possible for you by the love and sacrifice of countless Christian women of our Southland."[124] One student urged her classmates to follow regulations as an expression of Christian commitment: "No matter how many rules we have, if we do not have loyalty to Jesus, they will do no good."[125]

Regulations gave concrete expression to accepted Southern Baptist definitions of appropriate behavior for women. Although student handbooks continued to forbid certain actions, there is evidence that students challenged the rules, sometimes in open discussion as in the example of the "Findings Committee" and sometimes covertly through disobedience of regulations. Training School women attempted to be a part of the larger changes of the 1920s by bobbing their hair, sneaking out to the cinema, and negotiating regulations that allowed more contact with Seminary men. Maude McLure did not choose to make accommodations to the changes and retired, disappointed that newer students no longer upheld the ideals of a previous generation of students. The new principal, Janie Bose, increased the number of rules to be followed, perhaps as an expression of anxiety over the new behaviors of resistance emerging from the student body.

The Ideal Training School Girl

Both students and administrators understood the Southern Baptist ideal for women. This image was described in the portrait of

---

[124]Board of Managers to WMUTS students, [1924?], TSC, SBTS.
[125]SGA Minutes, WMUTS, November 9, 1926.

"The Ideal Training School Girl" who demonstrated her love for Christ not only by studying the Bible and evangelizing others, but also by being a lady. She would develop "those attributes of personal charm which will express themselves in graciousness of manner, gentleness of speech, [and] reverence of conduct."[126] By creating a domestic atmosphere in which a woman learned to be housekeeper, hostess, and leader of women's mission societies, the Training School assured the denomination that a graduate would stay in the sphere to which she had been appointed by God. Her chief responsibility would be to care for the home. She might demonstrate her leadership skills among other women, but in church organizations that included men, she would take a secondary role. The social curriculum, transmitted through the daily life of the Training School, taught women to stay in their limited domain within the Southern Baptist denomination.

---

[126]"The Ideal Training School Girl," [1920?], TSC, SBTS.

5

THE GOSPEL AND GOODWILL
The Baptist Training School Settlement House

The Training School prepared women for denominational service using the formal curriculum of the classroom and a second curriculum to instill the cultural expectations of Southern Baptists. Both formal and second curricular learning were joined together in field work, as students practiced what they were taught. While doing field work in the local community, students passed on to other women and children the values and skills learned at the Training School.

Field work gave students the opportunity to provide Christian service to the community under the supervision of Training School faculty. It was a chance for the novice missionary to "try her wings" by bringing the theories of the classroom to meet the challenges presented by real life situations. The Baptist Missionary Training School at Chicago also required students to do field work. Working among immigrant populations in Chicago, students in the Northern Baptist school learned to lead programs of recreation, worship, story telling, and crafts. They also practiced friendly visiting in a desperate section of the city called "The Black Hole."[1] The influence of the Chicago school may have provided the inspiration for McLure to bring the practical element of field work to the Training School curriculum.

Initially, Training School students did field work in the churches, missions, and social work agencies of Louisville. Then in 1912, under the direction of Maude McLure, the school opened its own settlement

---

[1] Faith Cox Bailey, *Two Direction*, (Rochester, NY: Baptist Missionary Training School, 1964) 20-22.

house in which students gained practical knowledge of classroom theories. McLure spent the summer of 1912 in New York studying social work methods in preparation for the new venture. Her summer training introduced her to two important trends in the emerging profession of social work: the charity organization movement and the settlement movement.

The Charity Organization Movement

The charity organization movement that emerged in the late nineteenth century was founded on three basic assumptions: that urban poverty was caused by the moral deficiencies of the poor, that poverty could only be eliminated by the correction of these deficiencies in individuals, and that various charity organizations would need to cooperate to bring about this change. Inspired by a similar movement in Great Britain, the charity organizations flourished in the United States.

By the 1890s, over a hundred American cities had charity organization societies. Journals like *Lend-a-Hand* (Boston) and *Charities Review* (New York) created a forum for ideas; annual meetings of the National Conference of Charities and Corrections provided opportunities for leaders to discuss common concerns.[2] Supporters of the movement believed individuals in poverty could be uplifted through association with middle and upper class volunteers. Privileged women employed the technique of "friendly visiting" to establish relationships as well as investigate the circumstances of families in need. Charity organization societies did not usually give money to the poor; rather they coordinated various charitable resources and kept records of those who had received charity in order to prevent "duplicity and duplication" by "having the wealthy keep an eye on the poor."[3] The case method, later used by the social work

---

[2]Paul Boyer, *Urban Masses and Moral Order in America, 1820-1920* (Cambridge, MA: Harvard University Press, 1978) 146-150.

[3]Lori Ginzberg, *Women and the Work of Benevolence: Morality, Politics, and Class in the Nineteenth Century United States* (New Haven: Yale University Press, 1990) 196-97.

profession, is rooted in charity organization philosophies, which focus on the individual, change through relationship, and investigation.[4]

The New York City Charity Organization Society, sponsor of the school where McLure completed summer study, was founded in 1882 and directed for twenty-five years by Josephine Shaw Lowell. One of the movement's well-known national leaders, Lowell articulated her conviction that workers were responsible for "moral oversight" of people in poverty. Those who would help the poor must guard against random almsgiving that not only was inefficient but in fact could "do fatal moral injury" to those who might come to believe that society would cushion them from their failings.[5] Lowell and her followers also rejected church-related approaches to charity. Stephen Humphreys Gurteen, a clergyman and author of A *Handbook of Charity Organization* (1882), warned that no one connected with the movement should "use his or her position for the purpose of proselytism or spiritual instruction." Mary Richmond, leader of the Baltimore Charity Organization Society argued that church-related relief work was usually a form of bribery for church attendance.[6]

Edward T. Devine, leader of the New York City Charity Organization Society was willing to include church-related organizations in charity work although he insisted that "friendly visiting should be done strictly for the sake of the family rather than as a means of winning converts, however desirable that also may be."[7] Devine was the director of the New York School of Philanthropy in 1912 when McLure enrolled in the summer course.[8] Established in 1898 as the first school to provide formal training in charity work, the School of Philanthropy taught basic charity organization principles. However, Devine also demonstrated his sympathy with the emerging settlement

[4]Rhonda Connaway and Martha Gentry, *Social Work Practice* (Englewood Cliffs, NJ: Prentice Hall, 1988) 11-13.

[5]Ibid., 147-149.

[6]Boyer, *Urban Masses*, 148.

[7]Edward T. Devine, *The Practice of Charity* (New York: Lentilhon and Company, 1901) 99.

[8]Paul Klein, *From Philanthropy to Social Welfare* (San Francisco: Josey Bass, 1968) 220-223.

movement by working closely with the settlements in New York.[9] By exposing students like McLure to both the charity organization and settlement movements, Devine provided an opportunity for learners to experience different perspectives. McLure respected Devine and later used his writing as a text in Training School classes.[10] McLure and other Training School faculty would teach charity organization tenets emphasizing the changing of individuals. Training School students would also adopt the technique of friendly visiting to be used in field work.

The Settlement Movement

While supporters of the charity organization movement emphasized changing individuals, the settlement movement stressed societal reform and attempted to help those in need by changing institutions. The movement spread to the United States from England in the late 1800s when the country was dealing with questions of immigration, industrialization, and urbanization. Leaders of the movement like Stanton Coit, Robert Woods, and Jane Addams created settlements after visits to London's first and most important settlement, Toynbee Hall, located in East London. Toynbee and the first American settlements, held strong ties to the local university; students lived among the poor as residents while professors offered the benefits of lectures and stimulating discussions. Although the movement in England was largely masculine, settlement leadership in the United States included both men and women. In 1889, a group of women, many of them graduates of Smith, founded the College Settlement Association in New York City. In that same year, Jane Addams and

---

[9]Allen F. Davis, *Spearheads for Reform: The Social Settlements and the Progressive Movement 1890-1914* (New Brunswick, New Jersey: Rutgers University Press, 1984) 22.

[10]*Catalogue, Woman's Missionary Union Training School*, 1914, WMU Training School, Carver School Collection, Southern Baptist Theological Seminary, Louisville, KY. (Hereafter cited as TSC, SBTS).

Ellen Starr opened Hull House in a poverty-stricken area of Chicago.[11]

Settlements were established in urban areas, particularly where immigrants tried to find work. The settlement's chief purpose was to establish communication between the well-to-do and the working class. It was based on a democratic ideal or, as Jane Addams expressed it, "on the theory that the dependence of classes on each other is reciprocal."[12] As neighbors living together, people of the settlement worked to improve city conditions. Settlements focused their energies not on reforming individuals but on addressing urban problems. Research on economic and social conditions carried out by residents informed social action taken on behalf of city dwellers. In fact, settlements carried out the first systematic attempts to study immigrant communities in American cities. They used their insights to initiate reforms in the area of child labor, sanitation, and women's working conditions. Other activities of the settlement included education and recreation for neighbors of all ages. Settlements offered college extension courses, vocational training, demonstrations of domestic skills, kindergartens, and playgrounds to improve the lives of neighbors. Courses in the English language prepared immigrants for life in the United States.[13]

A portion of McLure's summer training was the experience of living in a settlement. Allen Davis estimates approximately eighty-two settlement houses in New York City when McLure was a student, and there is no record to indicate in which house she took residence. However, one Baptist paper reported that she lived in New York's East Side, probably indicating that she chose a settlement with a religious focus. Some likely choices may have been East Side House or Union Settlement. McLure shared the philosophy of Clarence Gordon who had been head resident of East Side House from 1894 to 1903. In his essay, "The Relation of the Church to the Settlement,"

[11]Allen F. Davis, "Settlements: History" in Encyclopedia of Social Work, edited by John B. Turner (Washington DC: National Association of Social Workers, 1977): 1266-1271.

[12]Davis, Spearheads for Reform, 19.

[13]Davis, "Settlements: History."

Gordon stated, "Humanitarians, socialists, philanthropists, may do settlement work and do it well . . . but only on the foundation of Christ . . . and His example, and grace to inspire and direct, can the settlement realize its highest possibilities."[14]

Another religious East Side settlement, which might have hosted McLure that summer, was the Union Settlement. Although it was connected with the all-male Union Theological Seminary, the majority of workers in the settlement were women. In addition, the head resident of the Union Settlement was a lecturer at the School of Philanthropy.[15]

Two Baptist settlements may have been of interest to McLure. The Children's Home Settlement was located on the East Side and was organized "to demonstrate the merits of a religious social settlement."[16] The Amity Baptist Church and Settlement House was located in a different neighborhood on the West Side and attempted to provide a "union of the religious and industrial forces in the salvation of mankind." In addition to the typical daily activities of a settlement, the Amity House provided religious services and a Bible School.[17]

After her summer in New York, McLure brought back to Louisville a basic understanding of the settlement movement and ideas about activities and services that such an establishment might provide. However, neither McLure nor the WMU ever embraced the foundational tenets of the American settlement movement, which involved workers living in poor neighborhoods and working with neighbors for social reform. The workers at Louisville's Baptist settlement did not concentrate on reform activities, nor did they work to reduce the gap between themselves and the poorer classes. Although they utilized many of the methods of the settlement movement, the women of the Training School did not work with

---

[14]Davis, *Spearheads for Reform*, 14.

[15]Robert A. Woods, and Albert J. Kennedy, eds., *Handbook of Settlements*, (New York: Charities Publication Committee, 1911) 225-227.

[16]Woods and Kennedy, *Handbook of Settlements*, 239

[17]Ibid., 234.

neighbors for social reform. The major goals of the Baptist Settlement house were to evangelize the neighborhood and to socialize Louisville immigrants into American Protestant life.

WMU and Personal Service

Operating within the charity organization philosophy, women of the WMU worked to change society by reforming the individual. The phrase used by WMU to describe its program of social welfare was "personal service," a term reflecting the focus on individual persons. The Personal Service program was launched by WMU in 1909 with Lulie Wharton of Baltimore in charge. WMU called upon members for "the Christian up-building of their own communities, acknowledging a spiritual duty to the poor, neglected, and outcast of their own neighborhood."[18] However, the purpose was not simply help for the needy but evangelization of the poor. Personal Service had "the gospel as its motive and conversion as its aim."[19] Like the leaders of the charity organization movement, WMU members intended to "rebuild the diseased social climate" by reforming individuals. For Southern Baptist women this meant religious conversion, using the technique of friendly visiting as an opportunity to evangelize. WMU women were warned against placing "the ministry to the body before or apart from the ministry to the soul."[20]

The emphasis of WMU on conversion of the individual rather than societal reform was in line with the thinking of most Southern Baptists of the early twentieth century. Although a few individuals embraced the Social Gospel movement, which promoted the general improvement of society through church action, most Southern Baptists rejected the notion, claiming that individual conversion was the answer to society's ills. The minority of Southern Baptist leaders who believed that secular reform goals were proper religious concerns

---

[18]Catherine Allen, *A Century to Celebrate: History of Woman's Missionary Union* (Birmingham: Woman's Missionary Union, 1987) 215.

[19]Ibid., 216.

[20]Ibid., 215.

envisioned social improvement as a method of advancing the kingdom of God on earth.[21] These leaders, both men and women, became involved in social reform groups such as the Southern Sociological Congress. Created in 1912, the Southern Sociological Congress brought together Southern leaders in education, social work, religion, and government. Its social program called for prison reform, the abolition of child labor, compulsory education, and solving of the race problem. In the 1913 Congress meeting, Walter Rauschenbusch, the best known theologian of the Social Gospel movement, urged Southern leaders to involve churches in reform efforts. Fannie Heck provided the link between WMU and the Southern Sociological Congress; in 1914 Heck served as the second vice president of the congress while maintaining the presidency of WMU. Other WMU leaders, including Maude McLure and Lulie Wharton, attended congress meetings as well.[22]

Fannie Heck was one of the few WMU leaders to balance secular social reform efforts with the decidedly evangelical aims of WMU. Heck was founder and first president of the Associated Charities organization in her hometown of Raleigh, North Carolina. She also served as the first president of the Woman's Club of Raleigh, leading members to become involved in community health and sanitation concerns. WMU women did not follow the example of their president in seeking societal reform through secular groups. WMU leaders typically focused their energies on church-sponsored efforts aimed at the conversion of the individual. As Allen notes, "WMU seldom responded to need by marching on the halls of government . . . most often WMU went to work alleviating distress in small groups."[23]

Although WMU did not embrace the aims of progressive social reform, leaders used the methods developed by reformers and social scientists in striving for evangelistic goals. They identified with social workers, modifying the tradition of the charity organization move-

---

[21]Billy F. Sumners, *"The Social Attitudes of Southern Baptists Toward Certain Issues, 1910-1920* (Masters thesis, University of Texas at Arlington, 1975) 17.

[22]Allen, *Century to Celebrate*, 213.

[23]Ibid., 214, 216.

ment and stressing reform of the individual through religious conversion.

The Training School, like its parent WMU, emphasized evangelism in its approach to personal service. Agencies in which students did field work were typically missionary in purpose. Organizations such as the Hope Rescue Mission and the Salvation Army provided students with experience in personal evangelism to people in poverty.

A Settlement of Their Own

While local agencies provided some opportunities for field work, Training School faculty and the local board of managers wanted the school to have an agency of its own. In 1912, McLure created the Baptist Training School Settlement to provide service to the community while training students in missionary methods. McLure saw the Baptist Settlement's purpose as twofold: to provide practical training in social work and missions to Training School students and to evangelize the neighborhood.[24] It is interesting to note that the Training School chose the term settlement to describe the new enterprise, thus aligning itself with that movement. However, the purpose of the new venture was closer to the purposes of the charity organization movement with reform of the individual as the clear objective. The Baptist Settlement emerged as a hybrid, using the methods of the settlement movement to reach objectives that were commonly held by charity organization supporters. Perhaps McLure created this combination in response to the twofold training she received in New York. In 1913 McLure described the aims of the Baptist Settlement:

1. To reach the little children that their tiny feet may be started in the upward path

---

[24]Maude McLure, "A Glimpse of Settlement Work," (Baltimore: Woman's Missionary Union, 1913) 2.

2. To inspire the older boys and girls with ideals that shall help them to improve their environment and shall give them strength against the awful temptations that sweep over them.

3. To interest the young people in sane and wholesome pleasures that their energies may be rightly directed

4. To help the women to be better home makers, more careful wives and mothers, better Christians

5. To give Christ to the neighborhood.

To attain such ends, the settlement house, even without resident workers, remained open every day of the week and several nights.[25]

This statement of purpose reflects three distinct features of the Baptist Training School Settlement. First, it did not include men within the population it served; the settlement provided services primarily to women and children. Another feature of the Baptist settlement was that workers did not live in the neighborhood but came in daily from a more prosperous setting. Finally, the overarching purpose of the entire program was not societal reform but to convert the neighbors to the Baptist faith and engage them in a local church. McLure wrote that the settlement was "opened in the belief that, with Christianity as a foundation, a settlement may be a feeder to the church and a mighty force in the coming of the Kingdom."[26] McLure modified the settlement methods she learned in New York to meet the goal of evangelizing individuals in the neighborhood.

In the summer of 1912, while McLure was studying in New York, the Training School's board of managers rented a building on Madison Street, within five blocks of the school, where the new settlement could be housed. Five rooms were used for activities of the

---

[25]McLure, "A Glimpse," 2.
[26]Ibid.

settlement and two apartments upstairs, were sub-rented to tenants.[27] This house was used until another building in the same block was purchased one year later.

The students canvassed the neighborhood to inform families about the services of the new center and invite them to attend an "Open House" event on October 25. The language used to describe the planning and execution of the event reflects the cultural practices of Training School women. Carrie P. Porter described the event:

They (students) gave personal invitations to all the mothers and children in the neighborhood, and few, if any, regrets were evident when the auspicious occasion arrived. So cordial a welcome was given to this "house warming" that all callers felt that they had a share in the good cheer that this under-taking stood for.[28]

Congruent with domestic values passed on from the WMU elite, Porter's words describe an event that is more like a ladies tea than provision of services to needy families.

Emma Leachman, city missionary in Louisville and teacher of Applied Methods, located her office in the settlement and served as the director of its activities. Leachman had been working with Louisville's poor neighborhoods in connection with local Southern Baptists for about ten years when the settlement opened. She supervised the students in the settlement work and taught classes in social work methods.[29]

The majority of settlements in the United States were established in the northeastern and midwestern regions of the nation. According to Allen Davis, there were only two important settlements in the South: Kingsley House in New Orleans and Neighborhood House in

[27]Carrie Porter, "The Baptist Woman's Missionary Union Training School and Its Settlement Work," clipping from Western Recorder, 1913, Historical Scrapbook, TSC, SBTS.

[28]Ibid.

[29]Carrie Littlejohn, History of Carver School of Missions and Social Work (Nashville, TN: Broadman Press, 1958) 65.

Louisville Kentucky.[30] The Baptist Training School Settlement was very proud to be the first Southern Baptist Settlement in the nation.

Louisville's Neighborhood House

Training School students did field work at Neighborhood House before their own settlement opened. Students and faculty were familiar with the programs and philosophy of this settlement. Two theological students, Archie Hill and W. E. Wilkins, founded Neighborhood House in 1896. They invited two noted Settlement workers—Graham Taylor of Chicago Commons and Jane Addams of Hull House—to address a group of Louisvillians interested in the settlement idea. A local philanthropist, Lucy Belknap held organizational meetings in her home that led to a decision "to establish in the less favored district of the city a settlement where educated men and women could share with their neighbors what was best in each other's lives." Lucy Belknap donated the funds and property, which would enable Louisvillians to participate in the settlement idea.[31]

In the formation years of Neighborhood House, Archie Hill was the primary settlement worker. Activities were centered on clubs and classes for boys. The settlement was so popular among the neighbors that it outgrew its original quarters within a year and Belknap donated a new building. Soon the programs were expanded to include activities for all ages.[32] The neighbors were mostly immigrants: Syrians, Jews, Greeks, and Italians. Neighborhood House made an effort to help the neighbors preserve the traditions of the homeland by sponsoring concerts and festivals where native customs were shared. Songs, stories, and dances of the immigrants were a regular part of Neighborhood House entertainment.[33]

---

[30]Davis, *Spearheads for Reform*, 23.

[31]Minutes of Neighborhood House, "A Tribute to Miss Lucy Belknap," April 1914, Neighborhood House Archives, Louisville, KY. (Hereafter cited as NHA). See also "A Tie That Bound Famous Jane Adams to Louisville," *Louisville Courier Journal*, January 20, 1955.

[32]"History of Neighborhood House," n.d., NHA.

[33]*Neighborhood House: A Social Settlement*, 1914, NHA.

Classes in the English language and American government were also offered as part of an Americanization effort. Practical skills like sewing, cooking, and weaving were taught in classes for women and girls. Boys learned to work with wood, copper, and clay. There were also athletic activities such as basketball teams for boys and girls, as well as a gymnasium and playground. Academic endeavors were also a part of Neighborhood House activities. A branch of the public library was housed in the settlement as well as a picture loan system in which neighbors checked out art prints to take home on loan. A group of boys organized a debating club, young girls took piano lessons, and a few young women studied French.[34]

One of the more festive activities was the regular dance held in the gymnasium. An average of a hundred adults attended this weekly event, which was known as the "Social Evening." During summer months, Neighborhood House transported children to Louisville parks for picnics and hikes and cooperated with other agencies in sponsoring The Fresh Air Home: a residence in the country where city-dwellers could spend one or two weeks. The Baptist Training School Settlement referred some of the families to the Fresh Air Home.[35]

In addition to the management of daily activities the residents of Neighborhood House researched social problems and lobbied for local and state reforms. Head Resident Mary Anderson convinced Louisville's City Council that a public bath was needed and secured funds to build it. Neighborhood House also cooperated with the Consumer's League in investigations that led to the enactment in 1908 of the Child Labor Law and in 1912 of the Ten Hour Law for Women.[36]

The Baptist Settlement

Although its aims were different from those of the Neighborhood House, the Baptist settlement worked with a similar population. Many

---

[34]*Neighborhood House Report, 1914*, NHA, 6-9.

[35]*Neighborhood House Report, 1914*, NHA; "Louisville Fresh Air Home," n.d., NHA, 9-12.

[36]*Neighborhood House Report, 1914*, 4-5, NHA.

of the neighbors served by the Baptist Settlement were immigrants from Eastern and Southern Europe working in Louisville's industrial district. While the activities of the Baptist Settlement may at first glance appear similar to those of Neighborhood House and other settlements, the unique aims of the Baptist Settlement required a modification of the typical settlement house program.

Perhaps the most obvious difference was that the Baptist Settlement did not focus on societal reform or engage in cooperative programs with other agencies. Although both Neighborhood House and the Baptist Settlement had clubs and organizations, the activities and goals of these groups were very different. Neighborhood House's Saturday evening dances were not considered an acceptable activity for Southern Baptists at that time. Traditions of the homeland were not emphasized at the Baptist Settlement; rather pageants and plays focused on missionary activities in foreign lands. The songs sung in the Baptist settlement were not traditional tunes from the Old Country but Baptist hymns, which were taught to the newcomers.

Evangelism was the goal, and the success of the Baptist Settlement was measured accordingly. After visiting Hull House in 1915, McLure reported to Fannie Heck "without the love of Christ as the dynamic such a work is a failure."[37] By combining the methodology of the settlement movement with the goal of evangelism, the Training School created a resource that was unlike the conventional settlement.

The Baptist Settlement provided library services, a bathhouse and a playground, as well as weekly clubs and organizations. Descriptions of club activities reveal the values and attitudes that the Training School was teaching the neighbors. Women students were leaders of the children's clubs, a male Seminary student led the older boys, and Emma Leachman managed the mother's club. Each organization met weekly.[38] Although some of the club names were changed over the years, the goals and activities remained fairly constant.

---

[37]Allen, *Century to Celebrate*, 221.
[38]McLure, "A Glimpse, 3, 4.

"The Friendly Circle" was a club for women of all ages, which expressed in its organizational meeting in 1913 a desire for "development of physical, moral, and spiritual life" and a cultivation of "Friendliness, cleanliness, honesty, and Christlikeness." Meetings were held in the settlement chapel and usually opened with a song and a prayer. The weekly programs involved lessons on social and personal hygiene, community betterment, homemaking, co-operation with the schools, and religious and devotional topics. The women of the neighborhood did not serve as officers for the club. Instead, Emma Leachman and her student assistant, Miss Olive, were chosen by motion as president and secretary of the club.[39]

Ten years after the club's first meeting, a faculty member gave an assessment of the club's success, based on the school's goals for the neighbors:

> The vilest homes have become homes where love is, the dirtiest homes have been cleaned up and made habitable, the dependent have been made self-respecting and self-supporting, the dreariest of lives have had something of joy put into them, the sinner has been reclaimed for Jesus Christ.[40]

This statement reveals not only that the Training School attempted to teach these women a particular set of values including cleanliness, independence, and most importantly, Christian faith, but also that they believed the lessons taught to the immigrants made a positive difference in their lives.

For young children, ages three to eight, there was a story hour in which fairy tales, poems, and Bible stories were read aloud. A Training School student taught songs, games, and handwork.[41]

Boys ages six to sixteen were involved in the "Good Will Heroes" club. The junior club was led by a woman student and included ages

---

[39]"Training School," clipping from *Royal Service*, 1923, TSC, SBTS.
[40]Ibid.
[41]McLure, "A Glimpse," 4.

six to ten; the senior club, led by a male seminary student, included boys aged ten to sixteen. Maude McLure compiled a report of the settlement's experiences with club activities to serve as a model for other groups of Baptist women working with boy's clubs. Her suggestions reveal attitudes about appropriate gender roles both for the children and for their leaders:

> Boys between the ages of nine and fifteen are usually considered difficult to control and interest and for this reason are often neglected. The very fact that a boy is "bad" is a sufficient reason for getting him into a club. He needs the club because he is bad. If the boy is properly dealt with, turning his energy into the right channel, he will become just as energetic in doing something worthwhile as in mischief. . . . Order is absolutely indispensable but the leader must not try to make girls of boys. She must be able to distinguish between fun and misbehavior. The boy loves noise, excitement and enthusiasm and should be given as much freedom as can be allowed without the club becoming rowdy.[42]

McLure also suggested that the theme of "heroes" would teach lessons of bravery and honor to boys. She recommended using stories of animals and various Bible heroes, as well as a motto such as "Brave and True." Patriotism was also an important value to be taught, according to McLure, and this could be learned through ceremonies honoring the flag and by singing patriotic songs. McLure also emphasized "neatness of person," suggesting that it become a requirement for admission into the club.

There were particular gender qualifications for leaders of these clubs. McLure emphasized, "It is always preferable to have a man as a leader of boys clubs. . . ." She suggested that women may teach boys

---

[42]The Preface to A *Handbook of Personal Service*, (Baltimore: Woman's Missionary Union, [1915]), notes that McLure wrote the section on Good Will Center Work; quote 20-21.

basketry and simple forms of woodwork, but if a carpenter's shop was a part of the Good Will Center equipment, then a man should teach.[43]

Although she probably did not use the phrase "hidden curriculum," McLure was very aware of the concept and summarized her understanding of the educational process in this way: "In a good club the boy unconsciously absorbs ideals and ambitions which never entered his head before, and which will surely have a part in bringing him to Christ and in helping him to develop into the right kind of a man."[44]

Activities of the girls' clubs emphasized particular concepts of appropriate attitudes and behaviors for women. The Good Will Center designed its clubs for younger girls in accordance with the national Camp Fire Girls Organization, adapting its principles to include a religious element.[45] Club meetings opened with a devotional message and a hymn in addition to the Camp Fire's usual recitation of the motto, roll call, and collection of dues. McLure notes the values learned by girls who memorize "the law of the Camp Fire":

Seek Beauty
Give Service
Pursue Knowledge
Be Trustworthy
Hold on to Health
Glorify Work
Be Happy.[46]

While describing the club for girls ages nine to thirteen, McLure noted that "no formal instruction is given on 'being good' or 'keeping clean,' for children of this age learn best at play." Girls were being prepared for future domestic roles. McLure suggested that girls bring

---

[43]Ibid.
[44]Ibid., 22
[45]*Social Work Yearbook* (New York: Russell Sage, 1935) 443-444.
[46]*Handbook of Personal Service*, 33.

their dolls to club meetings where they might learn to care for the dolls by singing to them, sewing for them, and furnishing their dolls' houses. "In this way," McLure suggested, a love for home is created and the motherly instinct is developed."[47]

The younger girl's club was called the "Bluebirds," who typically advised, "Sing whenever tempted to scold or be cross; wear a smile and answer bravely when disappointed." The club's motto was "Purity," because the bluebird "seems to say 'Purity' when he sings." McLure described the girls' lessons thus: "Cooking, sewing, laying the table, hygiene, singing, beadwork, basketry, games and gymnastics . . . are all taught in such interesting ways that 'ere she is aware, a girl has emerged from a state of incompetence into a useful member of the family."[48]

The club for girls ages sixteen and older was called the Cheer-All Club, designed specifically for the young working woman. The Club held meetings on Friday evenings and included such activities as stories, games, handicrafts, and demonstrations of domestic skills.[49] Cheer-All girls, like the Training School students, presented pageants with missionary themes and did personal work such as visiting the sick in hospitals. The purpose of the club was "To develop a symmetrical young womanhood; to band together for the purpose of bringing happiness into the lives of others and to give the gospel message to all."[50]

Women and Children

Southern Baptists saw the evangelization of women and children as the woman missionary's special task. The women of the Training School asserted their need for training by reminding others that women could engage in particular "womanly" activities that were necessary in Christian service. Anna Eager, one of the school's

---

[47]Ibid., 34.
[48]McLure, "A Glimpse," 4.
[49]*Handbook of Personal Service*, 26-29.
[50]Ibid.

founders, stated that women students must learn "lessons which train soft voices and supple hands of women to lead in God's praise, to bind the broken limb, to prepare the tempting meal and meet the problems of women's lives in a woman's way."[51]

While the majority of settlement houses involved all members of a neighborhood family, the settlement of the Training School served mainly women and children. This reflects Southern Baptist beliefs about women's proper role in Christian service to serve women. Since Southern Baptist women were not teaching men in Sunday School or praying aloud with them in their own churches, it is not likely they would work with men in the settlement. A male Seminary student was asked to be the leader of the older boys club. Direct experiences between women students and immigrant men or older boys were seldom mentioned. Men only related to the settlement indirectly in their roles as fathers and husbands. The majority of the settlement's activities were planned for women and children.

From Outside the Neighborhood

The second unique feature of the Baptist Settlement was that it did not utilize resident workers living in the neighborhood. Instead, the students and faculty of the Training School walked to the settlement each day from another, more prosperous neighborhood. College women involved in settlement work typically lived in the "college dormitory in the ghetto" in order to experience "the reality of life." The organization of the typical college settlement was similar to that of a dormitory. Residents shared bedrooms and dined together sharing intellectual discourse. Guests came from the town or from the university for dinner, lectures, and formal discussions.[52]

Pamphlets and articles that describe the Baptist Settlement do not explain why Training School students or faculty did not take up

---

[51]Anna Eager, "A Great Vision, A Great Task," [1920?], TSC, SBTS.

[52]Sheila Rothman, *A Woman's Proper Place: A History of Changing Ideals and Practices, 1870 to the Present* (New York: Basic Books, 1978) 112-113.

residence in their settlement. However, one may postulate several reasons for this decision. First, the Training School faculty did not embrace the basic philosophy of the settlement movement, which was grounded in the idea that settlement workers were to live among the poorer classes in order to "reduce the mutual suspicion and ignorance of one class for the other."[53] The main goal of the Training School women was not to have solidarity with the poor but to offer something to them: salvation through education.

Secondly, the curriculum of the Training School attempted to form a particular kind of woman who was trained to serve others "in a woman's way."[54] To accomplish this, women students lived together in the carefully constructed environment of the Training School home where lessons of domesticity complemented the formal curriculum of the classroom. Such a controlled environment, intended to shape the lives of women students, would not have been possible if some of the women had lived at the settlement. In addition, the home in which the Training School students lived was much more appealing than the ordinary gray structure of the settlement house. The stark contrast between the two buildings reinforced differences between the women of the Training School and the poorer immigrants of the settlement neighborhood.

Finally, there may have been concerns for the safety of the students in the tenement neighborhood. A local Baptist woman refers to the neighborhood as a "rather submerged district," a euphemism for an unpleasant and even dangerous residential setting for a group of women. In the dialogue of a dramatic production written by a Training School student, one of the women characters expresses fear of visiting in the homes of the Baptist Settlement neighborhood:

---

[53]Davis, *Spearheads for Reform*, 6.
[54]Eager, *A Great Vision*.

That's a splendid place for work, but when I first began to visit there last winter and had to go up dark stairs into unlighted houses, I was scared.[55]

Christian Americanization

The women of the Training School came into the neighborhood daily attempting to educate and socialize the immigrants. "Christian Americanization" was their end and evangelism was the means.[56] As Edith Campbell Crane, corresponding secretary of the WMU, put it, "God is bringing to us at our very doors, whole communities of people whom we may help to become not only good Americans but citizens of the Kingdom of God."[57] This is the third and perhaps most significant characteristic of the Baptist Settlement: rather than aiming to reform society, women workers attempted to reform individuals through religious conversion.

Although socialization of the immigrant to American customs and values was the goal for many settlement houses across the nation, the Baptist Settlement adopted the additional task of socializing immigrants to American evangelical Protestantism. This was particularly challenging since the immigrant populations in the settlement neighborhood were from primarily Catholic or Jewish regions of Europe. Training School literature recounted numerous stories in which a rabbi or priest became outraged when a parishioner attended Bible studies at the Baptist Settlement. Training School women considered this a victory, particularly when the neighbors were converted in spite of opposition from their cultural group.[58]

Before 1880 most immigrants had come from northwestern Europe and settled on farmlands throughout America. However, between 1880 and 1920, the "new immigrants" came from southern

---

[55]"Building in His Name at the Training School: A Playlet," [1915], TSC, SBTS.

[56]Allen, *Century to Celebrate*, 217.

[57]*Baptist World*, May 14, 1908.

[58]"Doers of the Word" clipping from *Royal Service*, [1916], Historical Scrapbook, TSC, SBTS.

Europe and settled in the cities, congregating in tenement neighbor-hoods that perpetuated the customs of their native lands. While settlement workers tended to blame the wealth, corruption, and prejudice of old-stock Americans for the problems of the city immigrants, many groups blamed the unfortunates themselves. Social Gospel advocates spoke out against the high rates of crime and immorality among newcomers, labor unionists complained about unemployment and lower wages due to the immigrants, and politi-cians worried about corruption of the immigrant vote by city bosses.[59]

Southern and eastern Europeans were generally seen as a different species that was morally, socially, and intellectually inferior. Old-stock Americans feared that if immigrants were not Americanized they would destroy the cities and threaten the middle-class, Anglo-Saxon way of life.[60] The nation attempted to control immigrants by socializ-ing them to American customs and values. Settlement houses assisted immigrants by sponsoring classes in the English language and American citizenship. Public schools began offering special classes in English to immigrant children. Teachers found themselves giving baths to children as well as teaching lessons on manners, cleanliness, and dress.[61]

Maxine Seller writes that the education of immigrant women in schools, settlements, and churches focused on home economics, preparing them exclusively for roles as wives and mothers. Commonly held beliefs that women were created for domesticity were fused with stereotypical beliefs about the intellectual inferiority of the new immigrants. The result was an emphasis on vocational rather than academic learning for immigrant women. Educators intended to give the immigrant woman a little English and an understanding of American customs so she might reinforce the Americanization of the

---

[59]Lawrence Cremin, *The Transformation of the School: Progressivism in American Education, 1876-1957* (New York: Vintage Books, 1964) 66-70.

[60]Maxine Seller, "The Education of the Immigrant Woman, 1900-1935," *Journal of Urban History* 4 (May 1978): 307.

[61]Cremin, *The Transformation*, 70-72.

rest of the family. This was seen as critical to the health and safety of the whole nation.[62]

Southern Baptist views of immigrants matched those of other white Protestant Americans, but the emphasis was placed upon religious conversion as a means of socializing the new immigrants. Many Southern Baptists held that immigrants must not only learn American values and customs, but must also embrace the Protestant faith, in particular the Southern Baptist version of it, in order to keep from becoming a danger to society. Even persons who professed to be Christians, but were of the Catholic faith, were considered a threat to Southern Baptists. Victor Masters wrote in 1910, "In considering the city problem it is only fair to say that the Catholic population is on the average to be rather a liability than an asset. Perhaps there is no one element in our city life in which the forces of disintegration and corruption find material more suited to their wishes than is furnished by a large part of this population."[63]

In 1909 the annual meeting of the Southern Baptist Convention was held in Louisville. A report of the committee on "Cities and Foreigners," presented by Dr. O. C. S. Wallace of Baltimore exemplifies the attitude of Southern Baptists toward the urban immigrant:

> In the beginning these foreigners will be poor . . . with many temptations to immorality, exposed to the wiles of the devils of lawlessness, godlessness, and all manner of corrupting and blasting wickedness. They will be but inadequately fortified against these attacks upon them. No puritan traditions will restrain them, no lofty standards of virtue and right will inspire them . . . their religious knowledge fragmentary and streaked with lies, they will be from the first like sheep scattered upon the mountains, having no shepherd, and the wolves not far away.[64]

---

[62]Seller, "The Education of Immigrant Women," 307-330.

[63]Victor Masters, "Shall Southern Baptists Save Their Cities?" *Baptist World*, November 3, 1910.

[64]"The Salvation of the City," *Our Home Field* (July 1909): 28-29.

This sketch portrays the immigrant as a child-like innocent who, if not looked after, would easily be drawn into corruption and vice. Southern Baptists intended to save these "scattered sheep." Wallace warned that Southern Baptists must not be indifferent to the problem, and that "to ignore the duty of saving the foreign-born . . . and of evangelizing those whom God has placed next door to us would be ignoble." Wallace also reminded listeners that immigrants posed a threat to American citizens. Southern Baptists shared the responsibility "of protecting our families from the proximity of a great godless element in our population." He predicted "the sections of our cities in which the recently arrived foreigners congregate and huddle together will become spots of plague and peril."[65]

Yet Wallace, and many other Southern Baptists of his day, believed that the attitudes they were expressing were ultimately about love and caring. After painting a picture of the immigrant as an ignorant person who is easily corrupted and dangerous, he adds an ironic warning to Baptists: "We must not take a scornful attitude towards the people whose presence, character, and environment create this problem. Others may speak contemptuously of the foreigners. This we may not do. We are Christians."[66]

A Settlement or a Mission?

The women of the Training School believed their attempt to socialize immigrants into American Protestantism was an act of love. They took the methods developed by the settlement movement and modified these for their own evangelical purposes. The goal of reforming individuals through a religious conversion replaced the goal of the traditional settlement, which was social reform. However, Southern Baptist women were not the only workers to form a settlement with clear missionary aims. Other groups, including

---

[65]"Salvation of the City," 29.
[66]Ibid.

Methodist women's missionary societies, were inspired by religious motives to create similar neighborhood centers, making it difficult to distinguish between a religious settlement and a mission.

The 1897-1898 annual report of Unity House, a Minneapolis settlement, delineated differences between a mission and a settlement: "A mission is sectarian, devoted to propagating the faith of some church, but a social settlement has no creed but the golden rule and works for man. . . ."[67] John Gavitt, editor of the early settlement movement's most important journal, *The Commons*, noted that a mission did not become a settlement just by adding clubs and classes. "A mission in the ordinary sense of the word comes from *outside* to a neighborhood or community which it regards as 'degraded.' . . . The settlement bases its existence, its hope, its endeavor on the firm foundation of Democracy—on the thesis that the people must and can and will *save themselves*."[68]

The Training School women also believed their efforts were based on democracy. They imagined they could provide immigrants with the tools they needed to have better lives in America. In their way of thinking this included a faith in Christ and involvement in a Christian community. Yet they did indeed come from outside the community, literally and metaphorically, and held themselves apart from the neighborhood by residing several blocks away. The primary purpose of the Baptist Settlement was decidedly missionary, and leaders of the settlement would have classified the enterprise as a mission rather than a settlement.

Allen Davis notes that the majority of settlement workers in the nation were religious persons. In 1905, a poll of 339 settlement workers showed that eighty-eight percent were active church members and nearly all stated that religion had been a major influence on their lives.[69] Therefore, the discussion about the relation

---

[67]Howard J. Karger, The Sentinels of Order: A Study of Social Control and the Minneapolis Settlement House Movement, 1915-1950 (Lanham, MD: University Press of America, 1987) 16.

[68]Davis, *Spearheads for Reform*, 15.

[69]Ibid., 27.

of the settlement work to religion was kept alive in the settlement literature. In the early 1920s, Mary Simkovitch argued from the Christian perspective that a settlement cannot be a mission because its purpose is not to pass on a particular conviction to others, as missions do, but to work out its own common conviction: a faith in democracy.[70] In a discussion entitled "Problems of Religion," Arthur Holden advised that settlements did not need to talk about religion or attempt to teach it. He argued that by simply living a life in service to others, the settlement worker embodied Christian principles.[71]

Graham Taylor, Congregationalist minister and founder of a Chicago settlement, notes that while religious individuals may be involved in settlements, the church and the settlement have two very different purposes. Taylor believed that a church must press the tenets of its faith, and if it does not, it ceases to be a church of that faith. A settlement, on the other hand, may not embrace any cult or creed lest it forfeit its place as being a common ground for all.[72]

Good Will Centers

Although excluded by those who set the standards for classification as a "true settlement," the Baptist Settlement was in the company of many other centers that would have been classified as missions. Women of the WMU may have observed that their center was much closer to a mission than a typical settlement house. Two years after its opening, the name of the center was changed from "The Baptist Training School Settlement" to "The Good Will Center," a name proposed by Lulie Wharton, WMU director of personal service.[73] Her vision was that WMU groups would organize many such

---

[70]Mary Simkovitch, "The Settlement and Religion," in *Readings in the Development of Settlement Work* edited by L. M. Pacey (New York: Association Press, 1950) 136-142.

[71]Arthur C. Holden, *The Settlement Idea: A Vision of Social Justice* (New York: MacMillan, 1922) 132-144.

[72]Graham Taylor, "The Settlement's Distinctive Future," in *Readings in the Development of Settlement Work,* edited by L. M. Pacey (New York: Association Press, 1950) 196.

[73]Allen, *Century to Celebrate,* 221.

centers across the South in line with the model created by the center in Louisville. She convinced the Woman's Missionary Union that these centers should share a common name that would be "more appealing and uniquely Southern Baptist."[74]

Methodist women of Kentucky had taken similar action in 1906 when they changed the name of their Louisville Settlement Home to the Louisville Wesley House, a name used by other Methodist institutions honoring the denomination's founder. The Wesley House served a population similar to the Good Will Center, with a similar statement of purpose: "The work is evangelical and seeks not only to instruct, but to regenerate."[75]

The Good Will Center of Louisville continued to set the pace for other Southern Baptist centers. In 1925, the WMU authorized the construction of a model Good Will Center building in Louisville, complete with a domestic science laboratory in which neighbors would be taught housekeeping skills considered appropriate for them.[76] By 1930, approximately twenty-one Good Will Centers, funded by local and state WMU organizations, had been established across the Southern portion of the United States. Many of them were directed by Training School graduates. Eventually, Training School graduates traveled overseas to organize Good Will Centers in places like Italy and Brazil.[77]

Wherever they went, graduates took with them the Southern Baptist values, which had been reinforced by the Training School experience. They attempted to evangelize women and children in impoverished corners of the United States or in far away lands. As they spread the Christian message, graduates also transmitted to others the Southern Baptist cultural norms concerning woman's proper place in Christian service.

---

[74]Littlejohn, *History of Carver School*, 66.

[75]Woods and Kennedy, *Handbook of Settlements* 89-90.

[76]Allen, *Century to Celebrate*, 221.

[77]"Good Will Center Work," 1930, TSC, SBTS; Littlejohn, *History of Carver School*, 167.

6

"TAKE THE LIGHT"
Alumnae in Christian Service

There is darkness more deadly than death itself.
There is blindness beyond that of sight.
There are souls fast bound in the depths profound
Of unconscious and heedless night.

To their night, To the darkness and the sorrow
of their night
Take the Light. Take the Light.
Take the wonder and the glory of the light[1]

Women students of the Training School, like other women of their time, found that higher education had opened the door for a variety of vocational opportunities. While still limited to activities defined by Southern Baptists as "women's work," they found those definitions expanding as they began to professionalize the activities that they had previously engaged in as volunteers.

---

[1]"Take the Light" was sung at each commencement service, beginning in 1912. Carrie Littlejohn, *History of Carver School of Missions and Social Work* (Nashville: Broadman Press, 1958) 62; For lyrics see "Anniversary Alumnae Luncheon," June 1982, Training School Collection, Woman's Missionary Union Archives, Birmingham, AL.(Hereafter cited as TSC, WMUA).

The alumnae of the Training School sustained an extraordinary bond with each other.[2] Students and alumnae considered themselves linked together in a common enterprise: their mission to evangelize the world. The chain that bound them together was prayer. Students prayed for their predecessors doing the Lord's work, while those in the field prayed for the current students of House Beautiful. A group of former Training School students serving as missionaries in China wrote about how comforted they were by this linkage:

> Often our thoughts go back to our days in the House Beautiful, and often we five T. S. girls here talk of those dear days and of you. Every message we receive from you is passed around and greatly enjoyed by each of us. . . . It is an inspiration to know that we are part of the chain which extends around the world.[3]

Letters from alumnae were placed on a table in House Beautiful for students to read.[4] Training School alumnae visited the school often and missionaries home on furlough made speeches at the Training School about their work overseas. Also, those who were employed by WMU found occasions to visit the school in their travels.

The Alumnae Association, which had been organized by 1913, maintained a network of former students. The group met for a luncheon once each year at the WMU annual meeting and periodi-

---

[2]The word "alumna" does not always refer to a graduate, as many women attended the school for one year only. I have included them among the alumnae, just as they are included in the Training School Alumnae Association in the category of "Students Eligible to Wear the Training School Pin."

[3]*Annual Bulletin, Alumnae Association of Woman's Missionary Union Training School,* April, 1920, 10.

[4]Virginia Wingo to Carrie Littlejohn, 15 July, 1949, Unclassified Papers, Training School Collection, Southern Baptist Theological Seminary, Louisville, KY. (Hereafter cited as TSC, SBTS).

cally published the *Annual Bulletin* in which alumnae wrote brief accounts of their work and family lives.[5]

Although alumnae engaged in a variety of activities after leaving the Training School, three patterns were most common. As either an unmarried or married woman, an alumna might pursue a career in secular or church-related work. She might marry and do church work with her husband, typically describing her role as secondary; she was his helper. Some women married and focused primarily on domestic tasks, pursuing church work on a voluntary basis. A few reports from alumnae will exemplify these patterns.

Single women typically went to work immediately after leaving the Training School in order to support themselves. They were engaged in many different types of work, but a sampling of the *Annual Bulletin* reveals that a majority of single women pursued educational work, in both religious and secular settings.[6] Single women typically lived with other women or with families. Mary Hester, who graduated in 1922, described her living situation: "I live with a splendid Baptist family. . . . I prepare my own breakfast in their kitchen. . . . Two school teachers are in the home, one shares the living room with me upstairs."[7]

A few married women pursued careers independent of the spouse's work. However, the majority served as partners in the husband's ministry. An example is the typical foreign missionary family in which the husband received the paycheck while the wife who engaged in women's work was considered a volunteer.[8] Graduates who married pastors often described their marriage relationship

---

[5]The *Annual Bulletin*, published in 1916 by the Alumnae Association of the WMU Training School contains reports of the Association's fourth annual meeting, indicating that the Association was first organized in 1913.

[6]See *Annual Bulletin*, 1916, 1917, 1918, 1932.

[7]"Survey of Training School Graduates," 1941, Una R. Lawrence Papers, Southern Baptist Historical Library and Archives, Nashville, TN. (Hereafter cited as SBHLA).

[8]Ruth Tucker, "Women in Mission: Reaching Sisters in 'Heathen Darkness'" in *Earthen Vessels: American Evangelicals and Foreign Missions, 1880-1980*, edited by Joel A. Carpenter and William R. Shenk (Grand Rapids, MI: Willam B. Eerdmans Publishing Company, 1990) 226.

as a service commitment. One woman described her life after Training School in this way: "Married James H. Street and served as pastor's wife for more than fifty years."[9] Another wrote, "My work is that of a busy pastor's wife with some [Baptist] Associational work besides."[10] These statements imply a common understanding among the women that marriage to a pastor necessarily meant volunteer service in the church that employed him.

Some married women did not engage in paid employment but sent news of their children and husbands. They reported engaging in volunteer church work, often with the WMU. Their enthusiasm in writing about volunteer activities suggests that they considered unpaid service an important contribution to the goal of evangelizing the world. One graduate of 1922 wrote:

> My hands have been more than full with my household responsibilities, we have two small daughters, and the business of being a pastor's wife . . . but we have been fortunate enough to have entertained a District WMU meeting, a state student conference, an associational meeting . . . so we feel like we are still a link in the chain and are having some part in "girdling the world with light."[11]

Training School women used their own educational experience as a model for the church work they did after graduation. Perhaps the most striking example of the influence of the Training School is found in educational service overseas. According to W. O. Carver, training schools for women were established in nearly all the Southern Baptist foreign mission fields.[12] Reports of the South Brazil Mission describe the Woman's Missionary Union Training School of Brazil, which was also called "The Brazilian 'House Beautiful'"

---

[9]"Training School Anniversary Luncheon Survey," June 1982, TSC, WMUA.
[10]*Annual Bulletin*, November 1916, 16.
[11]*Annual Bulletin*, March 1928, 39.
[12]W. O. Carver, Address to WMU Training School, October 2, 1948, TSC, SBTS.

Practical activities have been emphasized along with the classroom work. The girls, while learning as much as possible, apply that knowledge through the opportunities afforded them by their field work. . . . The girls also speak at WMU meetings within the city.[13]

The South Brazil Mission also reported activities of a Goodwill Center in Mendoza:

We now have about 250 in the eight classes of our institution. These classes include a kindergarten . . . a handwork class for girls, [a class] in woodwork for boys . . . and a class in English for young people.[14]

The Training School experience shaped the vocational lives of women students. A closer look at the activities of three alumnae will demonstrate how women passed on the lessons of the Training School to the people they served. These three women were selected to exemplify the working lives of Training School women not only because they represent a range of periods of attendance and a variety of vocations, but also because they have left behind adequate materials to be explored. Jewell Legett Daniel served as a missionary in China, Juliette Mather was employed by Woman's Missionary Union, and Carrie Littlejohn worked in a settlement house before returning to work at the Training School, first as a teacher, and later as the school's principal.

Jewell Legett Daniel: Training School Student, 1908-1909

On the last night before she left to begin a missionary career in China, Jewell Legett gathered with her family in Texas to participate in:

---

[13]*Annual Report*, Southern Baptist Convention, 1951, 65.
[14]*Annual Report*, Southern Baptist Convention, 1948, 80.

. . . family prayers, as we had always had them, only with a poignancy never before experienced. Two young brothers, one seventeen, the other twenty-two; papa, mamma, me. Papa read the 23rd Psalm, then we knelt and he prayed. And when we arose from our knees mamma sang in her clear, sweet, soprano, "There are angels hovering round."[15]

A young woman like Jewell was a typical recruit for the mission field. A family living on a modest income reared her in a rural setting. Jewell's parents were missionaries on the frontier; she described her father as "an uneducated, powerful, cowboy preacher."[16] According to historian Jane Hunter, over forty percent of the women missionaries appointed by the American Board of Commissioners of Foreign Missions had fathers and mothers who did church work as missionaries or ministers. Hunter notes that these women were in some sense emulating both parents. However, they often drew vocational inspiration from a strong identification with their fathers, which encouraged the ambition, and assertiveness that could lead to a career on the mission field.[17]

Jewell had attended Baylor University, where she became involved in a group of students, male and female, who intended to become missionaries. After graduating in 1907, she headed to Louisville, Kentucky to attend the WMU Training School in the fall of 1908. The next spring, principal Maude McLure received a letter requesting that two women be sent to China. McLure asked two students, Lettie Spainhour and Jewell Legett, if they would like to apply with the Foreign Mission Board. At the close of her first year at the Training

---

[15]Jewell L. Daniel, "Jewell Daniel," mimeographed autobiography in author's possession.

[16]Jewell Legett Daniel to Woman's Missionary Union, September 5, 1980, Legett Papers, WMUA.

[17]Jane Hunter, *The Gospel of Gentility: American Women Missionaries in Turn-of-the-Century China* (New Haven: Yale University Press, 1984) 32-33.

School, Jewell interviewed with the FMB and was appointed to Pingtu in the Shantung Province of China.[18]

During the first twenty years of the century, China experienced a radical reversal of policy toward the West. This policy change mission activity to flourish. The Boxers, who opposed any foreign presence in China, had been defeated after killing 250 foreigners, including many missionaries, and 2,000 Chinese Christians. After 1900, China turned "from traditional dynasty looking backward to a reforming nation looking outward."[19] After the 1911 revolution, China became even more interested in the West, and this enhanced the status of Western missionaries. These years of honor and respect for missionaries would last until the early 1920s when anti-Christian sentiment grew steadily under an increasingly nationalist climate.[20] Jewell arrived in a period of rapid growth of missions in China. The Christian missionary force had doubled between 1890 and 1905, and doubled again by 1919 reaching 3,300 workers.[21]

In the United States, mission work in Asia was encouraged as expedient foreign policy. The women missionaries were charged with bringing Western ideals to Chinese women who would influence husbands and children. Cultural, rather than political, imperialism was seen as the hope for peace. Theodore Roosevelt wrote in 1908:

> Now is the time for the West to implant its ideals in the Orient, in such a fashion as to minimize the chance of a dreadful future clash between two radically different and hostile civilizations; if we wait until tomorrow, we may find that we have waited too long.[22]

---

[18]"Jewell Daniel, 100, "Remembers Service with Lottie Moon," *Baylor Line* (Feb, 1985) 44; Jewell L. Daniel, "Jewell Legett Daniel," unpublished autobiography, mimeograph in author's possession, 1.

[19]Hunter, *The Gospel of Gentility*, 3.

[20]Ibid., 3.

[21]Ibid., 5.

[22]Theodore Roosevelt, "The Awakening of China," *Outlook* 28 (November 1908): 665-667.

Jewell Legett did not speak about "yellow peril" or "minimizing future clashes" when she stated her reasons for serving as a missionary. She did not view her reasons for missionary service as political; she simply wanted to share the gospel message with the Chinese people. Jewell traveled to San Francisco in September 1909 to set sail for China. She sailed with three friends from the Training School: Lettie Spainhour, Floy White, and Janie Lide.[23]

Upon arrival in China, the new missionaries did not travel immediately to their posts but remained a few days near Tengchow in order to attend the wedding of the new missionary Floy White to Wayne Adams, a graduate of Southern Seminary. The couple had been engaged while Wayne began his work in China and Floy finished her studies at the Training School. While waiting for the wedding day, Jewell traveled a half-day's journey to the mission station at Hwanghsien where she observed mission work first hand. "It was lots of fun to the oldsters on a mission field to induct the new-comer into Chinese life, so these dear new friends enjoyed me too." Alice Huey, one of the "Big Four" early graduates of the Training School, stopped by Hwanghsien on her way to the wedding. Huey was stationed in Laichowfu and had been in China since 1907. At the wedding, Jewell and Jane Lide sang a benediction, based on Psalm 91 that they had learned at the Training School.[24]

Missionaries had to make many cultural adjustments and negotiated various levels of assimilation to their new surroundings. Veteran missionary Charlotte Diggs ("Lottie") Moon provided orientation for new missionaries. One of Jewell's most startling discoveries was the expectation that women would modify their Western attire. At the White-Adams wedding celebration Jewell and Jane Lide proudly dressed in new white dresses, which had been purchased for the Training School commencement ceremony:

---

[23]Daniel, Autobiography, 3.
[24]Ibid., 4-6, Virginia Wingo, "Pioneers, O Pioneers!," *Annual Bulletin* (August 1947): 2.

we hurried out . . . and met Miss [Lottie] Moon face-to-face. . . . and her face was aghast. . . ." You are not going out of my house in those clothes!" she burst out. "Why Miss Moon," we cried in dismay, "What's the matter with them? They're all we have!" we said. . . . Our dresses were form-fitting—very—whereas every line of a Chinese woman's dress is made to conceal the lovely body-lines. To Miss Moon and to the hundreds of Chinese neighbors and friends gathered in the street, our dresses would be utterly indecent and vulgar.[25]

Jewell would learn that women typically wore jackets in public to avoid offending Chinese custom. Moon spent much time and energy training new missionaries and was very strict about details of manners, dress, and grammar.[26] Jewell listened carefully to the advice of this well-respected veteran missionary.[27]

On another occasion Jewell met with disapproval from Miss Moon when she forgot to wear her pith helmet—standard equipment for women missionaries in a climate where sunstroke was a danger. Another missionary, Elsie Clark, described the obligatory pith helmet: "It looks very heavy and clumsy, but in reality is very light and cool; at any rate we must put looks aside and wear it." Clark also notes that Western women improved the appearance of their helmets by having embroidered covers made to wear over them.[28]

While she was still adjusting to her new surroundings, Jewell left Tengchow and traveled to Pingtu, the mission station in which she would serve. Pingtu was located about 120 miles inland from Tengchow, about a four-day trip by mule cart. Residents of this agricultural area were more affluent than in Tengchow, due to a

---

[25]Ibid., 5.

[26]Hunter, Gospel of Gentility, 138; Catherine Allen, The New Lottie Moon Story (Nashville, TN: Broadman Press, 1980) 264.

[27]The name Lottie Moon was known by all Southern Baptists at the turn of the twentieth century, as she wrote many letters published in mission literature and spoke to huge crowds when traveling in the United States on furlough.

[28]Daniel, Autobiography, 8; Hunter, 140.

profitable bean-oil trade. Approximately seven Christian churches had been established in the area, cultivated by Lottie Moon and a Chinese preacher called Pastor Li.[29] When Jewell arrived, Mrs. Cora Oxner took over the orientation of the new missionary. Two other missionary couples, the Searses and the Owens, were also stationed in Pingtu. Jewell was given an outfit of loose-fitting garments and a new Chinese name: Lan Jen Bao. She began the long and difficult study of the Chinese language.

Before she had mastered the language, Jewell was doing mission work with Mrs. Oxner. She felt vulnerable around the Chinese women unless a translator was nearby. She wrote in a letter:

I like to be among them when there's somebody near who can talk Chinese, some American I mean: but it takes courage to face them alone. I feel like Rebekah (Owen), baby girl of the station. . . . She likes to go among them with her mother, but when they find her alone and crowd about to feel her clothes and rub her hands and "jabber," Rebekah gets frightened and cries. I want to, too, sometimes![30]

In spite of her nervousness in the situation, Jewell was touched by the love and warmth she felt from the Chinese women, recording in her diary that an elderly woman "drew my hands into hers and rubbed them warm" during a Bible class:

It was in one of those classes that I understood my first sentence, in a prayer: "Heavenly Father, give Miss Legett sense!" Mrs. Oxner hastened to explain in a whisper, "Honey, it's idiom. She means understanding, ability to learn the language."[31]

---

[29]Allen, *Lottie Moon Story*, 151, 155; Daniel, Autobiography, 26.
[30]Daniel, Autobiography, 10.
[31]Ibid., 11.

In addition to language difficulties, missionaries found vast differences between American and Chinese foods. According to Hunter, missionaries in China replicated home menus and ordered staples from Montgomery Ward. Local Chinese vegetables seldom were a part of the missionary diet, and lemonade and postum were standard drinks rather than Chinese tea. Servants were trained to prepare meals in the American style.[32]

Jewell showed a willingness to try Chinese foods, though she didn't enjoy all the foods she sampled. Her 1910 diary entry describes a lunch enjoyed with a schoolteacher including millet, gruel, and potatoes. However, during the same lunch, she "couldn't swallow more than one egg," because they were not "this year's." Jewell was amazed that eggs were often kept as many as forty years. "When I am in the country [I] am in mortal terror of being offered one of these eggs. 'Twould be a great breach of etiquette to refuse." She also noted that a fellow missionary had been required to eat dried fish for breakfast, "the very smell of which is nauseating."[33]

Hunter points out that new missionaries sometimes found themselves disgusted by the different standards and facilities for personal cleanliness in China. When Jewell was visiting in a girl's school she met a "dear little trick . . . with the sweetest mouth and not a speck of a nose between her eyes." The novice missionary was simultaneously attracted and repulsed; "I would have hugged her if she hadn't been so impossibly dirty. . . ." she wrote in her diary.[34] Cynthia Miller, who had attended the Training School in 1905 and was stationed in Laichowfu, did not trust the Chinese dairy owner to observe what she considered proper hygiene. She wrote to her family in 1919:

At first I refused to take his milk for fear it was not clean, then when he told me he would come and bring his cow and

---

[32]Hunter, *Gospel of Gentility*, 134-135; and Allen, *Lottie Moon Story*, 3.

[33]Jewel Legett, Personal diary, 1910, quoted in Daniel, Autobiography, 14.

[34]Hunter, *Gospel of Gentility*, 163; Daniel, Autobiography, 14.

let me milk her I decided I would try. . . . Well, I have thought
of a good plan now to get out of it. For the last two or three
mornings I have just gone out there and take[n] my book or
paper and sit (sic) down and read and see[n] that the China-
man is clean about it. . . ."[35]

Since gender taboos barred Chinese women from hearing male
preachers, women missionaries entered the homes of Chinese women
to share the Gospel message. Access to elite women of the area was
difficult although considered a great victory. The well-to-do women
could influence their husbands and sons while their daughters were
sent to mission schools to be educated.[36] Christianizing daughters of
the elite was Lottie Moon's first intention when she created her first
school for girls at Tengchow. However, as Moon found out, village
women of the poorer classes were easier to approach, and these
women ultimately became the target of Moon's outreach efforts.[37]

Women missionaries traveled to villages accompanied by a "Bible
woman," who was a Chinese Christian trained by missionaries. Bible
women lent credibility to the missionary's words and provided
translation when necessary. The missionaries usually drew a crowd in
the village because of their unusual Western appearance and dress.
The Chinese often could not distinguish the gender of missionaries.
Western women who had "free ways, big feet, pale hair, and long
noses" confused them. Lottie Moon had to assure women that she was
also a woman before they would come near to her.[38] The village
women's curiosity opened the conversation, which led to a presenta-
tion of the Gospel message.

---

[35]Cynthia Miller to Brother, Sister, and Family, July 2, 1919, Cynthia Miller File, Foreign Mission Board Correspondence, SBHLA.

[36]R. Pierce Beaver, *American Protestant Women in World Missions: History of the First Feminist Movement in North America* (Grand Rapids, Michigan: Eerdman's Publishing Co, 1980) 119-120.

[37]Allen, *Lottie Moon Story*, 103,108.

[38]Hunter, *Gospel of Gentility*, 214; Allen, *Lottie Moon Story*, 108.

The missionaries were often invited into a woman's home to sit on the "kang," a mat-covered platform for eating and sleeping, and talk about Jesus while village women and children crowded in to listen.[39] The personal approach of women missionaries differed from evangelism techniques of men. Hunter notes that men typically preached to gathered crowds, while women used "an effusion of encouragement and love on the part of the missionary, manifested in soulful eye contact and frequently a held hand."[40] Jewell had seen these differences reinforced in the Training School curriculum. While her male counterparts at the Seminary had been studying Homiletics, Jewell was enrolled in a course for women called "Personal Work," which gave instruction in these methods.

The work of women missionaries in China fell into three categories: medical work, schooling for girls and young women, and evangelistic "country work," in rural areas. Jewell was primarily involved in educational work. Typically, primary schools for girls were run by Chinese Christians and maintained a local village flavor. Boarding schools for older girls, called "middle" schools, were based on Western methods of education and were managed by missionary women at the mission compound. Young women could choose to attend one of three women's colleges founded by American missionaries in the early twentieth century. A system of Bible training schools for native Bible women and pastor's wives was also in operation.[41]

In addition to a formal curriculum of literacy and Christian doctrine, the women missionaries taught ideals of hygiene and housekeeping. Women like Jewell intended to model Western perceptions of proper domesticity for Chinese converts. One report at the turn of the twentieth century declared success:

Let a European light down upon any village in Asia Minor, or the Chinese Empire, and the tidiest house there, with the

---

[39]Beaver, *American Protestant Women*, 120; Allen, *Lottie Moon Story* 103-104.
[40]Hunter, *Gospel of Gentility*, 183.
[41]Ibid., 16.

cleanest tablecloth and the most inviting bed, is the house of
a mission-school graduate. . . . As women rise they bring the
home up with them.[42]

Before leaving the United States, Jewell Legett had been offered
a curriculum at the Training School that included formal course work
and domestic training. In China, she would teach a curriculum that
emphasized the same priorities for women and girls.

In her first tour of a village school, the girls charmed Jewell. She
wrote in her diary in 1910:

Another dear little friend I made. Her name is Chang White
Flower. She had memorized a great many chapters of the book
of Matthew. Also, she read several pages to me out of the
little book whose characters she had so often traced with her
rough, red fingers that they were almost effaced.[43]

Jewell was fully prepared for the Chinese method of pedagogy in
which each child recites lessons aloud, independently of the others.
However, she was caught off guard by the method in which students
presented their lessons:

When two girls came up to recite, whisked about with their
backs to the teacher, and said their lessons so fast I could not
distinguish a syllable, I couldn't help it. I exploded with
laughter. From the sudden hush I gathered that I had blun-
dered and that an explanation was due. Got Mrs. Oxner to

---

[42]Ellen C. Parsons, "History of Women's Organized Missionary Work as Promoted by
American Women," in *Woman in Missions: Papers and Addresses presented at the Woman's
Congress of Missions*, comp. E. M. Wherry (New York: American Tract Society, 1894) 107-
108, in Patricia Hill, *The World Their Household: The American Woman's Foreign Mission
Movement and Cultural Transformation, 1870-1920* (Ann Arbor: University of Michigan
Press, 1985) 58.

[43]Daniel, Autobiography, 14.

say that Lan-Mang-me she was sorry she laughed but that in America she had never seen it done that way.[44]

After serving in Pingtu nearly four years, Jewell Legett married her friend from college days, Carey Daniel, who was also stationed in North China. As a single woman, Jewell Legett had been able to devote most of her time and energy to mission work. Married women missionaries, on the other hand, spent most of their time maintaining exemplary Christian homes, particularly if they had children. Believing that proper Western homes would serve as an appropriate example for Chinese women, married missionary women labored to maintain their homes as evangelistic tools. A married woman's domestic duties were considered primary by mission boards, missionary husbands, and missionary wives. According to Hunter, married women were often torn between a desire to do the mission work that had originally inspired them to sail overseas and the responsibility for daily chores of the household. Missionary wives and mothers used the feminine ideology of their day to reframe their situations as opportunities for further sacrifice and self-denial.[45]

Jewell Legett and Carey Daniel had been friends since their college days at Baylor and had attended Seminary classes together when Jewell was at the Training School. Jewell sometimes accompanied Carey to church or to the almshouse where he occasionally preached.[46] She later said that she and Carey had no special interest in one another during her college and Training School days, and her diaries of this period do not indicate any romance in their relationship. When she arrived in China one year ahead of Carey, she wrote letters to him and sent a photograph of her surroundings.[47]

Carey Daniel was stationed in Hwanghsien, four days journey from Pingtu. By 1913, he had moved to Laiyang to begin evangelizing in that community. The young missionaries may have visited together

---

[44]Ibid., 15.
[45]Hunter, *Gospel of Gentility*, 11, 128, 120; Hill, *The World Their Household*, 72.
[46]Legett Diary, March 15, 1909 and May 15, 1909.
[47]"Daniel, "100 Remembers Service,"; Daniel, Autobiography, 7.

during summer vacations when missionaries often headed for one of several summer retreats to avoid malaria, cholera, and other fevers that threatened Westerners in the hotter months. Jewell and Carey would have also seen one another at yearly gatherings of the entire Southern Baptist mission group of North China.[48]

Jewell Legett and Carey Daniel were married on February 25, 1914, in Pingtu. Invitations were sent by Jewell's "family"—Florence Jones and Ella Jeter, single women stationed at Pingtu.

> MISSES JONES AND JETER
> request the pleasure of your presence
> at the marriage of their sister
> MISS JEWELL LEGETT TO MR. J. C. DANIEL
> at the "House o' Joy" in Pingtu
> Seven o'clock, Wednesday Evening
> February Twenty-Fifth
> Nineteen hundred and fourteen.
> At Home, Laiyang City, Shantung, China, March First.

Both Chinese and foreign guests were invited to the celebration. In accordance with Chinese custom, the bride did not see the home, which the husband prepared until after the wedding. The couple traveled to their new home in Laiyang where Carey had renovated and furnished an old Chinese house. Perhaps the most pleasing piece of new furniture Jewell found in her new home was a desk that had belonged to Lottie Moon. Carey had purchased the thirty-year old desk after Moon died the previous year. The couple appreciated the orientation they had each received from Moon when they arrived as new missionaries and revered the desk as a reminder of the missionary they loved and admired.[49]

Like the homes of most missionary couples, the Daniel home imitated American homes in furnishing and decor. Jewell was thrilled

---

[48]Ibid., 8.
[49]Ibid., 20-21.

that the house had American rocking chairs and beds ordered from Montgomery Ward.[50] As mistress of the house, Jewell would also be in charge of the servants. Initially, this could be an uncomfortable experience for young women who grew up in near poverty themselves. However, due to the exchange rate, the low wages paid to servants were easily affordable.[51] In reviewing volumes of missionary correspondence, Hunter found that women missionaries enjoyed the luxury of servants and enjoyed the authority the mistress-servant relationship afforded them. One wrote, "it's rather fun, after all, to be running my own house and bossing my own servants." Hunter notes that missionary women managed domestic empires, based on paternalism and racial distinctions.[52] The authority over Chinese servants was often generalized to authority over Chinese persons, giving American women in China a sense of power that they lacked back home.[53]

The Daniels spent four months as newlyweds in Laiyang before Carey died tragically. On June 28, 1914, he attempted to cross a flooded river on horseback and was drowned. A servant found the old gray horse with soaked saddle. Chinese Christians searched several days for Carey's body. Jewell was pregnant and returned to the United States to deliver her son. Four years later, Jewell and her small son Carey headed back to China so that she could resume her work with the Chinese women. They went back to the Laiyang mission.[54]

It was not unusual for a woman to continue mission work after the death of her husband. She might remarry a widowed man or continue her work alone.[55] However, Jewell was a widow with a young child, and this was a more unusual situation on the mission field. Most missionary mothers of this era did not participate in full-time mission

---

[50]Hunter, *Gospel of Gentility*, 128-129; Daniel, Autobiography 20-21.
[51]Hunter, *Gospel of Gentility*, 161.
[52]Ibid., 167.
[53]Ibid., 164-165.
[54]Daniel, Autobiography, 22; "A Deplorable Accident" and "The Far Off Fields," *Foreign Mission Journal*, September 1914, 72-73, 84. The FMJ reported: "The North China Mission at its Annual Meeting on July 6 decided that Mrs. Daniel ought to come home at once."
[55]Beaver, *American Protestant Women*, 4.

work but made domestic responsibilities primary.[56] However, there was a precedent for Jewell's situation among Southern Baptists of the North China Mission. Robbers had murdered the husband of Lottie Moon's early colleague, Mrs. Sallie Holmes, when Sallie was pregnant with her son Landrum. After her husband's death, Sallie Holmes continued mission work while rearing her young son. She managed a girl's school and traveled through the villages of Shantung, sharing the gospel message.[57]

Jewell faced the problems of single motherhood and regretted having to leave young Carey with servants each day while she did mission work in and around Laiyang. Speaking of herself in third person she described:

> How on tip-toe he awaited the hour when "momio" would return and he might cuddle down beside her for his long bed-time stories. His day began when hers ended![58]

When he reached school age, young Carey went to a boarding school in Chefoo. Jewell continued with her work in Laiyang, bringing Carey to their home between school sessions.

In 1921, Jewell helped to organize a Woman's Missionary Union in Laiyang. Jewell described the Chinese women of WMU using the same frame of reference she used years earlier to describe the WMU royalty visiting the Training School. She notes their manners and charm:

> The little women were grand! No one of them except my dear Bible woman Mrs. Giang, had ever appeared in public before, but you'd never have known it, so perfectly poised they were![59]

---

[56]Ibid., 59.
[57]Allen, *Lottie Moon Story*, 89.
[58]Daniel, autobiography, 22.
[59]Ibid., 31, quote, 20.

Under Jewell's leadership, the WMU of China imitated the American version. Each local church had its own women's group and together they formed a larger body, comparable to the State WMU in the United States. The Chinese WMU did charity work for an orphanage and gave money to support missions.[60]

Jewell continued her work in China until 1926 when she and her eleven-year-old son, along with many other missionaries, were sent back to the United States "because of Communist dangers." When she reached home Jewell had a very special gift for the Training School sent from China. A WMU group in Texas helped her to retrieve the desk in her former home that had belonged to Lottie Moon. Jewell's cherished desk was taken to Louisville, Kentucky and placed in the prayer room of House Beautiful.[61]

Jewell Legett Daniel continued her mission work on a volunteer basis, evangelizing among Jews in the United States. She was invited often to tell stories of her experiences in China to various WMU groups in Texas. Jewell lived to be 106 years old, continuing her mission work by sharing the gospel message with residents of the nursing home in which she spent her later years.[62]

Juliette Mather, Class of 1921

Juliette Mather learned the ideals of WMU at the Training School and spent the following thirty-six years passing them on to young people in her work as a Woman's Missionary Union professional. She noted in later years that the Training School experience had instilled in her a love for the WMU organization:

I came to see the organization as a group of women dedicated. . . . to something that was big and wonderful. It never

---

[60]Ibid., 20.
[61]Daniel, "100, Remembers Service," 22-23.
[62]Daniel, "100, Remembers Service"; L. Ernsting to author, June 28, 1994.

occurred to me in those days that I would have any big part in it, but I just thought, "well this is just marvelous."[63]

She remained an active advocate for the Training School, recruiting young women to attend the school and visiting Louisville whenever possible. She also maintained correspondence with a professor and encountered other Training School graduates in her work. Juliette Mather's story illustrates how the lessons of the Training School were passed along through WMU professionals.

In 1896, Juliette was born in Chicago to a family of devout Northern Baptists. Her parents, William and Julia Mather, encouraged their children to take an interest in other cultures, especially to further the missionary cause. For example, Juliette's father, a ticket agent for the railroad, asked a train conductor who was traveling in the South to pick some cotton in bloom so he could show it to his children who had not seen the South. Juliette's mother, who was active in the missionary societies of Chicago, organized a missions club for girls in the neighborhood called "The Lightbearers":

Each girl had a notebook and a missionary, and as we read anything we could find about that missionary, we put it into our books. They were quite homemade books—scrapbooks. . . . I delighted to read the magazines . . . so that I could see if there was anything about [my missionary] in that literature. . . .[64]

Two of Juliette's siblings were missionaries with the Northern Baptist Convention. Her brother Asher served in Assam, while her sister Ruth went to China and Burma. Juliette intended to become a foreign missionary to China as well. After receiving her bachelor's (1917) and master's (1918) degrees from University of Arkansas and a brief

---

[63]Juliette Mather, interview by Catherine Allen, January 26, 1976, tape recording, transcript, 20, WMUA.

[64]Juliette Mather, interview by Gertrude Tharpe and Ethalee Hamric, September 17-21, 1979, tape recording, transcript, 46, WMUA.

period of teaching English at Central Baptist College in Conway, Arkansas, she headed for the WMU Training School in 1919 with this purpose in mind. However, a representative of the Foreign Mission Board who came to the Training School soon discouraged her:

> . . . when I went to talk to him he said, "You're too scrawny. They will never take you." So I didn't think "scrawny" was a nice word and I was sort of insulted. I didn't bother with the Foreign Mission Board anymore[65]

Juliette was small in stature, with "piercing dark eyes, and a quick step." She has also been described as "energetic, feisty, and inspiring."[66] At the Training School, Juliette became a leader among her peers, chairing the Social Committee. She was also a favorite of Mrs. McLure, becoming more intimately acquainted with McLure through her friendship with McLure's niece, Hannah Reynolds.[67] While a student at the Training School, Juliette demonstrated her talents as a writer by contributing articles to the WMU periodical *Royal Service*. She also wrote a pageant about missions that the Training School students performed in Washington DC at a WMU annual meeting.[68] Juliette was a gifted speaker and was selected by McLure to go to Elizabethtown, Kentucky to speak in a church about the Training School experience.[69]

As the end of her final year was approaching, Juliette became concerned about what she might do after graduation. Students were generally recommended by the principal for a position or placed by the Foreign Mission Board. However, no placement for Juliette had been secured. She later recalled that "there were several young

---

[65]Mather interview (Allen), 14.
[66]Rees Watkins, *A Backward Glance: History of Woman's Missionary Union* (Birmingham: WMU, 1987) 45; Allen, *Century to Celebrate*, 334.
[67]Mather interview (Allen), 20.
[68]Ibid., 1, 60.
[69]Ibid., 35-36.

women out of my WMU Training School class taken as state [WMU] young people's leaders, and I wondered why they didn't ask me to do that. I could have done that." Then one night Maude McLure asked her to come to the principal's office after the final light bell. McLure told Juliette that WMU wanted to offer her a job as Young People's Secretary:

> I remember saying, "Well, nobody has asked me to do anything, so I think I'll have to do that. But I don't know what it would be". . . . So I just felt, well this is what the Lord wants me to do. You certainly wouldn't say no to the only thing that anybody had ever asked you to do. So I said yes, I would do it. She said, "Well, you pray about it tonight", and so I thought, "Well it's not necessary to bother the Lord, He's already got it fixed". But anyway I said alright I would. Then I told her in the morning, I wished I knew more about what they were supposed to do.[70]

Juliette Mather completed her final term at the Training School, but before leaving she received a visit from Kathleen Mallory, the corresponding secretary of WMU who would supervise Miss Mather in her new job. Mather remembered a special moment with Mallory:

> . . . I remember the guest room at the Training School has a little low dresser and stool by it. And so we knelt on either side of the little stool to pray together. I remember how gentle and tender her prayer was for a young woman coming into the work of Woman's Missionary Union.[71]

Mather admired Mallory's leadership, although she noted that Mallory "had her little quirks." Descriptions of Mallory note that she had a frugal, efficient nature, and was well-organized. "She would

---

[70]Ibid., 3.
[71]Mather interview (Allen), 39.

have nothing on her desk but the papers she was working with, and she sat ram-rod straight."[72] Mather, Mallory, and another Training School graduate, Mallory's assistant Ethel Winfield, lived together in a humble Birmingham apartment near the WMU headquarters. The three employees ate dinner each evening at the house of Mrs. Moore who lived around the corner. Mather and Mallory walked together to work and to church. Although the two women spent a great deal of time together, they always addressed one another as "Miss" rather than using first names.[73] Mather said that she loved Mallory dearly, and although she knew that Mallory was not a very affectionate person, Mather wished for a more personal friendship with her supervisor. After Mallory's death she learned that Mallory had referred to her as "my beloved Juliette." Mather commented: "I could have been much freer with Miss Mallory if I'd known that she really loved me in that way. I knew she loved working with me. I don't recall anything I suggested that she didn't go along with."[74]

The Birmingham location was a new one for WMU. The organization had been located in Baltimore since its founding in 1888. In 1920, the executive committee made plans to move headquarters to a more central location, in response to complaints that Baltimore was too far from the hub of Southern Baptist life. In addition, the Baltimore Baptists were known for their involvement in ecumenical work, a notion that was strongly opposed by most Southern Baptists of this era.[75]

Southern Baptists in four cities invited WMU to establish headquarters there: Atlanta, Memphis, Nashville, and Birmingham. A vote was taken at the 1921 annual meeting. Before her appointment to the new position had been announced, Juliette Mather played an important part in the decision of where to relocate. The vote was tied, with 203 for Nashville and 203 for Birmingham.[76] The

---

[72]Mather interview (Tharpe and Hamric), 23.
[73]Ibid., 40.
[74]Mather interview (Tharpe and Hamric), 23.
[75]Allen, *Century to Celebrate*, 63-64.
[76]Ibid., 64.

officers of WMU were asked to break the tie, but those connected to either Birmingham or Baltimore declined to vote, leaving Mather and the treasurer to cast deciding votes. Mather had been instructed by her superiors to vote for Birmingham so she and the treasurer stood up to break the tie. Mrs. McLure overheard someone in the audience say "You know, I don't think it's quite right to have that little girl up on the platform to decide such an important matter."[77]

WMU employees worked in crowded conditions. "We were so crowded we didn't have an extra chair . . . we were just filled," Mather recalled. Her tiny office included a desk, a bookcase and a chair. "There was nothing handsome about them," she said in describing the offices.[78] Salaries were exceedingly low in keeping with WMU ideals of self-sacrifice. Mather earned approximately $1800-$1900 per year when she began her job in 1921. Her supervisor Mallory earned $2,000 that year, a mere 35 percent of the wages earned by her male counterpart at the Foreign Mission Board.[79] Known for her frugal nature, Mallory set the tone that allowed only subsistence wages. In later years, Mather implied that although she understood Mallory's reasoning, she would have enjoyed earning more money: "Miss Mallory never wanted her salary to go above that of the missionaries. Consequently, she didn't realize that nobody else's salary could go above that of a missionary."[80]

Juliette Mather brought a great deal of creativity to her responsibilities as young people's secretary and college correspondent. According to historian Patricia Hill, the education of young Christians was an important responsibility for women's mission societies who saw themselves as world mothers. Involving the young in the missions cause was seen as an important tool for recruiting future missionaries and beginning patterns of financial contribution at an early age.[81] When Mather arrived in Birmingham in 1921, there were

[77]Mather interview (Allen), 18.
[78]Ibid., 10.
[79]Allen, *Century to Celebrate*, 64.
[80]Mather interview (Allen), 37.
[81]Hill, *The World Their Household*, 65.

no Southern Baptist missions publications for children. In her first year she created *World Comrades*, a quarterly magazine with the motto, "to girdle the world with friendliness." Mather refined the age-graded system for children and adolescents, creating a program of achievement similar to that of Girls Scouts or 4-H clubs. Children completed readings and tasks related to missions and received promotion certificates. Over the years, Mather helped to create a distinctive character for the various youth missions organizations by publishing a unique magazine for each one. For example, *The Window of YWA* was designed for young women ages sixteen through twenty-four. while *Tell* was for girls, ages nine through sixteen. Boys of all ages subscribed to *Ambassador Life*, which was edited by a male missions leader.[82]

Another innovation Mather developed was the summer camping program for young women and girls. Although some states were holding summer camps as early as 1919, Mather helped to develop new methods and train leaders. The camps were initially more formal events. Young women attended conferences and church services in dresses, wearing informal attire only for afternoon recreation.[83] While assisting with a seaside camp, Mather was reprimanded by another WMU employee for taking off her stockings at the beach. Over the years, recreational dress became more accepted for other events of the camp.[84]

Mather initiated the model YWA camp in 1924 at Ridgecrest Baptist Assembly in the mountains of North Carolina.[85] The slogan was "Fellowship, Friendship, Frolic, and His Spirit Over All."[86] Mather assured leaders that a state camp could be held almost anywhere with a little ingenuity and flexibility. In Arkansas she assisted with a camp held at the county fairgrounds:

---

[82]Allen, *Century to Celebrate*, 204-205.
[83]Ibid., 207-208.
[84]Mather interview (Tharpe and Hamric), 13.
[85]Allen, *Century to Celebrate*, 207-208.
[86]Mather interview (Allen), 93.

I remember how the men got up and went and caught fish so
that we could have fish for breakfast the last morning. . . . The
mothers came and did the cooking for us there at the fairgrounds . . . and proved that you could do a YWA camp very
happily at the county fair building. It didn't have to be all
beautifully arranged.[87]

The YWA camps were an important feeder for the mission field, as
many young women publicly dedicated their lives for service, inspired
by the emotional and spiritual climate of the camp experience.[88]

In the same way Maude McLure had helped her secure a job,
Mather helped the young women she encountered to plan their
futures. In 1926, she wrote to another Training School alumna, Una
Roberts Lawrence, about a woman who hoped to be a teacher but was
unable to find a position at the last minute:

I want to talk just a minute about Virginia Mae. She is
another " girl with a year on her hands." . . . I suggested going
to Training School for a year . . . it would help her even when
she was doing regular teaching. . . . I am telling you so that if
you think wisely of it you can write her that I just casually
mentioned the matter. . . . Virginia Mae is all right even
though she did shock Mrs. Newman by saying that perhaps
there is something to this evolution business.[89]

In addition to her editorial and camping duties, Mather trained
the lay leadership of youth organizations. This activity, along with her
responsibility to inspire young women in Baptist colleges, kept her
traveling almost constantly. Her private correspondence with friends
and colleagues reveals that Mather was overworked and fatigued from
the beginning of her career in 1921 until her retirement in 1957. She

---

[87]Mather interview (Tharpe and Hamric), 30.
[88]Mather interview (Tharpe and Hamric), 54; Allen, *Century to Celebrate*, 208.
[89]Mather to Una Roberts Lawrence, September 2, 1926, Lawrence Papers, SBHLA.

carried editorial work to complete as she traveled. "Many an issue of *World Comrades* was put together on someone's guest bed," she remembered.[90]

At times, Mather was overwhelmed by her workload, as revealed in a letter to her friend and WMU colleague in Arkansas, Una R. Lawrence:

> Someway I'm feeling unusually inadequate to the situation just now. We know how one thing leads to another snowball fashion. . . . W. C. [*World Comrades*] keeps getting farther into debt—policies on hand to be "thunk" out for years ahead, spring work around the corner, College Bulletin, etc. . . .[91]

Mather felt free to be candid with Lawrence, temporarily releasing the WMU image that was sometimes a burden for her. She wrote to Lawrence in 1926:

> I've always loved the freedom you've given me in your home and I've been grateful for it. I feel myself slip out of my have-to-be-nice-whether-I-want-to-or-not" professional garb and just be Julie with you.[92]

Eventually, the stress led to a physical breakdown in 1930. Mather was given a year's leave of absence from WMU and went to live with family members in Granville, Ohio. In spite of the doctor's orders to rest, Mather could not keep her hands out of WMU work. She wrote to her former professor from the Training School:

> You may be interested to know that the Woman's Missionary Union has arranged for me to pick up the editing of my

---

[90]Watkins, *A Backward Glance*, 47.
[91]Mather to Una Roberts Lawrence, [1928?], Lawrence Papers, SBLA.
[92]Mather to Lawrence, July 28, 1926, Lawrence Papers, SBHLA.

magazines . . . and to do the work from here at home . . . I made the serious mistake of having a doctor named Leach for my physician and he seems as good as his name in not letting me escape.[93]

Mather recuperated from her illness and returned to WMU. But by 1936, she was discouraged with her job and began contemplating a career change. In a letter to W. O. Carver she articulated some of her frustrations:

I do love my work exceedingly but there are increasing obstacles which seem too big to buck against. I realize that life is not all easy and pleasant but I've been wondering if perhaps some things are to lead me to make a change. . . . I have gone all these years without a stenographer's help except for part of a day some days and the work piles up so it's sometimes unbearable. If our work is to grow as it should we should have some more workers. . . . Someway lately I have felt sort of baffled and frustrated and wondered if it were the Lord's leading me to seek some other work.

Mather asked Carver if he knew of a Baptist college in which she might teach Bible and missions courses. She warned, however, that she would not be willing to work in a college where smoking and dancing were allowed because she has opposed these practices all her life as "evidences of worldliness." Mather urged Carver to keep her plans a secret, as she had not told WMU of her wish to resign.[94]

The next year a job offer came from the denomination of Mather's childhood: Northern Baptists The Woman's American Baptist Foreign Mission Society was offering Mather a $400 per year increase to work for them. "I really thought that when I changed it would be

---

[93]Mather to W. O. Carver, April 12, 1930, Carver Papers, SBHLA.
[94]Mather to W. O. Carver, October 5, 1936, Carver Papers, SBHLA.

to a settled down sort of task, not just another travel and talk one," she wrote to Carver.

Mather turned down the job with Northern Baptists and continued her work with WMU. She confined her complaints to private audiences of close friends. In later years, she noted that Mrs. McLure had been a model of professionalism for her:

> She had over her desk [a sign that instructed] never to call attention to the burdens of the office or something like that. And so I thought "I'll never do it, I'll never say I worked too hard and I'll never say I haven't done this because I have been too busy." Never call attention to the burdens of the office.[95]

In 1948, Mather became editorial secretary of WMU, leaving behind the tiring work of traveling and youth camping. "GAs [girls ages nine through sixteen] were greeting me at camp with 'My mother remembers you were the speaker when she was a GA.' That made me feel old and I stopped trying to be the young people's secretary. . . ."[96] Mather edited the youth missions publications she had created as well as the women's periodical *Royal Service*. Mather served in this position until her retirement at age sixty.

In 1957, after her retirement from WMU, Mather realized her lifelong dream to become a foreign missionary. She had traveled overseas while working for WMU. In 1934 Mather traveled in Europe, and in 1953 she visited mission stations in Asia. Seinan Gakuin, a Baptist university in Japan that she visited, invited her to teach English for two years. When that assignment was complete, Mather left for Taiwan to teach for another five years. She returned to the United States for a brief visit and then went to Hong Kong to assist with publications. She served a total of ten years on the mission field until age seventy.[97]

---

[95]Mather interview (Allen), 146.
[96]Juliette Mather, "If on Life's Highway," *Tell*, May, 1963.
[97]Watkins, *A Backward Glance*, 49.

In her seventies, Mather reflected upon her role as a woman in Southern Baptist denominational work. She noted that women did not seem conscious of ways in which their leadership was connected to progress for women. She emphatically opposed the notion that mission work may have been used as a vehicle for enlarging women's roles in denominational life:

> [WMU asked me] to develop the young people's missionary education organization. They didn't say, "well we're reaching out for women's rights" . . . we were a missionary organization and that was our job and I don't think we sat down to talk [about] what women's rights were or whether women were leaders. . . . I think we attribute falsely if we attribute to women pioneers . . . the idea that "I'm going to get in." . . . That, I think, would be totally wrong in the mind and heart of the pioneers of Woman's Missionary Union. And I think it would be a betrayal of everything they said and did. [98]

When asked if she ever considered being a "homemaker rather than a career woman," she replied, "I never decided on being a career woman; I did what the Lord led me to do step by step." She said she received marriage proposals several times, "but I didn't think that was for me . . . because I was doing something else that seemed to be what the Lord wanted me to do."[99] Mather was frustrated with modern day women who seem less dedicated to the missions cause:

> . . . it always troubles me that women are saying "I have to find myself." Well, where have they been all these years? . . . I've never stopped to find myself. I was always busy about doing what was to be done, I guess. . . . Our purpose is a missionary purpose and . . . the woman who finds herself

---

[98]Mather interview (Allen), 61, 64-65.
[99]Ibid., 143.

would find herself best if she read the Word of God and prayed.[100]

Juliette Mather lived to age eighty-seven, spending the last years of her life in St. Petersburg, Florida. She remained devoted to the Training School and made a special effort to attend a reunion for the school's alumnae at Ridgecrest in North Carolina where she had begun the first national camp for YWA's. She was in poor health and nearly blind when she made the trip.[101] Reflecting later in life, she summed up the contribution the Training School made:

> It was Dr. Carver's mission classes. It was the living together with all these young women . . . it was the prayer times we had together, it was the chapel services we had in the morning . . . It was all of that together . . . What they gave to me was a passion for missions . . . Of course I was brought up with it . . . but it was intensified. Nobody knows how much.[102]

Carrie Littlejohn, Class of 1915

When Carrie Littlejohn left the Training School in 1915, she went to Dalton, Georgia to do mission work with the people employed by the local mills. The school's principle, Maude McLure, had recommended Littlejohn for the job, and the young graduate was thrilled.[103] She had thought about such work in her childhood, growing up in South Carolina where:

> . . . the state mission board employed women missionaries to work in the cotton mills that were dotted around over the

---

[100]Mather interview (Allen), 143-144.

[101]Alma Hunt, *Reflections from Alma Hunt* (Birmingham: Woman's Missionary Union, 1987) 20.

[102]Mather interview (Allen), 148.

[103]Carrie Littlejohn, interview by Doris DeVault, April 16 1979, tape recording, transcript, 8, WMUA.

state. . . . As a child ten years old, I would read the articles that these women missionaries would write about their work in these mill towns. That was my first compelling desire to do similar things.[104]

Carrie Littlejohn grew up in Spartanburg, South Carolina in the heart of cotton mill territory. Although hers was a farming family, rather than a mill family, she probably had opportunities to interact with mill personnel in her childhood. She attended Converse College, a woman's school organized in 1889 by Spartanburg's leading mill owners and named for the most prominent manufacturer in the town.[105]

After one year at Converse College, and a brief career in teaching, Littlejohn headed for the Training School in 1913 and received theological and practical training to prepare her for church-related service. After graduation, she was employed by the First Baptist Church of Dalton, Georgia to provide various religious activities for mill workers. However, she was soon frustrated with the expectations of the job:

[The mill workers] were very sensitive about that First Church in Dalton getting a missionary to work with them. Oh, me! So, it put me in a very difficult position . . . the wife of the pastor there at the First Church who had been the moving spirit in getting this work started . . . did not know enough of the background of mill people to realize it wasn't the thing to do, that they resented it. . . .[106]

Pastors in mill town churches sometimes expressed similar frustrations with religious work. One minister serving in the 1920s said he found

---

[104]Ibid., 2.

[105]"Carrie U. Littlejohn," Baptist Biography Files, SBHLA, Converse College Catalogue, 1992, 6-12.

[106]DeVault, Littlejohn interview, 8.

mill people hard to approach, noting that they were generous with one another, but suspicious of others.[107]

Life in a Southern mill town was based on the division between laborers of the mills and "town people" of the business and professional classes. David Carlton notes the social conflict arising in the mill towns of South Carolina as town people took a paternalistic stance in their efforts to solve what was called "the mill problem". Mill workers were white southerners from the poorer classes. In contrast to mills of the north, African Americans and immigrants were rejected as potential laborers in southern mills.[108] However, white supremacy was not the same as white equality. The impoverished white workers came to the factories with cultural practices considered by mill owners to be ill-suited to industrial life. Town people sought paternalistic control over mill workers using education, both public and religious, as a means of regulating workers and their children.

Mill owners and presidents, typically men from commercial or professional backgrounds, made benevolent contributions to establish churches, schools, and amenities of town life. The entire mill industry itself was often defended as a philanthropic enterprise, as it gave employment to poor whites who needed work.[109] Furthermore, a social improvement theme was sometimes heard in mill promotion. John V. Stribling told South Carolinians of the benefits of "assembling [the South's] indigent, unemployed, labor in villages, where through the influence of churches, schools, and factories, they could be improved mentally, morally, and physically [and] saved from vicious lives."[110] Town people with an educational agenda proposed to use mill villages as "acculturating institutions with schools as missions

---

[107]Lois MacDonald, *Southern Mill Hills: A Study of Social and Economic Forces in Certain Textile Mill Villages*, (New York: Alex Hillman Publisher, 1928) 99.

[108]David Carlton, *Mill and Town in South Carolina, 1880-1920* (Baton Rouge: Louisiana State University Press, 1982) 112-114.

[109]Ibid., 9-12, 72.

[110]Ibid., 78.

designed to teach 'habits of regularity, neatness, kindness, obedience, and self control' to factory children."

Religious instruction was part of the educational agenda. Mill town churches were typically erected after local ministers, missionaries, or evangelists had established a congregation. Mill owners were obliged to at least donate property for the church so they would not be counted among the "heathen"; some contributed to the support of the church itself.[111]

Lois MacDonald, a researcher of the 1920s working in a mill and observing mill town society, provides a description of the religious life of three mill villages. MacDonald noted that mill towns typically had one church from each of the three mainline denominations in the southern Bible Belt: Baptist, Methodist, and Presbyterian. In one village MacDonald studied, the Baptist church was the oldest and had the largest membership. It was built in 1909, seven years after the mill had opened and the mill had contributed to the building and a portion of the minister's salary. The three churches in this village maintained activities including Sunday worship, Sunday school, prayer meetings, young people's societies, and women's missionary societies.[112]

When Carrie Littlejohn was employed in 1915 to work among the mill folk, she encountered a resistance from the workers that she described as a sensitivity or resentment toward missionaries. Perhaps some of the same frustrations she experienced were those articulated by the ministers in MacDonald's study. In addition to the feeling of being regarded with suspicion, these mill town pastors complained that it was difficult to maintain continuous work among a migratory population. They also noted a lack of initiative in church work on the part of mill villagers. "They are good people," the pastors asserted, "but they take it for granted that everything will go along without their making any effort."[113] The exact nature of Littlejohn's activities

---

[111]Ibid., 183, 104.
[112]MacDonald, *Southern Mill Hill*, 55-57.
[113]Ibid., 58, 99.

among the mill folk at Dalton is not known. Presumably she evangelized among women and children, organizing mission societies and religious activities for children and teenagers.

After one year at Dalton, Littlejohn was contacted by a church at Sibley Mills in Augusta Georgia, and employed to do mission work with the mill workers of that town for four years. She described her situation thus:

> They had a settlement house which was a joint project between the mill heads and the First Baptist Church. It was supposed to be the women of the association, but really the First Baptist Church there did most of it. . . . [The mill owners] needed all the mill workers they could get so it was to their advantage to go in with the church people who would supervise and operate this settlement house.[114]

The first floor of the settlement house was used as a nursery for children of mill workers, while the second floor housed the nursery manager and Littlejohn, who directed the other settlement activities.[115] Littlejohn did not specify what sort of activities she supervised at the settlement house. However, MacDonald observed that mill towns of the 1920s sometimes provided, medical facilities, recreational activities, boys and girls clubs, women's associations, and related activities classified under the term "welfare work."[116]

There is some indication that mill workers may not have perceived a need for the services that were offered. In his 1930 study of Southern cotton mill workers, Jennings Rhyne questions the benefit of welfare work:

> The opinion of teachers, welfare workers, mill superintendents, and inspectors is that "as a rule the mill help does not

---

[114]DeVault, Littlejohn interview, 9.
[115]Ibid.
[116]Macdonald, *Southern Mill Hills*, 33.

greatly value, or appreciate in either sense of the word the efforts for their entertainment or for their advancement. First, they do not respond with any feeling of gratitude because they argue that all the money being spent on them is due them anyway as wages. . . ." In brief, the attitude of the worker toward welfare activities resolves itself into a general spirit of indifference.[117]

In contrast to her previous employment situation, Carrie Little-john enjoyed this work and did not experience the frustration she had felt at Dalton. She remembered her Sibley Mills days as "a wonderful experience . . . one I have always looked back to and enjoyed."[118] Perhaps the fact that mill owners had an investment in the project caused Littlejohn to feel more supported. Perhaps she benefitted from having the nursery worker as a colleague, helping to ease the burden of a difficult project.

The settlement idea was a familiar one for Littlejohn. As a student at the Training School, she participated in the activities of the Goodwill Center, which provided services such as mother's meetings, boys and girls clubs, story hour, and a playground for the immigrants in downtown Louisville. It is likely that Littlejohn used some of the methods she learned at the Training School in managing the settlement house for mill workers. Since mill owners described welfare work as a means to uplift the poor whites of the mills, it is likely that the settlement house which Littlejohn directed, like the original Good Will Center at the Training School, was designed for reform of the individual rather than societal change.

Littlejohn's work was reported in the Woman's Missionary Union periodical, *Royal Service*. Littlejohn likely organized Woman's Missionary Union events, such as the one described in a story by

---

[117]Jennings Rhyne, *Some Southern Cotton Mill Workers and Their Villages* (Chapel Hill, North Carolina: University of North Carolina Press, 1930) 35, quoting R. W. Edmonds, *Cotton Mill Labor Conditions in the South and New England* (Baltimore: Manufactures Record Publishing Company, 1925) 17.

[118]DeVault, Littlejohn interview, 9.

Juliette Mather. When a local WMU provided a reception for the girls of one mill village, the cultural expectations of WMU royalty required fancy attire. One young girl had no dress to wear to the event, but felt it was inappropriate to attend in the clothes she was wearing. A generous young friend attended a portion of the reception and ran back to where the girl was waiting. The two friends exchanged clothes, and the girl appeared in her friend's dress in time to socialize with WMU women.[119]

After four years in Augusta, Littlejohn went to another mill town, Gaffney, South Carolina where she served as a pastor's assistant. The job description of a Southern Baptist pastor's assistant varied according to need. Typically it involved clerical work, but also mission work with women and children, a domain that was considered better suited to a woman missionary than a male pastor. Elsie Ragsdale, a Training School graduate working in South Carolina, wrote that her position as pastor's assistant included "a little bit of everything pertaining to church work, except the preaching"[120]

After serving one year in Gaffney, Littlejohn was contacted in 1921 by the Training School and asked to manage the school's Good Will Center. Emma Leachman, who had been in charge of the Good Will Center since its beginning, had taken a job with the Home Mission Board, leaving the Center without a director. Littlejohn returned to Louisville to direct the Good Will Center, supervise the students' field work, and teach classes in personal work and social work.

When Littlejohn left the Training School in 1915, the Good Will Center was a relatively new enterprise, barely three years old, and methods of operation still were being refined. By the time she returned in 1921, however, the Good Will Center of Louisville was considered a model for Southern Baptist social work not only in the United States but overseas as well. Woman's Missionary Union groups had launched Good Will Centers all over the South, employing

---

[119]Mather interview (Tharpe and Hamric), 13.
[120]*Annual Bulletin*, March 1928, 59.

Training School graduates as directors.[121] By 1924, WMU reported that 103,000 persons were being reached by Good Will Centers and their influence was growing.[122] At the center of it all was the Training School Good Will Center directed by Littlejohn.

After Littlejohn served two years on the Training School faculty, Maude McLure resigned, leaving vacant the position of principal. Carrie Littlejohn was immediately appointed interim principal while the board of managers searched for the school's next leader. She gained important administrative experience that would be helpful to her in later years. After Littlejohn had served two years, Janie Cree Bose was appointed as the school's principal and Littlejohn returned to her position as Good Will Center director and teacher. After five years of service, Bose resigned in 1930 and Carrie Littlejohn once again assumed leadership of the school as interim principal. She had just returned from a year of sabbatical leave in which she studied at the Hartford School of Religious Education in Connecticut.[123] At the end of her first year, she was elected principal at the annual meeting of WMU in Birmingham Alabama. Littlejohn served as principal of the Training School for twenty-one years, the longest tenure in the school's history.

Carrie Littlejohn "maintained the strong pietistic flavor of the school" in her leadership. Upon election, she wrote to the WMU constituency:

> I am grateful for [the school's] sure foundations in the plan of God and I pledge my full cooperation in preserving its ideals and standards and distinctive atmosphere. My co-workers are one with me in their desire to adjust the program to the needs of the day without sacrificing those intangible qualities that have made the school a rare blessing to hundreds of students and visitors through the twenty-four years of its history.[124]

---

[121]Allen, *Century to Celebrate*, 222.
[122]Ibid., 223.
[123]Littlejohn, *History of Carver School*, 110.
[124]*Royal Service* 26 (November 1931): 31.

Carrie Littlejohn worked diligently to fulfill her promise to uphold the same ideals that had been in operation when she was a student. She was known as a strict disciplinarian with a stern demeanor. One graduate remembers being reprimanded severely by Littlejohn for walking down the marble stairway of House Beautiful that was reserved for Commencement services.[125] Littlejohn faced the same disciplinary questions that McLure dealt with in previous years concerning the social interaction of men and women. Following McLure's lead, Littlejohn maintained strict rules and regulations concerning dating.

Under Littlejohn's leadership, manners and social refinement were still parts of the Training School curriculum. Each month a lesson known as a "cultural program" was featured. Women students attended lectures and demonstrations, primarily given by local Christian women, on such topics as "Good Taste in Dress" and "Everyday problems in Table Etiquette."[126] As in McLure's day, these matters were still considered important learning for women.

While preserving Training School traditions concerning appropriate social behavior, Littlejohn also labored to raise academic standards. She proposed revisions to the curriculum that moved the school away from its original missions focus and toward a field that was opening new doors for women: the field of religious education. Religious education was a vocation pursued by both men and women and included such activities as Sunday school and Bible study, and work with children and adolescents. Within Littlejohn's first year as principal, the degrees of Bachelor and Master of Missionary Training were discontinued and the more standard degrees of Bachelor and Master of Religious Education (BRE and MRE) were substituted. The Sunday School Board of the SBC encouraged this new slant, and paid the salary of Gaines S. Dobbins, the professor of religious education

---

[125]Hugo Culpepper interview by Anne Davis, December 2, 1981, Davis Research Notes, WMUA.

[126]See SGA Minutes, 1938-1939, TSC, SBTS.

at the Training School. Southwestern Baptist Theological Seminary in Texas was already offering degrees in religious education, and the BRE degree had become the standard, which qualified women for missionary appointment and other church work.[127]

In addition to the new degrees being offered, admission standards were raised, with the Training School now requiring at least two years of college attendance before entering the Training School to pursue the BRE. Those wishing to pursue the MRE degree must have completed a bachelor's degree in arts, science, or religious education.[128] During Littlejohn's tenure the first librarian was employed by the Training School and volumes were catalogued for student use. The Training School began looking toward accreditation, although that goal was never fulfilled during Littlejohn's administration.[129]

Carrie Littlejohn took her position as an educator seriously. While she was working to improve the curriculum of the Training School, she was also pursuing further education for herself. Not only did she take a one year sabbatical leave to study at the Hartford School of Religious education, but she also enrolled in summer sessions at Boston University, George Washington University, and the University of Chicago. Between 1931 and 1933 she earned the degree Master of Science in Education from Northwestern University.

In 1936, Laura Dell Armstrong, president of WMU, began a campaign to rekindle the coordinate arrangement that had existed between the Training School and the Seminary prior to 1926. Training School women and Seminary men had attended theological classes together before the Seminary moved from its downtown location to the Louisville suburbs. Armstrong believed that a link with the Seminary was the key to academic strength and progress for the Training School. She succeeded in convincing the WMU Executive Board, the president of the Seminary, and the board of the Training

---

[127]Allen, *Century to Celebrate*, 277.
[128]Littlejohn, *History of Carver School*, 112.
[129]Ibid., 132, 141.

School to support her plan. Officials purchased property adjacent to the Seminary and made plans for a new building. Carrie Littlejohn would be supervising the move to the suburbs.[130]

Armstrong contributed an unusual amount of energy during the transition period. Nevertheless, the task was nearly overwhelming for Littlejohn. In later years, she described the moving years as the most difficult time of her twenty- one year tenure as principal.[131] However, in the fall of 1941 Littlejohn was pleased to be among the presenters at the dedication of the new Training School building located on Lexington Road, next to the Seminary. Littlejohn and the WMU women were soon disappointed, however, to learn that the Seminary would not admit Training School women to Bible classes, but would only allow their enrolment in electives or courses with small enrolment.[132]

The next year, Sampey retired as Seminary President, and Armstrong went immediately to negotiate with the new President, Ellis Fuller. Armstrong agreed that WMU would pay the Seminary $15,000 per year to allow the women to attend any Seminary classes. Thus, in 1942, Seminary men and Training School women resumed the arrangement of coeducation that had been in operation from the school's founding until 1926.[133]

In 1944, Carrie Littlejohn was awarded an honorary doctorate from Georgetown College in Kentucky. The title of Littlejohn's position was changed in 1948 from principal to president. She was treated as an employee of Woman's Missionary Union and was the first Training School head to serve on the WMU's Executive Committee. WMU paid Littlejohn a lower salary than male faculty of the Seminary, although she did receive higher compensation than Kathleen Mallory, chief administrative officer of WMU.[134]

---

[130]Ibid., 130-132.
[131]DeVault, Littlejohn interview, 16.
[132]Littlejohn, *History of Carver School*, 157.
[133]Ibid., 158.
[134]Ibid., x.; Allen, *Century to Celebrate*, 60, 273.

In her final year as president, Littlejohn was shocked and hurt by a movement among the students proposing the merger of the Training School and Seminary so that women could enroll directly in Seminary courses. Her anger is evident in a letter to the trustees of the Training School recounting the events. She reported that six women students had approached members of the Seminary faculty with the idea:

> if that were not so pathetic (in its revelation of the spirit, the immaturity and utter lack of understanding of basic ethics in human relationships) it would be funny. . . . For a group of students to be so presumptuous as to think they could *give away* an institution with assets worth around three-quarters of a million dollars or to initiate plans to change its basic policies without so much as "by-your-leave" from the owners, would raise the blood pressure of a calmer person than I am! . . . One girl naively said to me that if the women realized it was what the girls wanted, she believed they would be willing to make the change.[135]

Littlejohn was appalled at the denigration of the academic program she had worked so hard to establish. The students told the Seminary president "they were interested in Bible, theology, and such courses, but had no interest in the 'little study courses at the Training School.' " One student expressed a desire for equality with Seminary men and the few women who had enrolled in the Seminary's music school, "We are looked down on here on the campus as Training School girls. The Music School girls are part of the Seminary and we are not."[136]

Littlejohn immediately called a convocation of the students and confronted them on the matter. She gave a stern warning and reminded them of their debt to the WMU:

---

[135]Littlejohn to Board of Trustees, WMUTS, May 1, 1950, Littlejohn Papers, WMUA.
[136]Ibid.

I reminded the girls that they chose to come here in the beginning, that if they were not happy here nor satisfied with what they were getting, they were certainly not forced to stay, that if they chose to stay, we had the right to expect their cooperation. I have tried to make them see that to accept all that the School is doing for them and to attempt at the same time to undermine its work is ingratitude of the worst type, and unethical from every point of view.[137]

Littlejohn assured herself and the trustees that after the convocation, the problem was over: "I am glad to report that bringing the matter out into the open cleared the atmosphere. The 'movement' in its aggressive form seemed to disintegrate."[138] In reality, this movement was a prelude to the changes that would take place in the 1950s. When the Seminary began to allow women to matriculate as students, the enrolment of the Training School began to decline and never recovered.

Carrie Littlejohn spent her prime years of productivity in service to the Training School. She reflected on this period in her later years: "That's the best years of anybody's life. Thirty out of the middle."[139] In 1951, after thirty years of employment at the Training School, Carrie Littlejohn retired at age sixty-one. She returned to Spartanburg, where she cared for her mother and served as a WMU leader in her church. She remained involved in the life of her alma mater and devoted herself to the overwhelming project of writing a history of the Training School. It was published in 1958 and entitled: *History of Carver School of Missions and Social Work*. In her final years, Littlejohn lived in a retirement home surrounded by keepsakes and souvenirs from foreign countries given to her by Training School graduates who had served overseas.[140]

---

[137]Ibid.
[138]Ibid.
[139]Ibid., 15.
[140]DeVault, Littlejohn interview, 23, 27.

The Training School experience altered the lives of women students. As employees or volunteers in Southern Baptist work, women of the Training School maintained a deep loyalty to WMU. Jewell Daniel, Juliette Mather, and Carrie Littlejohn continued to associate with other Training School women and serve the WMU organization throughout their careers, and even after retirement. By teaching others in Chinese schools, through a WMU publication, or in Training School classrooms—the lessons of House Beautiful were not forgotten, but were reinforced and passed on to future generations. The Training School experience enriched the lives of women students, and these women contributed greatly to the ministry of Southern Baptists. In the twenty-first century, the future looks bleak for Southern Baptist women seeking full participation in the church's ministry, particularly in the area of preaching. Yet Southern Baptist women of today share a rich heritage with a group of pioneering women whose stories provide inspiration for continuing to knock on the doors of ministry that have remained closed to women.

7

EPILOGUE
1926-1999

B_y 1926, the Training School was experiencing a sharp decline in enrollment due to the halt in missionary appointments, both at home and abroad The Foreign Mission Board was deeply in debt due to over expenditures in the 1920s. Between 1926 and 1929, ninety-one missionaries died or retired but only twelve new missionaries were appointed.[1] The Home Mission Board also was suffering from financial loss due to over expenditures and the embezzlement in 1928 of nearly one million dollars by the board's treasurer.[2] Women were not preparing for home or foreign mission service, as they did not expect to be employed.

In addition, the Training School made a drastic change to its daily routine in 1926. That fall, students did not walk to the Seminary for theological course work, but took classes at their own building without male students. The Seminary had moved from its location in downtown Louisville to a suburban property called "the Beeches" because of its wealth of beautiful beech trees. For the next fifteen years the two schools would be fundamentally gender-segregated, although a few women traveled to the Beeches for graduate level courses after 1932.[3]

---

[1]See Baker James Cauthen, *Advance: A History of Southern Baptist Foreign Missions* (Nashville, Broadman Press, 1970) 33-37.

[2]J. B. Lawrence, *History of the Home Mission Board* (Nashville, Broadman Press, 1958) 115-119.

[3]Carrie Littlejohn, *History of Carver School of Missions and Social Work* (Nashville: Broadman Press, 1958) 133.

The Training School faced the challenge of continuing to provide a quality theological education for its students. C. L. McGinty was employed to teach Old and New Testament courses, while a few Seminary professors traveled downtown to the Training School to teach classes. The practical and performance skills taught by women faculty continued as usual. Carrie Littlejohn, president of the Training School during this era, noted the new arrangement was advantageous to the women who asked more questions in the smaller single-sex classes.[4] Ten years later, under the direction of WMU president Laura Dell Armstrong, the Training School made plans to resume a coordinate relationship with the Seminary and relocate near the Beeches. Armstrong noted, "the future progress of the school will be promoted by the return of the relationship with the Seminary that existed in the early years of the school." Five years later, in 1941, the Training School moved to a newly built property adjacent to the Seminary. By 1942, arrangements had been made for women students to join the Seminary men in the classroom once more. The Training School made a yearly contribution to the Seminary of $15,000 to supplement professors' salaries.[5]

In 1951, Carrie Littlejohn resigned her post, and the school launched a reevaluation of its purpose and direction. Emily Lansdell, whose mother sat quietly in the Seminary classroom at the turn of the century, was elected president of the Training School. Lansdell came to give the school new direction at a time when the school's purposes were growing uncertain. Women had begun matriculating directly into the Seminary in pursuit of the Master of Religious Education degree causing enrollment at the Training School to decline steadily. The WMU explored several options for redirection, including a proposal from the Seminary that the school serve as its religious education school for both men and women.[6] At the 1952 WMU

[4]Ibid., 98-99.

[5]Ibid., 130-131, 157-158.

[6]Kay Bigham interview by Catherine Allen, August 2, 1985, Louisville, KY, videotape, Southern Baptist Theological Seminary; Catherine Allen, A Century to Celebrate: History of Woman's Missionary Union, (Birmingham, AL: Woman's Missionary Union, 1987) 278.

annual meeting in Miami, the final plan was announced. Three important changes were made: the curriculum was altered to include a focus on social work as well as missions, the school would begin admitting students without regard to race or sex, and the name was changed to the Carver School of Missions and Social Work, honoring longtime supporter of WMU and the Training School, W. O. Carver.[7]

These changes did not stabilize declining enrollment, and in 1957, with WMU unable to support it financially, the school became the property of the Southern Baptist Convention. Emily Lansdell resigned, noting that she thought the school would have a better future if a man were president.[8] The SBC employed Booz, Allen, and Hamilton, a Chicago consulting firm, to study the school and make recommendations concerning its future. The report noted that the school was not achieving the goals set in 1952. Enrollment was dropping, and the report implied that this was due to lack of accreditation and the public perception that Carver School was exclusively a woman's school. Although it was promoted as a professional school, many graduates were serving as church volunteers and pastors' wives. On the basis of this study, the SBC recommended at the annual meeting of 1958 that the Carver School improve and expand its programs and pursue accreditation for its programs.[9]

While the Booz, Allen, and Hamilton study was being completed, Nathan Brooks became the school's first male president. Brooks would lead the school in its pursuit of accreditation by the Council on Social Work Education. However, it was soon apparent that accreditation would not be forthcoming, as Carver School did not meet the requirement stating that it must be housed in a college or university. It was becoming clear that the school would not survive in its present

---

[7]Littlejohn 174; C. Anne Davis, "The Carver School of Church Social Work," 1987, WMU Training School/Carver School Collection, Southern Baptist Theological Seminary, 8 (hereafter cited as TSC, SBTS).

[8]Allen, 280; Olive B. Martin to Trustees of Carver School, July 1, 1954, TSC, SBTS.

[9]Allen, 280; Cindy Russ, " The History of the Merger of Carver School of Missions and Social Work with Southern Baptist Theological Seminary, 1955-1963," 1980, 7-10, Training School/Carver School Collection, Woman's Missionary Union Archives, Birmingham, AL (hereafter cited as TSC, WMUA).

configuration. Therefore, in 1963, by action of the Southern Baptist Convention, the Carver School of Missions and Social Work was merged with the Southern Baptist Theological Seminary. The WMU turned over its real estate and other assets to the Seminary, but with a proviso that would become crucial in the 1990s. The agreement stipulated that if the Southern Baptist Convention ceased to operate a school for missions and social work, the agreement would be terminated and the funds would be returned to WMU.[10]

Through the 1960s and '70s, Seminary professors taught missions classes within the School of Theology and social work classes housed in the School of Religious Education. By 1970, over 100 students were pursuing the social work specialization within the Masters of Religious Education degree. That year Anne Davis, graduate of the Carver School, was employed to teach social work classes and became one of the early female faculty members at the Seminary.[11]

In 1979, a self-study of the social work program was conducted, leading to the formation of the Carver School of Church Social Work at the Seminary. Anne Davis was elected Dean of the new school in 1984. In 1987 the Council on Social Work Education (CSWE) accredited the Carver School to offer the Master of Social Work degree. By 1995 the school was enrolling over 100 students and was the only CSWE accredited Master of Social Work program in the United States that was housed in a theological seminary.[12] Anne Davis retired in 1993 and Diana Garland became the second dean of the school. The Carver School of Church Social Work thrived for twelve years, until it was closed in 1996 following controversy between leaders of the Carver School and Seminary president Albert Mohler. Because of conflict over faculty hiring processes, Mohler removed Garland from her position as Dean in 1995, though she remained a tenured faculty member. Garland objected to what she

---

[10]Davis, 13-14; Mark Wingfield, "WMU reclaims nearly $1 million from Southern," *Baptist Standard*, March 1, 2000.

[11]Ibid., 17.

[12]Ibid., 25-26; Enrollment Records, Fall 1994, Carver School of Church Social Work, Southern Baptist Theological Seminary, Louisville, KY.

called "the covert hiring criteria"—that Mohler applied to a faculty candidate. In an aberration of institutional hiring policies, Mohler required a faculty candidate to provide a written statement of his beliefs about abortion, homosexuality, the role of women, and the inspiration of Scripture. As Garland later reported on the events of 1995:

> [the faculty candidate] prepared thoughtful responses. Nevertheless, the President chose to reject [his] candidacy based on his response concerning the role of women in the life of the church. [The candidate] had in essence said that God can choose to do what God chooses to do; who are we to put limits on what God can do?[13]

The candidate's statement allowed for the possibility that a woman may be called into the preaching ministry. Mohler refused to hire the candidate. In a student/faculty forum Dean Garland publicly raised objections to the aberration of institutional hiring policies that led to the candidate's rejection. Within days of the forum, Mohler accused Garland of "a breach of personal and confidential communication" and fired her. Mohler then initiated plans to close the Carver School. In 1996, ninety-two years after President Mullins opened the Seminary doors to Southern Baptist women preparing for missions and social work, President Mohler closed the Carver School because he believed that the arena of service for Christian women should be limited. In 1998, the Seminary sold the Carver School name, library, and other assets to Campbellsville University, a Baptist school in Kentucky. By selling the Carver School, the Seminary ended the long tradition begun by the WMU Training School. The Seminary also broke the terms of the 1963 merger, which stipulated that the Seminary would continue operating a school for social work and missions or return the assets given by the Women's Missionary Union.

---

[13]Diana R. Garland, "When Professional Ethics and Religious Politics Conflict: A Case Study *Social Work and Christianity* 26 (Fall 1999): 60-76.

After the closing of the Carver School, WMU asked the Seminary to return nearly one million dollars in endowment funds, but did not request the return of its land or building adjacent to the Seminary. In 1999, after a long battle settled in mediation, the Seminary quietly returned to WMU $928, 451, which included a general endowment fund, the Margaret M. Norton fund, the W. O. Carver fund, and nine scholarship funds.[14] These funds represented the sacrificial giving of many WMU women who, since 1907, had sent all they had—their pennies, their homemade preserves, and their prayers—for the education of women seminary students in missions and social work.

Women Seminary Students

At the turn of the twentieth century, when Southern Baptists opened theological education to women, they did so with a clear understanding that women were preparing for different vocations than male ministers. Those who supported the creation of a school for women in connection with the Southern Baptist Theological Seminary offered assurances that "the object of the Training School is in no sense of the word to prepare women for the Christian ministry," but to prepare women for the "many other spheres of practical effort entirely outside the ministry."[15]

Although they allowed women the advantage of attending Seminary classes taught by a faculty of first rate scholars, Southern Baptists excluded women from certain forms of Christian service, first by narrowing the curricular choices available to them and eventually by creating a separate women's school which would provide a curriculum to reinforce the denomination's conservative views of appropriate vocations for Christian women. Yet women gained access

---

[14]Mark Wingfield, "WMU reclaims nearly $1 million from Southern," *Baptist Standard*, March 1, 2000.

[15]"A Statement Regarding the Women's Training School in Connection With The Southern Baptist Theological Seminary," [1906?] microfilm, Southern Baptist Historical Library and Archives, Nashville, TN.

to theological and biblical studies that would prepare them for leadership of other women and children.

The strict division of gender roles was quietly challenged in the late 1920s as women began learning church management and supervision skills in the "Course for Church and Educational Secretaries" offered at the Training School. Although the course maintained a title that suggested that women were being trained as secretaries rather than church administrators or ministers of education, it nevertheless gave women practical training in roles which had previously been reserved for men.[16]

In the 1950s, half a century after women had been invited to listen quietly to lectures, the Seminary graduated its first women students, women who typically pursued graduate degrees in the areas of music and religious education. Like the turn-of-the-century pioneer women students, these women had the freedom to select any Seminary courses they found interesting. In contrast to the first women students, they were allowed to participate in class discussions and were enrolled as students of the Seminary. After nearly fifty years of a separate formal curriculum, Southern Baptist women had come full circle, once again participating in a curriculum originally designed to prepare male ministers.

The first woman to graduate from the Seminary, Helen D. Armstrong, received the Bachelor of Divinity degree, usually pursued by students preparing for the pastoral ministry. Armstrong graduated from the Training School in 1949 with the Masters in Religious Education and then enrolled in the Seminary to pursue further studies. Armstrong recalled that she was not preparing for pastoral ministry but hoped "to teach or do counseling or both." She described the Seminary classroom as "pleasant . . . the students were friendly; the professors devoted." However, she did note that "some of the professors and some of the [Training School] women (both teachers and students) showed signs of being a bit threatened at times about

---

[16]*Catalogue*, Woman's Missionary Union Training School, 1928.

having a woman in this position."[17] "Brother Armstrong," as she was affectionately called by fellow students, married a seminary graduate, Carroll Wright, and later earned a Ph.D. from the University of California, pursuing a career in counseling and college teaching.

By the 1960s, women were not an unusual sight in the Seminary classroom. However, in 1964, the fears of opponents to women preachers were realized as Addie Davis became the first woman to be ordained by Southern Baptists. The Watts Street Baptist Church in Durham, North Carolina ordained Davis after she completed theological training at the nearby Southeastern Baptist Theological Seminary. A great deal of protest was raised but soon subsided when Davis accepted a pastorate outside the Southern Baptist denomination. No more ordinations of women were recorded until 1971, when Shirley Carter was ordained in Columbia, South Carolina. Under pressure, the church rescinded the ordination one year later. Leon McBeth estimates that fifty or more women were ordained between 1964 and 1977, although many were employed by non-Southern Baptist churches or served in non-preaching roles such as a hospital chaplaincy.[18]

Whether or not they were ordained, women of the 1970s began using the title "minister" to describe the church work they had been doing for many years. McBeth notes that after World War II Southern Baptists began to broaden their use of the term "minister" to refer to other church workers besides the pastor. In the 1970s, Southern Baptist women began to fill such church positions as Minister of Music or Minister of Education.[19]

Women seminary students of the 1970s struggled to understand the relationship between their calling, preparation, and service opportunities. While the Seminary was encouraging women in

---

[17]Armstrong may have been the object of tensions between Littlejohn and three students recounted in Chapter 6 of this study; Helen D. Wright to Marilyn Helton, April 23, 1978, Appendix of "The Feminine Touch: Women at the Southern Baptist Theological Seminary," Southern Baptist Theological Seminary, 1978, Photocopy.

[18]Leon McBeth, *Women in Baptist Life*, (Nashville: Broadman Press, 1979) 153-163.

[19]Ibid., 164.

theological studies, the denomination did not employ them in the work for which they had prepared. Anne Davis, professor at Southern Seminary, observed in 1976:

> Many women students have related to me that this reason leads to their most painful paradox. It is hard to handle the difference between the encouragement one received up to the point of seminary graduation and the mixed responses she then receives in her attempts to secure employment.[20]

The decade of the 1980s brought about a deep schism among Southern Baptists that drew a great amount of attention to the matter of woman's role in church work. Throughout the 1970s, a group of Southern Baptist conservatives organized a plan to gain control of the more moderate SBC in order to make the belief in Biblical inerrancy normative among Southern Baptists. The SBC annual meeting of 1979 became a turning point in the battle as busloads of fundamentalist supporters arrived in Houston, Texas to elect Adrian Rogers president of the SBC. From that point forward, conservative candidates have continuously held the SBC presidency, ensuring that only inerrantists will be appointed to boards, which manage the denomination's agencies and seminaries.[21] Southern Baptist historian Bill Leonard points out that although fundamentalists insisted that clarification of Biblical authority was the primary goal, "the line between inerrant Scripture and inerrant dogma is a thin one," and fundamentalists were promoting doctrines that they viewed as inseparable from the inerrancy issue. These doctrines were concerned with controversial issues such as the role of women and the nature of ministry. Debates over these issues, in addition to differences in belief concerning inerrancy, further divided Southern Baptists in the 1980s.[22]

---

[20]Anne Davis, "Women at Seminaries," *Contempo* (January 1976): 15.

[21]Bill J. Leonard, *God's Last and Only Hope: The Fragmentation of the Southern Baptist Convention* (Grand Rapids, MI: Eerdmans Publishing Company, 1990) 136-139.

[22]Leonard, *God's Hope*, 151.

As the SBC moved in a more conservative direction, Southern Baptists made a public statement of protest against women in ministry. In 1984, the SBC passed a resolution opposing the ordination of women, basing the resolution on selective references to Scripture, particularly the Pauline letters. The resolution stated that while Paul "commends women and men alike in other roles of ministry and service (Titus 2:1-10), he excludes women from pastoral leadership (1 Tim. 2:12) to preserve a submission God requires because the man was first in creation and the woman was first in the Edenic fall (1 Tim. 2:13ff). The conclusion stated, "we encourage the service of women in all aspects of church life and work other than pastoral functions and leadership roles entailing ordination."[23] Such statements echo opinions expressed at the turn of the century as the idea of a training school in connection with the Louisville seminary was being considered.

In spite of this statement of opposition, Southern Baptist women of the 1980s continued to be ordained by local churches. The willingness of some churches to ordain women while the denomination generally refused to employ them as pastors indicates the diversity of belief and practice among Southern Baptists. According to records of the Southern Baptist Women in Ministry organization, 232 women were ordained to Southern Baptist ministry by 1986. Even if a woman found support in a local church, other Southern Baptists might present obstacles to her ministry. In 1987, when the Prescott Memorial Baptist Church in Memphis, Tennessee, employed Nancy Sehested, a woman, as pastor, the church was "disfellow-shipped," meaning that the church's membership in the local association was terminated by that association.[24] The SBC discouraged women from entering the preaching ministry throughout the 1980s and '90s and at the annual meeting in June 2000, the Convention approved a formal prohibition of women pastors. Along with

---

[23]Leonard, 152, citing SBC Annual, 1984, 65.

[24]"Opening Doors: A Brief History of Women in Ministry in Southern Baptist Life, 1868-1993," (Louisville, KY: Southern Baptist Women in Ministry, [1993]).

sweeping revisions to its 1963 confession of faith, *The Baptist Faith and Message*, the SBC approved this statement: "While both men and women are gifted for service in the church, the office of pastor is limited to men as qualified by Scripture."[25]

While Southern Baptist women continue working to develop networks of support, opposition to women in the preaching ministry permeates the SBC at the beginning of the twenty-first century. Seminaries of our time, including the Southern Baptist Theological Seminary at Louisville, have been enjoined by the denomination to discourage women from entering the preaching ministry. At the turn of the last century, when Southern Baptists feared that women students at the Seminary would become preachers, they were assured that women were being trained only for those activities considered to be women's work. In our time, Southern Seminary is still expected to train women only for church vocations considered appropriate for their gender. The majority of women seminary students continue to cluster in the areas of music, social work, education and other ministries not requiring ordination. Few women study for the preaching ministry, since they will have no chance of being employed by Southern Baptist churches.

Current Seminary president R. Albert Mohler played a key role in the 2000 revisions of the *Baptist Faith and Message*, which reflects his convictions about biblical authority and the role of women in theological education. When he took office in 1993, he stated that while he did not oppose women attending the Seminary, he could not support women entering the preaching ministry. He found "the service of women in the pastorate or in certain offices of the church incompatible with Scripture."[26] Just as Training School students of the 1920s were required by their principal literally to "step to the side of the sacred desk," women seminary students of today are being told that a woman's proper place is beside, rather than behind, the pulpit.

---

[25] Article VI, *Baptist Faith and Message*, cited in press release, Associated Baptist Press, June 14, 2000.

[26] Mark Wingfield, "Mohler cites Abstract as Seminary's Doctrinal Border," *Western Recorder*, March 30, 1993.

Woman's Missionary Union in the 1990s

How have these events affected the Woman's Missionary Union whose Training School provided a way for women to receive a theological education while staying confined to a limited sphere of service? The WMU has not publicly entered the debates over the ordination of women, although some of its members have privately voiced their support.[27] This response parallels that of the WMU of the 1910s, which did not openly support suffrage for women, although some of its members privately worked for the cause. Today's WMU has shown support to women in all types of ministry by sponsoring an annual Women in Ministry session each year since 1982. Meanwhile, the WMU has entered into its own struggle with the SBC as it begins to act more independently than in previous years. As Southern Baptist agencies such as the Foreign Mission Board, Home Mission Board, and six seminaries become dominated by Southern Baptist fundamentalists, WMU has found advantages in the independence afforded it by the auxiliary arrangement. WMU is connected to, but not controlled by, the SBC as Delanna O'Brien, then executive director of WMU, made clear in 1992:

> WMU is an autonomous body and the Southern Baptist Convention does not exercise authority over it . . . Because WMU is a women's organization, it is important for women to direct its work.[28]

Using metaphors expressing traditional notions that women should be obedient to men, conservative SBC leaders objected to the independent actions of WMU. When WMU voted to support mission endeavors of other groups outside the SBC, a trustee of the FMB

---

[27]Grady Cothen, *What Happened to the Southern Baptist Convention?: A Memoir of the Controversy* (Macon, GA: Smyth and Helwys Publishing, 1993) 358.

[28]Dellanna O'Brien, "Auxiliary: A 104-Year-Old Relationship That Has Worked," *Royal Service* 87 (July 1992): 14.

called the WMU an adulteress.[29] Other Southern Baptist groups, in addition to the FMB, have expressed discontent with the WMU. The executive committee of the Southern Baptist Convention adopted a resolution to give thanks for WMU's good work, but also expressed "concern about the current relationship between WMU and the SBC."[30]

Women of the WMU continue to describe the auxiliary relationship in terms of traditional gender roles, while emphasizing their independence. June Whitlow, associate executive director of WMU stated in 1993 that "being a helper for the cause of missions is perhaps the best way to describe WMU's role within the SBC." However, she also emphasized that the auxiliary status means that WMU is self-governing and that "the SBC does not exercise authority over it." In addition, WMU is financially self-supporting.[31] Whitlow's description of the relationship of the WMU to the SBC reflects changing relationships between men and women throughout the past century. In 1888, when WMU was organized, women leaders assured the SBC that they intended to be proper helpmates and noted in the WMU constitution that they were "disclaiming all intention of independent action." Annie Armstrong, earliest executive secretary of WMU, rarely acted without first asking the advice of male leaders of the SBC agencies.[32] A century later, women of the WMU are emphasizing their self-governance and financial independence.

In spite of accusations of betrayal, WMU members continue to focus on missions and de-emphasize political struggles among Southern Baptists. O'Brien asserted the peacemaking role of WMU and called for renewed attention to the missions cause in a statement reminiscent of the rally cries of early WMU leaders:

---

[29]"WMU called adulteress, O'Brien Canceled," *Western Recorder*, February 2, 1993, 2.
[30] "WMU Report Spring 1993," Birmingham, AL: Woman's Missionary Union 2.
[31]Ibid.,7.
[32]WMU Constitution cited in Ethlene Boone Cox, *Following in His Train*, (Nashville: Broadman Press, 1938) 67; Bobbie Sorrill, *Annie Armstrong: Dreamer in Action* (Nashville: Broadman Press, 1984).

Even now, it is our desire that WMU be the entity that can relate to all Southern Baptists, no matter where they might find themselves along the political spectrum within the denomination. Surely it is possible for one entity in our convention to embrace all Southern Baptists! Is it not possible for one entity to relate to all—conservatives, moderates, undeclared, and confused?

WMU is committed to raising high the flag of missions. We invite you: If you believe in God's command to go and teach and make disciples, then go with us. Give total allegiance to missions—not to people, not to agencies, not to discreet groups—but to all expressions of Southern Baptist missions![33]

O'Brien's desire that Baptist groups continue to work together in spite of differences may seem naive to those who have been immersed in the recent controversy of the SBC. However, until 1993, the WMU was able to remain remarkably neutral and perhaps may continue cordial relations with both camps, although many fundamentalist leaders do not support WMU nor have allowed WMU organizations in their churches.[34]

A Place of Service for All Who Are Called

Baptist women continue the struggle to define their places of service. Many left the denomination to find employment by other denominations. Others have found acceptance among alternative Southern Baptist groups such as Alliance of Baptists or the Cooperative Baptist Fellowship, formed in the 1980s in response to changes in the SBC leadership. These organizations, composed of former and current members of the SBC, support women in all forms of church leadership including the preaching ministry. In the same way the

---

[33]WMU Report, 3.
[34]Cauthen, 358.

Training School provided a place for women to pursue theological studies when the Seminary did not admit women as students, these groups are nurturing Baptist women ministers who have been excluded from the Southern Baptist Convention. These Baptist sisters continue to search for places in which they may, without persecution, fulfill their calling to serve the Lord.

BIBLIOGRAPHY

Primary Sources

Most of the material on the Training School is found in four Southern Baptist depositories:

The Southern Baptist Historical Library and Archives (SBHLA), Nashville, TN:

This archive contains the papers of alumna Una Lawrence Roberts, professor W. O. Carver, and Foreign Mission Board Correspondence and Records of alumnae. Biographical sheets in the "Operation Baptist Biography" files, as well as copies of Baptist World, Foreign Mission Journal, Home and Foreign Fields, and Royal Service are also very useful. The SBHLA has microfilmed copies of the majority of materials available at SBTS, including the Annual Bulletin of Baptist WMU Training School Alumnae Association.

The Southern Baptist Theological Seminary (SBTS), Louisville, KY:

This depository contains the largest collection of Training School materials in its WMU Training School/Carver School collection. Correspondence, published pamphlets, historical scrapbooks, and photographs of the Training School, as well as minutes of the school's Board and student organizations provide an abundance of information. Some of the materials are still unclassified, and most are available on microfilm. Historical materials relating to the Seminary are also available from this depository. The *Western Recorder* and *Annual Bulletin of Alumnae* are available in the main library of SBTS.

The Sunday School Board Archives (SSB), Nashville, Tennessee

This archive contains the correspondence between J. M. Frost and Annie Armstrong, as well as additional materials on Armstrong. The paper "History of Movement to Begin a Training School" is located here.

Woman's Missionary Union Archives (WMUA), Birmingham, AL:

This depository contains copies of some material available at SBTS, but has a wealth of pamphlets and other publications not available in other archives. The WMU Minutes, collection of diaries, scrapbooks, photographs, oral histories, faculty, students and alumnae, Mather papers, Littlejohn Papers, and Legett Diary were most useful for this study.

Secondary Sources

Agee, Bob *A View from Bison Hill* OBU, Shawnee, OK 1985.

Alband, Jo Della. "History of the Education of Women in Kentucky." (Masters Thesis, University of Kentucky, 1934).

Album of Foreign Mission Board, Southern Baptist Foreign Missionaries. Richmond, VA: Foreign Mission Board of the Southern Baptist Convention, 1926.

Allen, Catherine. *The New Lottie Moon* Story. Nashville: Broadman Press, 1980.

_____. "Concerns Beyond Feminism," in *God's Glory in Missions* ed. John Jonson. Louisville, KY: privately published, 1985.

_____. *Laborers Together with God.* Birmingham: Woman's Missionary Union, 1987.

_____. *A Century to Celebrate: History of Woman's Missionary Union.* Birmingham: Woman's Missionary Union, 1987.

Ammerman, Nancy Tatom. *Baptist Battles: Social Change and Religious Conflict in the Southern Baptist Convention.* New Brunswick, NJ: Rutgers University Press, 1990.

_____ ed., *Southern Baptists Observed: Multiple Perspectives on a Changing Denomination.* Knoxville: The University of Tennessee Press, 1993.

Anders, Sarah Frances. "Woman's Role in the Southern Baptist Convention and Its Churches as Compared With Selected Other Denominations," *Review and Expositor* 72 (Winter 1975): 31-39.

Bailey, Beth. *From Front Porch to Back Seat: Courtship in Twentieth Century America.* Baltimore: Johns Hopkins University Press, 1988.

Bailey, Faith C. *Two Directions,* Rochester NY: Baptist Missionary Training School, 1964.

Bailey, Raymond. *God's Unfinished Dream: One Hundred and Twenty-Five Years in Review,* chief researcher, Bill J. Leonard. Alumni Chapel, 1984.

Bailey, Kenneth K. *Southern White Protestantism in the Twentieth Century.* New York: Harper and Row, 1964.

Baker, Eugene W. *To Light the Ways of Time: An Illustrated History of Baylor University, 1845-1986.* Waco: Baylor University, 1987.

Baker, Robert. *The Southern Baptist Convention and Its People: 1607-1972.* Nashville: Broadman Press, 1974.

Banner, Lois. *Women in Modern America: A Brief History.* New York: Harcourt Brace Jovanovich, 1974.

Barlow, H. M., ed., *Higher Education and the Social Professions.* Lexington, KY: College of Social Professions, University of Kentucky, 1973.

Barr, Pat. *To China With Love: The Lives and Times of Protestant Missionaries in China, 1860-1900.* Garden City, NY: Doubleday, 1973.

Beaver, R. Pierce. *American Protestant Women in World Missions: History of the First Feminist Movement in North America.* Grand Rapids, Michigan: Eerdman's Publishing Co 1980.

Bentley, Eljee. "Personal Responses to the Call to World Missions," *Baptist Heritage and History* 27 (October 1988): 34-43.

Berkin, Carol Ruth, and Mary Beth Norton. "The Paradox of 'Women's Sphere'," *Women of America: A History*. Boston: Houghton Mifflin Co., 1979.

Bledstein, Burton. *The Culture of Professionalism: The Middle Class and the Development of Higher Education in America*. New York: W. W. Norton, 1976.

Boyer, Paul. *Urban Masses and Moral Order in America, 1820- 1920*. Cambridge, MA: Harvard University Press, 1978.

Brackney, William H. *The Baptists*. New York: Greenwood Press, 1988.

Breul, F.R. and S. J. Diner. *Compassion and Responsibility: Readings in the History of Social Welfare Policy in the United States*. Chicago, Illinois: The University of Chicago Press, 1980.

Briney, Melvill O. *Fond Recollection: Sketches of Old Louisville*, Louisville, KY: The Louisville Times, 1955.

Brumberg, Joan Jacobs. "Zenanas and Girlless Villages: The Ethnology of American Evangelical Women, 1870-1910." *Journal of American History* 69 (September 1982): 347-371.

Brumberg, Joan Jacobs. *Mission for Life: The Story of the Family of Adoniram Judson*. New York: Free Press. 1980.

H. Button and E. F. Provenzo, *History of Education America* Englewood Cliffs, NJ: Prentice Hall, 1989.

Carlton, David L. *Mill and Town in South Carolina 1880-1920*. Baton Rouge: Louisiana State University. Press, 1982.

Carpenter, Joel A. and Wilbert R. Shenk, eds., *Earthen Vessels: American Evangelicals and Foreign Missions, 1880-1980*. Grand Rapids, Michigan: William B. Eerdmans Publishing Company, 1990.

Carson, Mina J. *Settlement Folk: Social Thought and the American Settlement Movement, 1885-1930*. Chicago: University of Chicago Press, 1990.

Cauthen, Baker James. *Advance: A History of Southern Baptist Foreign Missions*. Nashville: Broadman Press, 1970.

Chafe, William H. *The American Woman: Her Changing Social, Economic, and Political Role, 1920-1970.* New York: Oxford University Press, 1972.

Clifford, Geraldine J., *Lone Voyagers: Academic Women in American Coeducational Universities, 1869-1937.* New York: Feminist Press, 1988.

Connaway, Rhonda S. and Martha E. Gentry. *Social Work Practice.* Englewood Cliffs, NJ: Prentice-Hall, Inc., 1988.

Conway, Jill K. "Perspectives on the History of Women's Education in the United States," *History of Education Quarterly* 14 (Spring 1974): 1-12.

Cott, Nancy F. *The Bonds of Womanhood: "Woman's Sphere" in New England, 1780-1835.* New Haven CT: Yale University Press, 1977.

Cox, Ethlene Boone. *Following in His Train.* Nashville: Broadman Press, 1938.

Cremin, Lawrence. *The Transformation of the School: Progressivism in American Education 1876-1957.* New York: Random House, 1964.

Crumpler, Carolyn Weatherford. "The Role of Women in Baptist Missions," *Baptist History and Heritage* 23 (July 1992): 25-33.

Davis, Allen F. *Spearheads For Reform: The Social Settlements and the Progressive Movement 1890-1914.* New Brunswick, NJ: Rutgers University Press, 1984.

Davis, C. Anne. "History of the Carver School of Church Social Work" *Review and Expositor* 85 (Spring 1988): 209-220.

_____. "Liberation, Not Separation," *Review and Expositor* 72 (Winter, 1975): 63-69.

_____. "Women at Seminaries," *Contempo,* January 1976, 14-16.

DeBerg, Betty A. *Ungodly Women: Gender and the First Wave of American Fundamentalism,* Minneapolis: Fortress Press, 1990.

Devine, Edward, T. *The Practice of Charity.* New York: Lentilhon and Company, 1901.

Dillard, Badgett. "The Campus at Southern Seminary," *Review and Expositor* 81 (Fall 1984): 425-439.

Eighmy, John Lee. *Churches in Cultural Captivity: A History of the Social Attitudes of Southern Baptists*. Knoxville: University of Tennessee Press, 1972.

Epstein, Barbara L. *The Politics of Domesticity*. Middletown: Wesleyan University Press, 1981.

Faragher, John Mack and Florence Howe. *Women and Higher education in American History: Essays from the Mount Holyoke College Sesquicentennial Symposia*. New York: W. W. Norton and Company, 1988.

Fass, Paula S. *The Damned and the Beautiful: American Youth in the 1920's*. New York: Oxford University Press, 1977.

Faust, Drew Gilpin. *Mothers of Invention : Women of the Slaveholding South in the American Civil War*. Chapel Hill: University of North Carolina Press, 1966.

Flexner, Eleanor. *Century of Struggle: The Woman's Rights Movement in the United States*. New York: Atheneum, 1972.

Frankfort, Roberta. *Collegiate Woman: Domesticity and Career in Turn-of-the-Century America*. New York: New York University Press, 1977.

Fraser, Walter J., R. Frank Saunders, Jr., and Jon L. Wakelyn eds.,*The Web of Southern Social Relations: Women, Family, and Education*. Athens: The University of Georgia Press, 1985.

Friedman, Jean, *The Enclosed Garden*. Chapel Hill: University of North Carolina Press 1985.

Garland, Diana. "When Professional Ethics and Religious Politics Conflict: A Case Study." *Social Work and Christianity* 26 (Fall 1999): 60-76.

Ginzberg, Lori. *Women and the Work of Benevolence: Morality, Politics, and Class in the Nineteenth Century United States*. New Haven: Yale University Press, 1990.

Godbold, Albea, *The Church College of the Old South*, Durham, NC: Duke University Press, 1944.

Goodsell, Willystine. *The Education of Women: Its Social Background and its Problems*. New York: The Macmillan Co., 1924.

Gordon, Lynn D. *Gender and Higher Education in the Progressive Era*, New Haven: Yale University Press, 1990.

Hamilton, Frances D. and Elizabeth C. Wells. *Daughters of the Dream: Judson College 1838-1988*. Marion, Alabama, Judson College, 1989.

Hardesty, Nancy A. *Women Called to Witness: Evangelical Feminism in the 19th Century*. Nashville: Abingdon Press, 1984.

Hawks, Joanne and Sheila Skemp eds. *Sex, Race, and the Role of Women in the South*. Jackson: University Press of Mississippi, 1983.

Heck, Fannie E. S. *In Royal Service*. Richmond VA: Foreign Mission Board of the Southern Baptist Convention, 1913.

Helton, Marilyn. "The Feminine Touch: Women at the Southern Baptist Theological Seminary", photocopy Southern Baptist Theological Seminary, Louisville, KY, 1978.

Higginbotham, Evelyn Brooks. *Righteous Discontent: The Women's Movement in the Black Baptist Church, 1880-1920*. Cambridge, MA: Harvard University Press, 1993.

[Higginbotham], Evelyn Brooks. "The Women's Movement in the Black Baptist Church, 1880-1920." Ph.D. dissertation. Ann Arbor, MI: University Microfilms International, 1984.

Hill, Samuel S. Jr., ed., *Religion and the Solid South*. Nashville, Tennessee: Abingdon Press, 1972.

Hill, Patricia. *The World Their Household: The American Woman's Foreign Mission Movement and Cultural Transformation, 1870-1920*. Ann Arbor: University of Michigan Press, 1985.

Holden, Arthur C., *The Settlement Idea: A Vision of Social Justice* New York: MacMillan, 1922.

Hollis, E. V. and A. L. Taylor. *Social Work Education in the United States*. New York: Columbia University Press, 1951.

Honeycutt, Roy L. "Heritage Creating Hope: The Pilgrimage of The Southern Baptist Theological Seminary," *Review and Expositor* 81 (Fall 1984): 367-391.

Horowitz, Helen Lefkowitz. *Alma Mater: Design and Experience in the Women's Colleges from Their Nineteenth-Century Beginnings to the 1930's.* New York: Alfred A. Knopf, 1984.

Horowitz, Helen Lefkowitz. *Campus Life: Undergraduate Cultures from the End of the Eighteenth Century to the Present,* Chicago, University of Chicago Press, 1987.

Howe, Florence. *Myths of Coeducation: Selected Essays, 1964-1983* Bloomington: Indiana University Press, 1984.

Hunt, Alma. *History of the Woman's Missionary Union.* Nashville: Broadman Press, 1964.

Hunter, Jane. *The Gospel of Gentility: American Women Missionaries in Turn-of-the-Century China.* New Haven CT: Yale University Press, 1984.

Hyatt, Irwin. *Our Ordered Lives Confess: Three Nineteenth- Century American Missionaries in East Shantung.* Cambridge MA: Harvard University Press, 1976.

James, Mrs. W. C., *Fannie E. S. Heck: A Study of the Hidden Springs in a Rarely Useful and Victorious Life.* Nashville: Broadman Press, 1939.

Johnson, Charles D. *Higher Education of Southern Baptists: An Institutional History, 1826-1954.* Waco: Baylor University Press, 1955.

Johnson, Inman, *Of Parsons and Profs,* Nashville: Broadman Press, 1959.

Johnson, M. L. *A History of Meredith College.* Raleigh NC: Meredith College, 1956.

Karger, Howard J. *The Sentinels of Order: A Study of Social Control and the Minneapolis Settlement House Movement, 1915-1950* Lanham, MD: University Press of America, 1987.

Paul Klein, *From Philanthropy to Social Welfare.* San Francisco: Josey Bass, 1968.

Kerber, Linda K. "Separate Spheres, Female Worlds, Woman's Place: The Rhetoric of Women's History," *Journal of American History* 75 (June 1988): 9-39.

Kerber, Linda K., and Karen DeHart-Matthews, eds. *Women's America: Refocusing the Past*. 2nd ed. New York: Oxford University Press, 1987.

Kilman, Gail Apperson. *Southern Collegiate Women: Higher Education at Wesleyan Female College and Randolph Macon Women's College, 1893-1907*, Ann Arbor, MI: University Microfilms, International, 1984.

King, Joe M. *A History of South Carolina Baptists*. Columbia: South Carolina Baptist Convention, 1964.

Knott, Claudia. "The Woman Suffrage Movement In Kentucky, 1879-1920." Ph.D. dissertation, University of Kentucky, 1989.

Lane, Myrle Anderson. *Five Times Ten: A Child's story of Woman's Missionary Union*. Nashville: Broadman Press, 1938.

Laurence, J. B. *History of the Home Mission Board*. Nashville: Broadman Press, 1958.

Leonard, Bill J. "Student Life at Southern Seminary," *Review and Expositor* 81 (Fall 1984): 441-460.

_____. *God's Last and Only Hope*: The Fragmentation of the Southern Baptist Convention, Grand Rapids, MI, Eerdmans Publishing, 1990.

Littlejohn, Carrie. *History of Carver School of Missions and Social Work*. Nashville: Broadman Press, 1958.

Martin, Patricia, S. " 'Keeping Silence': Texas Baptist Women's Role in Public Worship, 1880-1920," *Texas Baptist History* 3 (1983): 15-30.

_____. "Ordained Work—Unordained Workers: Texas 'Bible Women,' 1880-1920, *Texas Baptist History* 8 (1988): 1-9.

MacDonald, Lois. *Southern Mill Hills: A Study of Social and Economic Forces in Certain Textile Mill Villages*. New York: privately published, 1928.

McBeth, Leon. *"Southern Baptist Higher Education" in The Lords Free People in a Free Land: Essays in Baptist History in Honor of Robert A. Baker*, ed. William R. Estep, Fort Worth, TX: South Western Baptist Theological Seminary, 1976.

_____. *Women in Baptist Life*. Nashville, Tennessee: Broadman Press, 1979.

McCandless, Amy Thompson, "Preserving the Pedestal: Restrictions on Social Life at Southern Colleges for Women, 1920-1940." *History of Higher Education Annual* 7 (1987): 45-67.

Meyerowitz, Joanne J. *Women Adrift: Independent Wage Earners in Chicago, 1880-1930*. Chicago: The University of Chicago Press, 1988.

Montgomery, Helen Barrett. *Western Women in Eastern Lands*. New York: The Macmillan Company, 1910.

Mueller, William. *A History of Southern Baptist Theological Seminary*. Nashville: Broadman Press, 1959.

Mullins, Isla May. *House Beautiful*. Nashville: The Sunday School Board of the Southern Baptist Convention, 1934.

Mylum, Dixie Bale, *Proclaiming Christ: History of Woman's Missionary Union of Kentucky 1878-1978*, Louisville, WMU of Kentucky, 1978.

Neil, Anne T. and Virginia Neely. *The New Has Come: Emerging Roles Among Southern Baptist Women*, Washington DC: Southern Baptist Alliance, 1989.

Newcomer, Mabel. *A Century of Higher Education For American Women*. New York: Harper, 1959.

Pacey, Lorene M., ed., *Readings in the Development of Settlement Work*. New York: Association Press, 1950.

Pearce, Betty M. *The Status of Women in the Southern Baptist Convention*, Louisville, KY: Center for Women in Ministry, 1984.

Porter, J. W., ed. *Feminism, Woman and Her Work*. Louisville: Baptist Book Concern, 1923.

Proctor, Robert A. Jr. *"The Classroom at Southern Seminary,"* *Review and Expositor* 81 (Fall 1984): 417-424.

Ragsdale, B. D. *Story of Georgia Baptists* Atlanta: Georgia Baptist Convention, 1932.

Rhyne, Jennings J. *Some Southern Cotton Mill Workers and Their Villages*. Chapel Hill: University of North Carolina Press, 1930.

Riley, Glenda. *Inventing the American Woman: A Perspective on Women's History, 1607 to the Present*. 2 vols. Arlington Heights, IL: Harlan Davidson, Inc., 1986.

Robinson, Mabel Louise. *Curriculum of the Woman's College*. U.S. Bureau of Education, Bulletin No. 6, (1918).

Rogers, James A. *Richard Furman: Life and Legacy*. Macon GA: Mercer University Press, 1985.

Rosenberg, Ellen. *The Southern Baptists: A Subculture in Transition*. Knoxville: The University of Tennessee Press, 1989.

Rosenberg, Rosalind. *Beyond Separate Spheres: Intellectual Roots of Modern Feminism*. New Haven: Yale University Press, 1982.

Rothman, Sheila M. *Woman's Proper Place: A History of Changing Ideals and Practices, 1870 to the Present*. New York: Basic Books, 1978.

Ruoff, John. *Southern Womanhood, 1865-1940: An Intellectual and Cultural Study*. Ann Arbor, MI: University Microfilms, 1976.

Scarborough, L. R. *A Modern School of The Prophets*, Nashville: Broadman Press, 1939.

Scharf, Lois. *To Work and To Wed: Female employment, Feminism, and The Great Depression*. Westport, CT: Greenwood Press, 1980.

Scharf, Lois and Joan M. Jenson, eds. *Decades of Discontent: The Women's Movement, 1920-1940*. Westport, CT: Greenwood Press, 1983.

Schuster, Marilyn R., and Susan R. Van Dyne, ed. *Transforming the Liberal Arts Curriculum*. Toowa, NJ: Rowman and Allanheld, 1985.

Schwager, Sally. "Educating Women in America." *Signs: Journal of Women in Culture and Society* 12 (Winter 1987): 333-372.

Scott, Anne Firor. *The Southern Lady from Pedestal to Politics, 1830-1930*. Chicago: The University of Chicago Press, 1970.

_____. "Women, Religion and Social Change," in Religion and the Solid South by Samuel S. Nashville: Abingdon Press, 1972.

_____. *Making the Invisible Woman Visible*. Urbana and Chicago: University of Illinois Press, 1984.

Seller, Maxine. "The Education of the Immigrant Woman, 1900-1935." *Journal of Urban History* 4 (May 1978): 307-330.

Shurden, Walter B. "Southern Seminary in the Life of the Southern Baptist Convention," *Review and Expositor* 81 (Fall 1984): 393-406.

Smith, Bertha. *Go Home and Tell.* Nashville: Broadman Press, 1965.

_____. *How the Spirit filled My Life.* Nashville: Broadman Press, 1973.

Solomon, Barbara Miller. *In the Company of Educated Women: A History of Women and Higher Education in America.* New Haven CT: Yale University Press, 1985.

Sorrill, Bobbie. *Annie Armstrong: Dreamer in Action.* Nashville: Broadman Press, 1984.

Southern Baptist Convention, The Missionaries of the Home Mission Board. Atlanta, GA: Southern Baptist Convention, 1936.

Spain, Rufus B. *At Ease in Zion: Social History of Southern Baptists, 1865-1900.* Nashville: Vanderbilt University Press, 1967.

Stetar, Joseph M. "In Search of a Direction: Southern Higher Education After the Civil War." *History of Education Quarterly.* Fall, 1985.

Stringer, Patricia and Irene Thompson, eds. *Stepping off the Pedestal: Academic Women in the South.* New York: Modern Language Association of America, 1982.

Sumners, Billy F. "The Social Attitudes of Southern Baptists Toward Certain Issues, 1910-1920." Masters thesis, University of Texas at Arlington, 1975.

Sumners, Bill, "Southern Baptists and Women's Right to Vote, 1910-1920," *Baptist History and Heritage* 12 (January 1977): 45-51.

Thompson, James L. *Tried as by Fire: Southern Baptists and the Religious Controversies of the 1920's,* Mercer University Press, Macon GA, 1982.

Trolander, Judith. *Professionalism and Social Change: From the Settlement House Movement to Neighborhood Centers, 1886 to the present. New York: Columbia University Press 1987.*

Tucker, Ruth A. *Guardians of the Great Commission: The Story of Women in Modern Missions*. Grand Rapids MI: Zondervan Publishing, 1988.

Tyack, D. O. *The One Best System: A History of American Urban Education*. Cambridge, MA: Harvard University Press, 1974.

Vesey, Laurence R. *The Emergence of the American University*. Chicago: University of Chicago Press, 1965.

Vickers, Gregory K. "Woman's Place: Images of Womanhood in the Southern Baptist Convention, 1888-1929" Master's thesis, Vanderbilt University, 1986.

_____. "Southern Baptist Women and Social Concerns, 1910-1929." *Baptist History and Heritage* 23 (October 1988): 3-13.

_____. "Baptists in America: 175 Years of National Organization." *Baptist History and Heritage* 24 (January 1989): 41-53.

Violette, E. M. *History of the First District State Normal School: Kirksville, Missouri*. Kirksville, MO: Journal Printing Company, 1905.

Watkins, Rees. *A Backward Glance: History of Woman's Missionary Union*. Birmingham: Woman's Missionary Union, 1987.

Weaver, B. H.,"Some Aspects of the Development of Liberal Arts Education for Women in the South", in *Trends in Liberal Arts Education for Women*. New Orleans: Newcomb College, 1954.

Wein, Roberta. "Women's Colleges and Domesticity, 1875-1918," *History of Education Quarterly* 1 (Spring 1974): 31-47.

Welter, Barbara. *Dimity Convictions: The American Woman in the Nineteenth Century*. Athens: Ohio University Press, 1976.

_____. "She Hath Done What She Could: Protestant Women's Missionary Careers in Nineteenth-Century America," in *Women in American Religion*, ed. Janet Wilson James. Philadelphia: University of Pennsylvania Press, 1980.

Woods, Robert A. and Albert J. Kennedy eds., *Handbook of Settlements*. New York: Charity Publication Committee, 1911.

Woody, Thomas. *A History of Women's Education in the United States* (2 vols.) New York: The Science Press, 1929.

Yater, George H. *Two Hundred Years at the Falls of the Ohio: A History of Louisville and Jefferson County* Heritage Corporation, Louisville, 1979.

Young, Elizabeth B. *A Study of the Curricula of Seven Selected Women's Colleges of the Southern States.* 1932; reprint, New York: Teacher's College Press, 1972. Arthur C. Holden, *The Settlement Idea: A Vision of Social Justice* (New York: MacMillan, 1922).

Interviews

Juliette Mather interviewed by Catherine Allen, January 26, 1976, tape recording and transcript, Woman's Missionary Union Archives, Birmingham, AL.

Juliette Mather interviewed by Gertrude Tharpe and Ethalee Hamric, September 17-21, 1979, tape recording and transcript, Woman's Missionary Union Archives, Birmingham, AL.

Carrie Littlejohn interviewed by Doris Devault, April 16, 1979, tape recording and transcript, Woman's Missionary Union Archives, Birmingham, AL.

Elsie Ragsdale interviewed by Catherine Allen, 1985, videocassette, The Southern Baptist Theological Seminary, Louisville, KY.

Kay Bigham interviewed by Catherine Allen, 1985, videocassette, Southern Baptist Theological Seminary, Louisville, KY.

INDEX